Palgrave Studies in the History of Economic Thought

Palgrave Studies in the History of Economic Thought publishes contributions by leading scholars, illuminating key events, theories and individuals that have had a lasting impact on the development of modern-day economics. The topics covered include the development of economies, institutions and theories.

More information about this series at
http://www.palgrave.com/gp/series/14585

Desmond McNeill

Fetishism and the Theory of Value

Reassessing Marx in the 21st Century

palgrave
macmillan

Desmond McNeill
Centre for Development and the Environment
University of Oslo
Oslo, Norway

ISSN 2662-6578 ISSN 2662-6586 (electronic)
Palgrave Studies in the History of Economic Thought
ISBN 978-3-030-56122-2 ISBN 978-3-030-56123-9 (eBook)
https://doi.org/10.1007/978-3-030-56123-9

Cover illustration: Hi-Story / Alamy Stock Photo

This Palgrave Macmillan imprint is published by the registered company Springer Nature Switzerland AG.
The registered company address is: Gewerbestrasse 11, 6330 Cham, Switzerland

Foreword

I first read Desmond McNeill's book around the millennium. It struck me then as a well written and original introduction to Marxian economics. He demonstrates forcefully that Marx's discoveries are not well served by insisting on a narrow economistic approach to them. Marx's theory of value has suffered in particular by neglect of concepts often judged by economists to be too 'philosophical', 'sociological' or 'immature' when compared with the achievements of *Capital*.

The notion of 'fetish' is central to these questions, and it takes up the first two sections of the book's five sections. McNeill branches out in the next two sections to consider first the implications of treating both money and language as the main means of human communication. This involves a critical assessment of structural linguistics and structuralist Marxism, both of which flourished in the 1960s and 1970s, the last time that Marx inspired genuinely new thinking. Second, he argues that the attribution of value just to social relations of production and labour is unnecessarily restrictive, extending the economic discussion to exchange and consumption also. The fifth section is entirely new to this edition, updating Marx's relevance for our century in the context of more recent Marxist-inspired literature on the pressing global issues of environment and financialisation.

This book, more than most, raises the question of its own and its subject's historicity, a question that is foreign to economic orthodoxy and is often neglected by twentieth-century Marxists, but not of course by Marx and Engels themselves. It started out as a London doctoral thesis in 1988. When I first encountered it two decades ago, I could not understand why it had not yet been published, since its scope and quality far surpass the promotion fodder that passes for academic publication these days. In desperation, its author resorted to private publication later. Now at last it has found its rightful place with a serious academic publisher, and I am delighted to introduce new readers to this exemplary work.

There are several reasons why the book might not have found an academic publisher for over three decades. The structuralist bubble burst around 1979–1980, when the neo-liberal counter-revolution against post-war developmental states was launched by Reagan and Thatcher. McNeill's thesis saw daylight just before the turning point of our world, 1989–1994—the end of the Cold War, the collapse of the Soviet bloc, the birth of one-world capitalism, China's and India's emergence as global powers, the internet going public and its transformation by the World Wide Web. Marxism went on the backburner for two decades, losing ground to writers like Karl Polanyi and Marcel Mauss. But the Lehmann crash of 2008 launched a revival of Marx's work, especially in Germany. Now, on the edge of what may be the next Great (or Greater) Depression and with internet optimism nullified by Big Tech and the banks, McNeill's timing may at last be right.

The current global crisis is a suitable moment to revive his intellectual project. Moreover, the author's integration of various literatures, including important nineteenth-century and twentieth-century sources, is a powerful antidote to the short-termism and parochialism of late academia. His approach has been unfashionable for too long. Some readers may be sceptical on two more fronts. First, they may imagine that this is a narrow specialist topic. I have already flatly contradicted this, and the rest of the Foreword expands on this view. Second, it may not be a suitable student textbook. This is true. It is mainly for mature academics who appreciate original scholarship, intellectual ambition and fine writing.

* * *

In Parts I and II, McNeill starts from the rather vague notion of fetishism that concludes the dense, synthetic introductory chapter to *Capital*'s first volume. With quick, precise strokes, he establishes the word's origins in European encounters with the indigenous populations of the Americas and Africa, shows how Marx translated Spanish greed for gold into a local German obsession with private property and charts its journey in Marx's writings from a word to a concept, culminating in the difficult but foundational idea of 'commodity fetishism' in *Capital*. It is typical of McNeill's vision and method that a term coined as a shaky tool for understanding primitive religion should be made the launching pad for grasping Marxian economics.

For he aims to show that Marx's ideas concerning value can only be understood through close examination of the notion that relations between men take the fantastic form of relations between things in societies dominated by capitalism. If Marx's concept of surplus value was, in his own eyes and McNeill's, his supreme theoretical achievement, the relationship of exploitation that it highlights is easier to understand than the theory of value that underpins it. The same might be said of the fetishism of interest on capital in relation to commodity fetishism. The dialectic of appearances and social reality is reproduced in Marx's concept of the value-form, the unity of use-value and exchange-value in the commodity under capitalism.

McNeill develops his argument through a triangulation of Marx with Bailey and Hegel, two of Ricardo's contemporaries after the Napoleonic wars. Samuel Bailey was a 'vulgar economist' who anticipated the marginalist revolution to a degree. Marx shared some of Bailey's criticisms of Ricardo, whose value theory was the immediate precursor to his own, but he rejected Bailey's (and later economists') reduction of value to price. On the other hand, Hegel offered a precursor of Marx's own dialectical method, but one which (in the latter's view, but not mine) reduced the material world's movement to abstract ideas. This chapter concludes the first two sections. More than any other, it reveals McNeill's originality and control as an intellectual historian.

Part III draws on an analogy between the economy and language. This entails an assessment of French structuralist Marxism, an intellectual bubble that burst soon after it came to dominate Anglophone critical discourse in the 1970s. McNeill considers three writers: Louis Althusser who was definitely a Marxist, Claude Lévi-Strauss who was perhaps *the* structuralist and Maurice Godelier who tried to synthesise the two. He concludes that Althusser was not a serious structuralist nor Lévi-Strauss a Marxist, and Godelier's familiarity with both, while promising, did not lead to an intellectual breakthrough. He might have added that none of these shared his passion for literate scholarship, but he does not. The main conclusion of his extension of the argument from economics into structuralism is that de Saussure's foundational *Course in General Linguistics* (published posthumously in 1916) is the best guide to the questions raised here. Last, McNeill makes a strong case for treating the commodity conceptually as a sign.

Somewhat surprisingly, Part IV suggests that Marx's reasons for privileging social relations of production and labour in his economic analysis were not strong enough. McNeill proposes that a general theory of value should also take in exchange and consumption as economic spheres of equal weight. Here his argument is more indicative than convincing, but it does point to possibly fruitful applications of the solid achievements of the earlier sections on fetishism and the value-form. The study of exchange leads into the rich anthropological literature on reciprocity for whom Marcel Mauss is usually taken as the key figure, even if Richard Thurnwald and Bronislaw Malinowski deserve more credit for launching the concept. Lévi-Strauss made it the cornerstone of his own approach, while attributing it to Mauss who hardly ever used it. McNeill draws out at length here Marx's sympathetic reading of Aristotle. Consumption opens up the issues of need and use-value that were revolutionised in the 1980s by the French sociologists, Pierre Bourdieu and Jean Baudrillard. In my view, Daniel Miller's synthesis of Hegel, Marx and Simmel, *Material Culture and Mass Consumption* (1987), would be a more useful source from nearer to home.

Part V covers a discursive literature linking Marx's theory of nature to theoretical work underpinning contemporary ecological politics ('the red-green alliance'). McNeill's treatment of these issues is far from superficial. There is, however, a tension between the Enlightenment concept of nature as whatever has ceased becoming (the property of life) and later usage referring to a physical environment that has not been modified by human intervention. Our author is right to say of Marxist geographers, as well as their economist counterparts, that Marx's theory of value plays only a peripheral part in this literature. Drawing on the idea of 'accumulation by dispossession' (David Harvey from Giovanni Arrighi), he turns from Marx's theory of rent to a sharp discussion of forces underlying the rape of the earth in our day.

The word 'financialisation' is now everywhere and sports a score of different definitions. This final chapter on finance, as with the one on production, exchange and consumption earlier, is a more hit-and-miss review than the core sections addressing value theory. It is nevertheless a useful introduction to a very diverse literature and McNeill's judgement is generally excellent. He spans the range from Marx's analysis of interest-bearing capital to 'the financialisation of everyday life' after having discussed speculative green finance in the previous chapter. He does not attempt to examine the financial crisis itself, preferring to stick to this book's focus on the theory of value. This is wise, since addressing the recent history of money and the debt crisis would have been a step too far. The chapter asks if finance is productive in Marx's sense and concludes with some more thoughts on the forms of appropriation.

This book seeks to correct the prevailing tendency to draw too tight a line around the 'economic' aspects of Marx's thought by privileging quantitative analysis over qualitative concepts. It is above all a passionate plea to view Marx's economics within the framework of a social ontology to which fetishism is the most appropriate point of entry. McNeill's rigorous scholarship and commitment to analytical clarity are not entirely compatible with his desire to update Marx through an approach that in some respects is more eclectic than *Capital* and consequently differs from it in significant respects. The resulting text, however, is an exhilarating read, one that has pushed me to explore the contemporary relevance of Marx's thought with renewed enthusiasm. I hope it might have a similar effect on some of you.

Paris, France
July 2020

Keith Hart

Acknowledgements

This book is the product of a three-stage process. The first and major stage was the preparation of my thesis, between 1984 and 1988, while I was registered for a part-time Ph.D. in economics at University College London. My initial intention was to address perhaps the most basic question in economics: 'What is value?' I thought I would compare neo-classical theory, which is what I had been taught at Cambridge, with Marxian theory, of which I knew nothing. It rapidly became apparent that in neo-classical economics the answer is all too brief: 'value equals price'. By contrast, Marx had much more interesting things to say, and I set out to try and get to grips with his struggles in addressing this crucial issue. I started the thesis while teaching in the economics department at the University of Edinburgh—and, from 1987, while working as free-lancer in Oslo, Norway.

For the parts that they played in this endeavour, my thanks go first to my wife Signe Howell for suggesting that I take on the challenge of a PhD. Next, to George Catephores, my supervisor for the first year, and to colleagues at the University of Edinburgh: Peter Vandome in Economics, Barry Barnes in Science Studies and Dori Scaltsas in Philosophy for valuable discussions. Also to Amartya Sen for noting the significance of Samuel Bailey and to G. de Ste. Croix for useful references on Aristotle. I am also grateful to those who commented on specific draft chapters or sections: Martin Fransman, Nigel Harris and Jerry Cohen, and on the complete thesis, Ådne Cappelen.

Encouraged by the comments of my examiners, I tried to have the thesis published, but without success; it was turned down by several major international publishing houses. There the story might have ended had it not been for Keith Hart who read it, enjoyed it and encouraged me to self-publish. Following his advice, I did so. I am enormously grateful to him.

That was the second stage in the process. The third was the result of a chance contact with my first tutor at Cambridge, Geoff Harcourt. He expressed interest in reading the self-published version, and having done so, he encouraged me to submit it to Palgrave Studies in the History of Economic Thought, of which he is an editor. The reviewers of the book recommended publication subject to substantial updating to engage with recent literature. This book is the result. I am very grateful to Geoff Harcourt, and to Ben Fine, one of the reviewers, who gave helpful advice in this updating process, and to my colleague Jostein Jacobsen, for his knowledge of recent literature on the environment. Finally, my thanks to staff at Palgrave Macmillan, especially to Rachel Sangster, Sristhi Gupta and Vanipriya Manohar who have been so helpful in bringing this long process to fruition.

About the Book

This book demonstrates the continuing relevance of Marx's critique of the capitalist system, in which value is simply equated with market price. It includes chapters specifically on the environment and financialisation, and presents Marx's qualitative theory of value and the associated concept of fetishism in a clear and comprehensive manner. Part I demonstrates how fetishism developed in Marx's writing from a journalistic metaphor to an analytical device central to his critique. In Part II, commodity fetishism is distinguished from other forms: of money, capital and interest-bearing capital. There follows an analysis of Marx's complex attempt to distinguish his argument from those of Ricardo and Samuel Bailey. The section ends with a discussion of the ontological status of value: as a social rather than a natural phenomenon. Part III considers the merits of understanding value by analogy with language and critically assesses the merits of Structural Marxism. Part IV challenges Marx's emphasis solely on production and considers also exchange and consumption as social relations. Part V critically assesses recent Marx-inspired literature relating to the two major crises of our time, finance and the environment, and identifies strong similarities between the key analytical questions that are being debated in each case.

Praise for *Fetishism and the Theory of Value*

"An outstanding and original book."

—Professor Emeritus Geoff Harcourt, *University of New South Wales, Australia*

"If you, like Joan Robinson and like me before I read this book, are inclined to dismiss Marx's theory of value and fetishism as 'gobbledygook', Desmond McNeill's beautifully written and very accessible book should persuade you otherwise. It deals with one of the most fundamental of social science issues: why we must distinguish (but generally don't) 'value' from 'price'. Without this distinction we are bound to superficial explanations of the basic structure of capitalist society, and of major current problems relating to the 'financialization of everyday life' and treatment of the environment as a commodity. McNeill shows how to go deeper."

—Robert H. Wade, *Professor of Global Political Economy, London School of Economics and Political Science*

"This book provides a compelling account of the qualitative nature of Marx's value theory, drawing upon a wide range of sources. The relevance for contemporary thought and debates is expertly addressed ranging, for example, over the role of value in understanding the environment and financialisation. Discussion throughout is extraordinarily accomplished, well-written, well-informed, a pleasure to read, insightful and of considerable synthetic originality, whilst also connecting the abstract conceptualisation of value to contemporary scholarship and issues."

—Ben Fine, *Emeritus Professor of Economics, School of Oriental and African Studies (SOAS), UK*

"Desmond McNeill's deep and broad learning brilliantly illuminates his exegesis of Marx's relevance to our understanding of the contemporary capitalist world of neo-liberalism. His application of the themes of fetishism, value, and rent to the understanding of financialization and the plundering of nature are subtle, lucid, and unsurpassed. If I had to choose a single 'local-tracker' to help me navigate the contemporary world system, he might well be the best guide."

—James C. Scott, *Sterling Professor of Political Science and Anthropology, 2020 recipient of the Hirschman Prize, Yale University*

"We live in a world of rampant fetishism and alienation, now as much as in the mid-nineteen century when Marx developed his path-breaking analysis of capitalism. Desmond McNeill reveals the enduring power of the fetish to conceal the social, spatial, temporal and environmental dynamics of the most destructive economic system ever created."

—Noel Castree, *Professor of Geography, The University of Manchester*

"This brilliant book shows what may still come of a careful reading of Marx and how important it is not to put aside works of genius in the illusion that we already know what they have to offer. Desmond McNeill's lucid and compelling exploration of Marx's idea of value demands to be read not only by economists, but by sociologists and anthropologists. It makes possible a new understanding of fetishism, and in so doing opens fascinating new pathways to social analysis - demonstrably so in respect of the financialisation of everyday life and the incorporation of the 'natural environment' into the world of economics."

—Christina Toren, *Professor of Social Anthropology, University of St Andrews, UK*

"Desmond McNeill's volume revisits and extends his earlier intellectual history of Marx's theory of labour value, basic to Marx's analysis of surplus value or capitalist exploitation. The unexpectedly etymological route of his defence begins with Marx's use of fetishism as metaphor for the social relations of capitalism. McNeill's extended epilogue considers the contemporary relevance of such analysis for nature and financialization, arguably the two Achilles heels of contemporary capitalism in the early 21st century."

—Jomo KS, *Malaysia*, winner of the 2007 Wassily Leontief Prize for Advancing the Frontiers of Economic Thought

"Today, more than ever, it is necessary to re-visit why and how our lives are increasingly lived through commodities real and fictitious. This erudite and astute reading of Marx's notion of fetishism is precisely what is needed in order to recover the experience of the social that lurks within the simulacrum of the thing."

—Erik Swyngedouw, *Professor of Geography, The University of Manchester, UK*

Contents

About the Author

Desmond McNeill (PhD economics, University of London) graduated from Cambridge University in 1969. He has been a lecturer at University College London and the University of Edinburgh, and recently retired from the Centre for Development and the Environment at the University of Oslo, Norway, where he had formerly been Research Professor and Director.

1

Introduction

In recent years, interest in Marx's works has experienced something of a revival. But his theory of value, which is, I believe, of abiding relevance for a critical understanding of capitalism, has not received the attention it deserves. My purpose in this book is to present a sympathetic critique of this theory, and especially his concept of fetishism that plays such a central role within it. Some of the subject matter that follows may be thought to lie outside the scope of economics as normally understood. My concern, however, is with the basic presuppositions of the discipline: the foundations that are too often unexamined. To define the boundaries of economics is also, to a large extent, to determine how it is to be studied. In economics, as Schumpeter observed, ideology "enters on the very ground floor" (Schumpeter 1954: 42).

> But suppose we did start from scratch, what are the steps we should have to take? … We should first have to visualize a distinct set of coherent phenomena as a worthwhile object of our analytic efforts. In other words, analytic effort is of necessity preceded by a preanalytic cognitive act that

---

This is a revised version of a chapter in McNeill, D (1988) *Fetishism and the Form of Value*. Unpublished thesis, University of London.

D. McNeill, *Fetishism and the Theory of Value*, Palgrave Studies in the History of Economic Thought, https://doi.org/10.1007/978-3-030-56123-9_1

> supplies the raw material for the analytic effort. In this book, this preanalytic cognitive act will be called Vision. (Schumpeter 1954: 41)

It is this "vision" which determines the scope of economics. At the same time it determines also its bias: "laying emphasis upon certain factors and relationships and excluding others or casting them into the shadows" (Dobb 1973: 7). Marxian economics lays its emphases very differently from "bourgeois" economics, giving recognition to "the priority of society over the individual, … the historical …, and the dominant part played by production" (Bukharin 1927). It does so self-consciously; it has the merit of questioning its own foundations. At these foundations, I suggest, is to be found a theory of value. It is reprehensible, but not perhaps surprising, that most neo-classical economists ignore the issue, treating value as identical with price, and expressing no further interest in it.

Sweezy asserted that "the marriage of the qualitative and the quantitative analyses was one of Marx's greatest achievements" (Sweezy 1979: 21). The latter, the quantitative analysis, has—since Bohm-Bawerk in 1896—been the subject of much, largely justified, criticism; and Marxian economists have, in response, devoted "a truly astonishing amount of energy to the 'transformation problem'" (Sen 1978: 179). I believe, however, that it is not the quantitative but the qualitative aspect of the theory of value that is Marx's important contribution to economics. This finds expression in the concept of fetishism, which both encapsulates his critique of economic categories and provides insights into the commodity—the foundation stone of the capitalist system.

Here, I believe, lies the major importance of Marx's critique. But Marxian economists have not, I suggest, made sufficient efforts to develop and propound this aspect of Marx's economics. Some, such as Joan Robinson, criticised his theory of value for being "metaphysical".[1] There has been a tendency to regard this aspect of Marx's work as falling outside the domain of economics proper: brilliant, perhaps—but to be classified as the work of "Marx the sociologist" or "Marx the philosopher". But

[1] To her it was "gobbledygook. She said 'It's great metaphysics for stirring the workers up, but it's not a theory. You don't need it'" (Harcourt and King 1995: 38).

some do assign a crucial place to the concept of value, and agree with Dobb that this necessarily shapes economic theory as a whole:

> Any theory of value necessarily constitutes an implicit definition of the general shape and character of the terrain which it has decided to call 'economic'. (Dobb 1973: 16)

There is thus a close link between the scope and method of economics. And bourgeois economics is severely limited in both respects:

> What characterizes bourgeois theory is that it takes the appearances of capitalism for granted and only studies the relationship between them. (Fine 1980: 9)

Marxian economics, by contrast, goes deeper; studying not only surface phenomena but also their foundations. Marx criticised both economic theory and the capitalist system that it sought to understand. In this book I shall argue that the importance of Marx's theory of value is precisely that it questions the categories on which economics is founded. It is not a theory of price-formation; that is not its strength, nor even its purpose. It is necessary to understand how the capitalist economy works, in its own terms; but it is important also to critique those terms—the categories which are used to analyse, and often to justify, the capitalist system.

While I believe that the major contribution of Marx to economics is his emphasis on social relations, this is not to suggest that Marx ignored the importance of the material. Indeed, his contribution to history lay precisely here. It is something of a paradox, and a source of permanent tension in Marx's work, that as an economist he stressed the social, while as an historian he stressed the material. It is never possible wholly to disentangle the two, but my own concern is with Marx the economist—and here, I suggest, his strength lay in his emphasis on the social: with the inner workings of capitalism, and the mystifying categories of bourgeois economics.

Interest in Marx's writings, which was rather limited in the period from the 1980s well into the twenty-first century, has now been revived—for two main reasons. The first is MEGA^2, the massive exercise to mark the 200th anniversary of Marx's birth by reproducing "basically all relevant material from Marx's literary remains, only parts of which were already known" (Kurz 2018: 792). Some new insights have emerged from these endeavours—for example with regard to Marx's writings on nature (Saito 2017). But this appears not to be the case with regard to the theory of value. In his recent article "Will the MEGA^2 edition be a watershed in interpreting Marx?" (Kurz 2018), he responds in the affirmative concerning topics such as technical progress and the rate of profit, but not with regard to the theory of value, which he describes as "the cornerstone of Marx's analysis of capitalism", concluding that Marx "unswervingly stuck to it till the very end of his life" (Kurz 2018: 793).

But it is not only the 200 year anniversary that has revived scholarly interest in Marx. His ideas have been found by many to be relevant to pressing problems of our day, as I demonstrate in the three concluding chapters of this book. These build on the twelve preceding chapters which provide a detailed and extensive exposition on fetishism and the theory of value. The first six chapters examine why and how Marx came to grant fetishism such a central place in his analysis, and include a discussion on the ontology of social relations. The next six chapters point up some limitations in his work, arguing the merits of structural Marxism, and suggesting that not only the social relations of production but also exchange and consumption are worthy of study.

In the final chapters of the book I review the quite substantial literature from recent years that draws on Marx's writings. I choose here to focus on works concerned with the environment and with financialisation. These two topics, and especially the former, have dominated the literature in quantitative terms; not surprising in view of the financial crisis of 2008 and the escalating problems of environmental degradation. The contributors come from a range of disciplines; only a minority are economists. Despite their very frequent references to Marx, many of these works, as I shall show, nevertheless pay scant attention to his concept of fetishism, or even his theory of value. But there are signs that this may be changing. I hope that this book may contribute in some small way to such a development.

Bibliography

Bukharin, N. (1927). *The Economic Theory of the Leisure Class*. New York: International Publishers.

Dobb, M. (1973). *Theories of Value and Distribution Since Adam Smith*. Cambridge University Press.

Fine, B. (1980). *Economic Theory and Ideology.* London: Edward Arnold.

Harcourt, G., & King, J. (1995). Talking About Joan Robinson: Geoff Harcourt in Conversation with John King. *Review of Social Economy, 53*(1), 31–64.

Kurz, H. (2018). Will the MEGA^2 Edition Be a Watershed in Interpreting Marx? *The European Journal of the History of Economic Thought, 25*(5), 783–807. https://doi.org/10.1080/09672567.2018.1523937

Saito, K. (2017). *Karl Marx's Ecosocialism: Capital, Nature, and the Unfinished Critique of Political Economy*. New York University Press.

Schumpeter, J. A. (1954). *History of Economic Analysis*. London: Allen & Unwin.

Sen, A. K. (1978). On the Labour Theory of Value: Some Methodological Issues. *Cambridge Journal of Economics, 2*, 175–190.

Sweezy, P. (1979). Marxian Value Theory and Crisis. *Monthly Review* 31, 20–35.

Part I

The Concept of Fetishism

2

The Origins of Fetishism in Marx's Writings

Fetishism, whatever that may mean!
(Max Müller, quoted in Aston 1912: 895)

In 1511 a certain Hatuey—a cazique, or native prince—heard that Admiral Don James Columbus had decided to sail from Hispaniola to neighbouring Cuba in order to establish settlements there. He therefore assembled his people,

> and putting them in Mind of their many Sufferings under the *Spaniards*, told them, 'They did all that for a great Lord they were very fond of, which he would show them', and then taking some Gold out of a little Palm-tree Basket, added, 'This is the Lord whom they serve, him they follow, and as you have already heard, they are about passing over hither, only to seek this Lord, therefore let us make a Festival, and dance to him, to the end that when they come he may order them not to do us harm'. Accordingly they all began to sing and dance, till they were quite tir'd. … When they were

This is a revised version of a chapter in McNeill, D (1988) *Fetishism and the Form of Value*. Unpublished thesis, University of London.

D. McNeill, *Fetishism and the Theory of Value*, Palgrave Studies in the History of Economic Thought, https://doi.org/10.1007/978-3-030-56123-9_2

> spent with Singing and Dancing before the little basket of Gold,[1] *Hatuey* bid them not to keep the Lord of the Christians in any place whatsoever, for tho' he were in their Bowels, they would fetch him out, and therefore they should cast him into the River, under Water where they could not find him; and so they did. (Herrera 1730b: 10)

This passage reveals, very graphically, the appalling greed of the sixteenth-century Europe for gold. But it does more than this. The description is especially powerful because the Spaniards are seen through the eyes of Hatuey, an outsider to their culture. He has the capacity, as an outsider, to perceive the behaviour of the Spaniards very differently. This certainly enriches his description of events; perhaps it also enlightens our understanding of them.

Karl Marx, in almost his first published work more than 300 years later, perceives the members of the Rhineland Assembly in somewhat similar terms. His famous attack on the views expressed in their debates concerning the theft of wood concludes with the words:

> The *savages of Cuba* regarded gold as a *fetish of the Spaniards*. They celebrated a feast in its honour, sang in a circle around it and then threw it into the sea. If the Cuban savages had been present at the sitting of the Rhine Province Assembly, would they not have regarded *wood* as the *Rhinelanders' fetish*? (Marx and Engels 1975a: 262)

The lengthy quotation cited above, from Herrera's History of the West Indies, is, certainly, the origin of this famous reference of Marx. He came across the story, however, not in Herrera but in the account by de Brosses in his *Du Culte des Dieux Fétiches* (first published in 1760), where the wording matches closely Marx's own.[2]

---

[1] This is printed as "God" in translation, but "**Oro**" in the original (Herrera 1730a: 232).

[2]

> Les Barbares de Cuba, sachant qu'une flotte de Castille alloit descendre dans leur île, jugèrent qu'il falloit d'abord se concilier le Dieu des Espagnols, puis l'éloigner de chez eux. Ils *rassemblèrent* tout leur or dans une corbeille. *Voilà*, dirent-ils, le Dieu de ces *étrangerss*; *célébrons une fête* en son honneur pour obtenir la protection; *après* quoi nous le ferons sortir de notre île. Ils dansèrent & *chantèrent* selon leur mode religieuse autour de la courbelle, puis la *jettèrent* dans la Mer. (de Brosses 1972: 53)

The only substantial difference between the versions of de Brosses and Marx is that the latter writes "fetish" where de Brosses, following Herrera, refers only to the God of the Spaniards. Nevertheless, the term "fetish" is frequently employed elsewhere in *Du Culte des Dieux Fétiches* and de Brosses is generally credited with being responsible for its adoption as an accepted category of comparative religion.

The word "fetish" comes originally from the Portuguese (Aston 1912: 894). Portuguese sailors first reached the coast of West Africa in 1481, and used the word "feitiços" to refer to the cult objects of the natives they encountered. Thus Purchas in his *Pilgrimages* (1613) described "strawen rings called Fatissos or Gods" (Marett 1932: 201). "Feitiços" in turn derives from the Latin "factitius" which simply means "skilfully made".

Diderot, in tracing the source of the word, attributes it to Dapper rather than to de Brosses. This may simply be due to his low opinion of *Du Culte des Fétiches*, which he described, in one of his letters, as "diffuse et plus de trois quarts trop longue" (Tourneux 1878: 231), adding that all the thoughtful material contained in it could be found in Hume's *Natural History of Religion*. Be that as it may, Hume did not himself use the word fetish, referring rather to the "savage tribes of America, Africa and Asia" simply as "idolaters" (Hume 1956: 23).

Seventy years after de Brosses, Comte, in his *Cours de Philosophie Positive*, adopted the term fetishism to refer to the first phase of theology (polytheism and monotheism being the next two). The aptness of the term in this context is indicated by an excerpt from J.S. Mill's commentary on Comte:

> The Theological … regards the facts of the universe as governed not by invariable laws of sequence, but by single and direct volitions of beings, real or imaginary, possessed of life and intelligence. In the infantile state of reason and experience, individual objects are looked upon as animated. (Mill 1866: 10)

After theology, in Comte's account of events, came metaphysics and positivism. Thus, again according to Mill in a most illuminating passage, the metaphysical was a transformation of the theological:

> The human mind, in framing a class of objects, did not set out from the notion of a name, but from that of a divinity. The realization of abstractions was not the embodiment of a word, but the gradual disembodiment of a fetish. … As soon as the voluntary agent, whose will governed the phenomenon, ceased to be the physical object itself … it seemed indispensable that the god, at a distance from the object, must act through something residing in it. … When mankind felt a need for naming these imaginary entities, they called them the *nature* of the object, or its *essence*. (Mill 1866: 21)

Writing fifty years later, the anthropologist Aston described fetishism as follows:

> Fetishism … rests on two principles. The first is what, in modern phrase, we call the immanence of deity; the second is the necessity which there is for the spiritual to be expressed in terms of the physical. (Aston 1912: 898)

At its richest, and most unspecific, the term fetish has been applied to many different classes of objects: personified natural objects and phenomena (the Sun, the Sky, and the Earth as a source of food); objects representing a nature-deity or deified man (such as a totem); objects serving as the abode of a spirit; charms or amulets which have a power quite independent of any spirits. Indeed, after Comte the term became increasingly debased, as theories of primitive religion changed. There was the nature-myth school, of which Max Müller was the most powerful representative. This in turn was criticised by Herbert Spencer and, independently but along similar lines, by Tylor who introduced the term "animism" which "virtually sounded the death knell of fetishism as a classificatory term" (Marett 1932: 202).

In summary, then, the term was first taken up and developed by students of comparative religion and anthropologists. They have generally abandoned it now, partly because its use became too indiscriminate, and partly because changes in the understanding of primitive religion rendered it obsolete.

Before moving on to consider Marx's own adoption and usage of the term, its application in psychology may be briefly considered (although, of course, this occurred much later). It was first used by the Frenchman and founder of experimental psychology, Alfred Binet, in an article in 1887. Krafft-Ebing, in 1906, took up what he regarded as an apt term "because this enthusiasm for certain portions of the body (or even articles of attire) and the worship of them, in obedience to sexual impulses, frequently call to mind the reverence for relics, holy objects etc. in religious cults" (von Krafft-Ebing 1939: 219). Havelock Ellis also favoured the term (Ellis 1933), but Freud used it only sparingly, for example, in a brief article of 1927, titled "Fetishism".[3]

Since the analogy is, at least in the case of Kraft-Ebing, rather loose, it is perhaps not surprising that little appears to be gained from detailed comparisons between the concept of fetishism in psychology and in Marx.[4] There is, however, a broad parallel between Marx and Freud which may be noted, one which is not reliant on Freud's limited, and rather different, usage of the term "fetishism". Both Marx and Freud were concerned with "false consciousness"; while Marx located this in society, Freud located it within the human subconscious. And both were in some respects reacting against a nineteenth century, mechanical view of the world in which appearance and reality were thought to coincide.

Contrary to what some have suggested (e.g. Urbanek 1969: 179) the above quotation from Marx does not constitute his first published use of the term fetishism. This is in fact to be found in an earlier article for the *Rheinische Zeitung*, dated July 10, 1842, in which he attacks a leading article in the *Kölnische Zeitung*, written by a Herr Hermes. The latter supported censorship and the limitation of scientific research, arguing that

[3] "The fetish is a substitute for the woman's (the mother's) penis that the little boy once believed in" (Freud 1927: 153). (Here Freud refers back to his 1910 article: "Leonardo da Vinci and a Memory of his Childhood".) In his much more substantial article "Totem and Taboo: Some Points of Agreement between the Mental Lives of Savages and Neurotics" he notes that: "As distinguished from a fetish, a totem is never an isolated individual, but always a class of objects" (Freud 1955: 103).

[4] The adoption of the term fetishism by psychologists may account for its subsequent popularisation and ultimate debasement. Certainly there are those who interpret Marx's commodity fetishism as if it meant no more than an unhealthy fixation on consumer goods (see, e.g., Ignatieff 1984).

"to spread philosophical and religious views by means of the newspapers, or to combat them in the newspapers, we consider equally impermissible" (Marx and Engels 1975a: 187). Marx demonstrates the internal inconsistency of the argument, since Herr Hermes is himself clearly trying to "combat religious views by means of the newspapers". He goes on to quote the writer's claim that religion "is the basis of the state and the most necessary condition for every social association which does not aim merely at achieving some external aim. … In its crudest form as *childish fetishism* it nevertheless to some extent raises man above his sensuous desires, which, if he allowed himself to be ruled exclusively by them, could *degrade him to the level of an animal* and make him incapable of fulfilling any higher aim" (Marx and Engels 1975a: 188).

Marx tries to show up the internal contradictions in this passage also, though with less success (and to little purpose). Thus, he argues that animal worship must necessarily "degrade man below the animal"—a conclusion which does not square with Herr Hermes' claim that fetishism, although the crudest form of religion, nevertheless raises man above the level of the animal. What is more interesting for our purpose is that Marx then continues as follows:

> And now, indeed, 'fetishism'! Truly the erudition of a penny magazine. Fetishism is so far from raising man *above* his sensuous desires that, on the contrary, it is 'the *religion of sensuous desire*'. Fantasy arising from desire deceives the fetish-worshipper into believing that an 'inanimate object' will give up its natural character in order to comply with his desires. Hence the crude desire of the fetish-worshipper *smashes* the fetish when it ceases to be its most obedient servant. (Marx and Engels 1975a: 189)

Marx's first usage of the term fetishism is thus a response to its employment by Herr Hermes, in what was, at that time its more literal meaning. It was some three months later that Marx wrote his article, in the same periodical, on the "Debates on the Law of the Thefts of Wood" in the Rhineland Assembly. Here his usage of the term is metaphorical, and merits further elaboration.

In general terms, what is at issue is the concept of property. More specifically, Marx is discussing whether the removal of wood which has fallen from the trees should be regarded as theft. One of the deputies has argued that if this were so, people who were otherwise honest would be set on the path of crime, by the severity of a prison sentence and the company of "inveterate thieves". Another deputy responds that in his region people cut small gashes in young trees which, when they soon die, are treated as fallen wood. This provides Marx with the opportunity to draw a forceful analogy with the lot of the poor people themselves. If the Assembly takes the harsh view of the matter, then "it is inevitable that many people not of a criminal disposition are cut off from the green tree of morality and cast like fallen wood into the hell of crime, infamy and misery". But the members of the Assembly are also the owners of the trees, and faced with the alternative possibility that some young trees may be damaged, "it need hardly be said that the wooden idols triumph and human beings are sacrificed" (Marx and Engels 1975a: 227).

This comparison with idols is recalled later in the same article, in Marx's reference to the "Cuban savages" cited above. He finds this analogy apt because it relates to a wider analogy with religion in general which he uses to express the power of ideas or modes of thought over men's actions. "The representation of private interests", he asserts "abolishes all natural and spiritual distinctions by enthroning in their stead the immoral, irrational and soulless abstraction of a particular material object and a particular consciousness which is slavishly subordinated to this object". He rails against "this abject materialism, this sin against the holy spirit of the people and humanity" (Marx and Engels 1975a: 262).

In the article in the *Rheinische Zeitung*, Marx confronts the category of property, and takes his first steps towards a fuller and more rigorous analysis of all that property involves. "Felled wood is wood that has been worked on. The natural connection with property has been replaced by an artificial one. Therefore anyone who takes away felled wood takes away property. In the case of fallen wood, on the contrary, nothing has been separated from property. It is only what has already been separated from property that is being separated from it." His understanding of the significance of property may here be inchoate, but what is forcibly conveyed by the earlier passage quoted is Marx's realisation that concepts such as property determine man's world-view and hence his actions. Such a world-view is analogous to—indeed is perhaps no less than—a religion.

And one of the effects of such a religion is to imbue things with powers over men and over their thoughts.

In the course of his writing in the next two years, after the articles in the *Rheinische Zeitung* and before the *Economic and Philosophic Manuscripts*, Marx does not employ the term fetishism itself, but makes frequent use of the religious analogy—most notably in the discussion of private property and primogeniture in the *Critique of Hegel's Doctrine of the State*. For example:

> Primogeniture is private property *enchanted* by its own independence and splendour, and wholly immersed in itself; it is private property elevated to the status of a *religion*. (Marx and Engels 1975a: 169)

These works are discussed below. But first it is interesting to record where Marx first came across the term fetishism and to enquire why it appealed to him as a metaphor. This may shed some light on the question of what precisely he meant to convey by the word, at least at this early stage in his writings. It appears from the Bonn notebooks (Marx and Engels 1975b: 1011), that Marx first read de Brosses' *Du Culte des Dieux Fétiches* early in 1842, very shortly before the article by Herr Hermes appeared, and it might reasonably be assumed that this was where he first encountered the term. If this is so, it seems rather unjust of Marx to dismiss Herr Hermes with a contemptuous: "And now, indeed, fetishism! truly the erudition of a penny magazine" (Marx and Engels 1975a: 189). Perhaps he was piqued by this evidence of Hermes' knowledge. It is, however, possible that Marx had come across the term earlier—for example in Comte, Hegel or Feuerbach, or perhaps in his reading for his doctoral thesis. In fairness to Marx these alternatives may be briefly considered.

It is unlikely that Marx found the term in Comte. Marx refers in a letter to Engels in 1866 that he is "studying Comte on the side", and implies that this is the first time he has done so. Indeed, it is commonly assumed that this is the case. He could, however, have heard of Comte's work from other sources. Comte was secretary to Saint-Simon, to whose works Marx's father-in-law was much attached; and it has been suggested that Comte wrote some of the works which are attributed to Saint-Simon (Lichtheim 1971: 73).

Hegel uses the word, but rarely (e.g. in an early and obscure work *Religion ist Eine* written when he was twenty-three). Feuerbach may have used the term, for he certainly discusses the concept. He espoused a more conventional theory of the development of religion than that of Comte, postulating two stages, polytheism followed by monotheism. Thus Comte's "fetishism" stage is excluded; but Feuerbach refers, for example, to the fact that "Primitive peoples … deify *particular* mountains, fields and streams. They invest them with *manitous* or spirits—they worship them not as inanimate objects but as they appear in human fantasies and imagination" (quoted in Kamenka 1970: 44). Indeed his views on religion, which exerted considerable influence on Marx, are most redolent of the concept of fetishism:

> Feuerbach defined the religious phenomena as such, as the projection and hypostasis of some element of human experience into an object of worship. (Hook 1936: 221)

Although Marx's interest in anthropology did not develop until many years later, he certainly read widely in the field of religion in his student days, and we find in his Doctoral Dissertation from 1841:

> In this sense *all gods*, the pagan as well as the christian, have possessed a real existence. Did not the ancient Moloch reign? (Marx and Engels 1975a: 104)

This quotation appears to contain in it the seeds of his later writing on fetishism, and to anticipate the parallels he was to draw between religion and the economic system, even if the term itself is not used. It is possible that he came across the word in the course of these early researches into religion. It is less likely that he encountered it in the course of his more general reading. It is not easy to establish to what extent the word was in use at this time. Although Diderot made reference to it in his famous encyclopaedia, it did not appear in the French dictionary until 1835, despite the fact that it was a Frenchman who coined it. The *Encyclopaedia Britannica* of 1842 does not include the word, which first appears in the eighth edition (1855). Nor does it appear in the contemporary German dictionary, although this may be attributable to the reluctance of the brothers Grimm to include words of manifestly foreign origin.

In sum, the evidence is inconclusive, but suggests that Marx did indeed come across the term only months, or weeks, before it appeared in Herr Hermes' article.

Why, then, to turn to our second and more important question, did the term appeal so strongly to Marx? To answer this, let us consider in more detail the context of his own article on the debates on the theft of wood. It is evident from the tone as well as the content that Marx is outraged. The focus of this outrage is the Rhineland Assembly, and the dangers of allowing laws to be made by "an Assembly of the Estates of particular interests" (Marx and Engels 1975a: 262). More generally, the article is an attack on property—not so much the concept as such, but on the right of the property owners to decide upon the definition of the term and hence to cast innocent men into the category of criminals. "The representation of private interests … abolishes all natural and spiritual distinctions by enthroning in their stead the immoral, irrational and soulless abstraction of a particular material object and a particular consciousness which is slavishly subordinated to this object." In such a context, the fetish appears as a most apt analogy, for here the object is imbued with the power of religion. "The wooden idols triumph and human beings are sacrificed."

I suggest that it was the connotations of the fantastic in the word "fetish" which initially appealed to Marx. When he first refers to it, he says: "Fantasy arising from desire deceives the fetish-worshipper into believing that an inanimate object will give up its natural character". On the next occasion, he observes the capacity of European culture to be equally deceived by the fantastic: "The savages of Cuba regarded gold as the fetish of the Spaniards".

To put it simply, Marx developed an interest in political economy from a sense of outrage at the institution of private property. He had the unusual capacity to stand outside his own culture and view the categories of thought of that culture as an outsider—seeing them as analogous to a religion (much as Hatuey observed the Spaniards in Cuba). In this religion he observed the importance of the material object imbued with a fantastic power derived from the strange beliefs of the society in which it was found. This explains the significance of the term fetish in its first famous appearance. He employs it in later works; first quite loosely, and then, as I shall describe below, to convey richer, and somewhat different meanings. Throughout his writings, however, we encounter the metaphor of the "veil", the "mist", the deceptive appearance which, like religion, prevents one from perceiving reality.

If we look now at the wider context, the intellectual currents of thought at the time, we will see that it is perhaps not surprising that Marx should have adopted the analogy with primitive religion. This was a period of intense interest in religion, and in exotic peoples of the world. It was also, of course, a period in which reason, and more specifically science, seemed to be all-powerful. And these two facts are not independent; a fascination with the primitive and the irrational precisely complements a secure faith in the superiority of those furthest along the path of evolution, and the power of rationality. Within this very dichotomous worldview the concept of the social was beginning to emerge. Marx, as a representative of his time—combining a confidence in the power of science with an interest in primitive religion—found it appropriate to compare society with the latter.

It is consistent, but nevertheless interesting, that another very famous figure of sociology drew on a remarkably similar analogy, albeit much later. In the section titled "The Origins of Religion" in his *Economy and Society* Max Weber writes as follows:

> Not every stone can serve as a fetish, a source of magical power. Nor does every person have the capacity to achieve the ecstatic states which are viewed … as the preconditions for producing certain effects in meteorology, healing, divination and telepathy. It is primarily, though not exclusively, these extraordinary powers that have been designated by such special terms as "mana", "orenda" and the Iranian "maga". … We shall henceforth employ the term "charisma" for such extraordinary powers … a gift that inheres in an object or person simply by virtue of natural endowment … (or) produced artificially by some extraordinary means. (Weber 1968: 400)

It is well-known that Weber coined the term "charisma". Less well known is that this quality could, according to him, inhere also in an object. In origin, then, it was remarkably similar to Marx's fetish, although the similarity does not extend much beyond this. It is nevertheless significant that Weber, as well as Marx, should find it appropriate to invoke an analogy with primitive religion in discussing social phenomena.

I move now to the question of what, more precisely, Marx intended to convey by the term fetish. This requires a detailed examination of his subsequent writings, which is the task for the next chapter.

Bibliography

Aston, W. G. (1912). *Encyclopaedia of Religion and Ethics* (Vol. V, J. Hastings, Ed.). New York: Charles Scribner & Sons.

de Brosses, C. (1972), *Du Culte des Dieux Fetiches* (MDCCLX, repr. by Gregg Intl.). Farnborough.

Ellis, H. (1933). *The Psychology of Sex*. London: Heinemann.

Encyclopaedia Britannica. (1842). Edinburgh: Adam and Charles Black.

Encyclopaedia Britannica. (1855). Edinburgh: Adam and Charles Black.

Freud, S. (1927). Fetishism. In J. Strachey et al. (Eds.), *The Standard Edition of the Complete Psychological Works of Sigmund Freud* (Vol. XIII). London: Hogarth Press.

Freud, S. (1955). Totem and Taboo: Some Points of Agreement between the Mental Lives of Savages and Neurotics. In J. Strachey et al. (Eds.), *The Standard Edition of the Complete Psychological Works of Sigmund Freud* (Vol. XXI). London: Hogarth Press.

Herrera, A. (1730a). *Historia de las Indias Occidentales*.

Herrera, A. (1730b). *The General History of the Vast Continent and Islands of America, Commonly Called, the West Indies, from the First Discovery Thereof* (Vol. II, Decad I, Book IX, J. Stevens, Trans.). London.

Hook, S. (1936). *From Hegel to Marx: Studies in the Intellectual Development of Karl Marx*. London: Victor Gollancz.

Hume, D. (1956). *The Natural History of Religion*.

Ignatieff, M. (1984). *The Needs of Strangers*. London: Chatto and Windus.

Kamenka, E. (1970). *The Philosophy of Ludwig Feuerbach*.

von Krafft-Ebing, R. (1939). *Psychopathia Sexualis*. London.

Lichtheim, G. (1971). *From Marx to Hegel*. London: Orbach & Chambers.

Marett, R. R. (1932). *Encyclopaedia of the Social Sciences* (Vol. 6, E. Seligman, Ed.). New York.

Marx, K., & Engels, F. (1975a). *Collected Works* (Vol. 1). Moscow: Progress.
Marx, K., & Engels, F. (1975b). *The Marx-Engels-Gesamtausgabe* (MEGA[1]). Berlin.
Mill, J. S. (1866). *August Comte and Positivism.*
Tourneux, M. (Ed.). (1878). *Correspondance littéraire philosophique et critique par Grimm, Diderot, Raynal, Meister etc* (Vol. 4). Paris: Garnier.
Urbanek, E. (1969). Roles, Masks and Characters: A Contribution to Marx's Idea of the Social Role. In P. Berger (Ed.), *Marxism and Sociology: Views from Eastern Europe*. New York: Appleton-Century-Crofts.
Weber, M. (1968). *Economy and Society.*

3

The Development of the Concept over Time

this false appearance and illusion … this personification of things and conversion of production relations into entities, this religion of everyday life.
(Marx 1959: 830)

The term fetishism is used in a variety of meanings in Marx's writings. As I shall seek to show in later chapters it is only in the mature works, and most especially the first volume of *Capital*, that it attains its full, rich and relatively rigorous meaning. In order to distinguish between the word in its early usages, and this final, more rigorous one, I shall refer to the latter as the "concept" of fetishism, as opposed to the mere "word" fetishism, whose meaning varies somewhat over time.

I suggest that we may distinguish three separate stages in Marx's writings. In the first, the word fetishism is used, but the concept is only in an embryonic state. In the second stage, the concept is developing without the word. On the few occasions on which the word is used in this stage, its meaning varies and often differs from the concept. In the third and final stage, the word and the concept come together.

D. McNeill, *Fetishism and the Theory of Value*, Palgrave Studies in the History of Economic Thought, https://doi.org/10.1007/978-3-030-56123-9_3

A second type of shift may also be noted in the development of Marx's use of the term fetishism—from an emphasis on property to an emphasis on the social relations of production. This too will emerge from the extracts from Marx's works that follow.

The first stage of my simple threefold division, where the concept of fetishism is only embryonic, ended in 1842, with the publication of Marx's article just discussed. The only pertinent point to add, in presenting the development in the use of the term in parallel with the development of his ideas in general, is to note that Marx identifies this period as the start of his concern with economics. As he put it, the subjects of these early articles for the *Rheinische Zeitung* "provided the first occasions for occupying myself with economic questions" (quoted in McLellan 1973: 11).

The second stage, with which this chapter is mostly concerned, extends from 1843 to 1859. Here the concept is developing without the word. Perhaps the most significant point to note is Marx's frequent use of the analogy of religion, and his concern with the power of private property. His writings in this period will now be very briefly examined, to bring out these aspects of his work, and to record those few occasions on which the word fetishism itself is used. (Since the major works have been analysed at great length by other commentators, relatively greater emphasis will here be placed on the minor works.)

It should be added, by way of introduction, that in Marx's early writings of this period the influence of Hegel and Feuerbach is very evident: Marx's treatment of the inversion of subject and predicate, alienation, hypostasis and so on. These concepts are applied mainly to politics (as in his critique of Hegel's views on the State) and to religion (as in *The Jewish Question*). But there is some application of these ideas to economics also, as appears most evidently in his critique of Mill.

Critique of Hegel's Doctrine of the State (1843)

This work is of interest in the present context both for its subject matter and for its critical method. With regard to the former, the concern with private property evident in Marx's discussion of the theft of wood in the

Rheinische Zeitung is developed further in relation to Hegel's views on property and primogeniture, where Hegel himself draws a comparison with religion.

And the argument is laden with instances of inversion. The estates of noble families are seen as an unusual form of private property, for this form of wealth is "*inalienable, entailed* and burdened by *primogeniture*" (Marx 1975b: 164). But whereas Hegel attributes this to the "*power of the political state over private property*, it is in fact the *power of private property over the political state*" (Marx 1975b: 167).

Primogeniture is "*the superlative form of private property, private property supreme*". Private property is "fortified against the *wilfullness* of its owner". Being inalienable, the property of the nobility becomes, in Hegel's words, in the context of his discussion of civil law, its "substantive characteristic", "its personality as such, its universal freedom of will, its ethical life, its religion". Thus, primogeniture is "private property elevated to the status of a *religion*" (Marx 1975b: 168). Marx asserts that Hegel is wrong, therefore, to claim, in the course of his discussion of the transition from property to contract, that "I hold *property* not merely by *means of a thing and my subjective will*, but by means of another person's will as well and so hold it in virtue of my participation in a *common* will" (Marx 1975b: 170). It is private property which is all-powerful:

> In primogeniture the fact that property is held not in virtue of *participation in a common will*, but only 'by means of a *thing* and a *subjective will*' is made an integral part of the law of the land. (Marx 1975b: 170)

Primogeniture is by no means "a determination of private property by the state". This brings Marx to his attack on Hegel's central claim that "[t]he state is the reality of the ethical idea" and that self-consciousness finds in the state "its substantive freedom". As Marx observes:

> The *reality* of the ethical idea becomes manifest here as the *religion of private property*. … The 'substantial will *manifest* and revealed to itself' becomes transformed into a mysterious will broken on the soil. … 'The confidence that my interest as an individual … is *independent* of another's

> (i.e. the state's) interest and end.' This is the nature of my consciousness of my *freedom from the state.* (Marx 1975b: 171)

This early criticism of Hegel, as Colletti has rightly noted, provides a key for understanding Marx's criticism of the method of bourgeois economics. "The Hegelian philosophy is upside-down; it inverts reality, making predicates into subjects and real subjects into predicates. Certainly, but, Marx adds, the inversion does *not* originate in Hegel's philosophy itself. The mystification does not primarily concern the way in which this philosophy reflects reality, but *reality* itself" (Colletti's Introduction to Marx 1975b: 33). This foreshadows very clearly the emerging concept of fetishism, and its subtle distinction from mere mystification. Indeed Colletti traces its origins this far, in his discussion of the concept of property:

> Property ought to be a manifestation, an attribute, of man, but becomes the subject; man ought to be the real subject but becomes the property of private property. Here we find the subject-predicate inversion and, simultaneously, the formulation through which Marx begins to delineate the phenomenon of *fetishism* or alienation. (Colletti's Introduction to Marx 1975b: 37)

A Contribution to a Critique of Hegel's Philosophy of Right: Introduction (1843–1844)

One of the most famous of Marx's early writings, this contains seeds of much of his later work, and the often-quoted sentence: "*Man makes religion*, religion does not make man. … This state and society produce religion, which is an *inverted consciousness of the world*, because they are an inverted world" (Marx 1975b: 244). Similarly, one might argue, society "produces" economic categories, and the world itself is, in a sense, inverted. This analogy, however, will not be drawn for some years—and the word fetishism is not used here by Marx.

Excerpts from James Mill's Elements of Political Economy (1844)

It was after Marx moved to Paris in 1843 that he began his serious study of economics, of which the first major product was the *Paris Manuscripts*. His notes on Mill written during the same period, though not often accorded such importance, also merit discussion in the present context. The comments on money are particularly significant:

> The nature of money is … that the *mediating function* or movement, human, social activity … is *estranged* and becomes the property of a *material thing* external to man. … The relation between things, human dealings with them, become the operations of a being beyond and above man. (Marx 1975b: 260)

> (For) the mediating movement of man engaged in exchange is not a social, human movement, it is no *human relationship*: it is the *abstract relation* of private property to private property, and this abstract relation is the *value* which acquires a real existence as value only in the form of *money*. (Marx 1975b: 261)

Already here we can see the seeds of ideas that will blossom in *Capital Volume I,* though the word fetishism does not appear. Alienation, however, does enter the debate:

> Economics … begins with the *relations between men* as relations between property owners. … If I cede my property to another it ceases to be mine. … I thus alienate my private property. (Marx 1975b: 266)

But, as Marx notes, the man, as much as the property, is alienated. The thing then becomes the property of another. What unites the two people who exchange, says Marx, is a common need:

> The bond which unites the two owners is the *specific nature of the object* which constitutes their private property. … The longing for these two objects, the need for them, shows each owner … that he stands in another

essential relation to the objects than that of private property … and … his needs stand in an *inner* relation to the products of labour of others. (Marx 1975b: 267)

The unifying bond that Marx here stresses is that of need; and this is manifested through exchange. "Thus *exchange* or *barter* is the social species-activity." Yet this is within private property, and "for that reason it is the external, *alienated* species-activity … the very antithesis of a *social* relationship" (Marx 1975b: 267). Thus, at this stage in his writings, exchange and shared needs are emphasised, rather than production and labour. Yet property is identified as the product of labour, and production at once enters the picture:

Private property itself comes into the category of *alienated* private property. For (1) it has ceased to be the produce of the labour and the exclusive, distinguishing personality of its owner, … (2) It has been related to and equated with other private property. … Its immediate identity with itself has given way to a relation to *another*. As an *equivalent* its existence is no longer peculiar to it. It thus becomes a *value*, in fact an immediate *exchange value*. (Marx 1975b: 267)

Although Marx defers discussion of this massive topic ("The problem of defining this *value* more precisely … must be dealt with elsewhere") he nevertheless provides some important insights, including reference to the central role played by money:

The reciprocal complementing and exchange of human activity itself appears in the form of: the *division of labour*. This makes man … an abstract being. … The individual no longer exchanges his surplus. … He no longer exchanges his product for something he *needs*. His equivalent now acquires its own existence as money. … In money the unfettered dominion of the estranged thing *over* man becomes manifest. The rule of the person over the person now becomes the universal rule of the *thing* over the *person*, the product over the producer. Just as the *equivalent*, value, contained the determination of the alienation of private property, so now we see that *money* is the sensuous, corporeal existence of that alienation. (Marx 1975b: 269, 270)

Economic and Philosophic Manuscripts of 1844

This is Marx's first major foray into the field of economics, but its importance for most commentators has been in its exposition of Marx's views on man, and most notably the important concept of alienation. The link between alienation and fetishism is close—as is already evident from Marx's comments on James Mill—and in some commentators the two are blurred. I will not attempt to define the distinction at this stage (the issue will be addressed in later chapters). Rather, I will begin by noting Marx's further shift in emphasis, from property to labour; and then simply examine his three explicit uses of the word fetishism, which serve to demonstrate, I suggest, that Marx's use of the term at this stage in his writings was far from its final meaning in *Capital*.

In the first manuscript, "Wages of Labour", Marx describes the various forms of man's alienation—from his product, from his productive activity, from his species-being, and from other men. Labour is clearly seen as the key to man's species-being: "It is just in his work upon the objective world, therefore, that man really proves himself to be a *species-being*" (Marx 1977: 74).

But Marx also notes the failure of political economy to explain private property, its starting premise. The economist (like the theologian) "assumes in the form of a fact … what he is supposed to deduce" (Marx 1977: 67).

> *Private property* is … the product, the result, the necessary consequence of *alienated labour*. … True, it is as a result of the *movement of private property* that we have obtained the concept of *alienated labour* … in political economy. But analysis … shows that though private property appears to be the reason, the cause of alienated labour, it is rather its consequence. (Marx 1977: 77)

Political economy has merely formulated the laws of estranged labour.[1] And it is estranged labour which gives rise to private property. Thus there

[1] An important point, that Arthur stresses, is that in the *1844 Manuscripts*, Marx uses the term "labour" to refer to alienated or estranged labour, not labour in its wider sense (Arthur 1986). (See Chap. 7.)

is here a further crucial shift. Marx finds alienated labour as the basis of private property. The word fetishism was first related by Marx to property; in his later works, it was related rather to labour. In this intermediate stage, however, the word is used somewhat differently. All the instances occur in the Third Manuscript titled "Private Property and Labour".

Marx praises the political economy of Adam Smith which recognised that the essence of private property is labour; and he contrasts Smith with "the adherents of the monetary and mercantile system, who look upon private property as an objective substance confronting men, (and) seem therefore to be *fetishists, Catholics*" (Marx 1977: 89).

The reference to Catholics draws on the analogy between Luther and Adam Smith, which Marx develops:

> Just as he (Luther) superseded *external* religiosity by making religiosity the *inner* substance of man … so wealth as something outside man and independent of him … is done away with. (Marx 1977: 89)

Marx is here criticising the erroneous view of the mercantilists identified by many subsequent historians of economic thought—"that wealth consists in money, or in gold and silver" (Smith's *Wealth of Nations*, quoted in Roll 1973: 64). The doctrine of the Physiocrats, who according to Marx effected the transition to Adam Smith, differed little from mercantilism, except that the language "is no longer feudal but economic. All wealth is resolved into *land* and *agriculture*. The land is not yet *capital* … but land is a universal natural *element*, whereas the mercantile system considered that wealth existed only in *precious metals*." Thus:

> The land is here still recognised as a phenomenon of nature independent of man—not yet as capital, i.e., as an aspect of labour itself. Labour appears, rather, as an aspect of *the land*. But since the *fetishism* (my stress) of the old external wealth, of wealth existing only as an object, has been reduced to a very simple natural element … the necessary step forward has been made in revealing the *general nature* of wealth and hence in the raising of *labour* in its total absoluteness (i.e., its abstraction) as the *principle*. (Marx 1977: 92)

The Physiocrats had made progress, but had still not taken the final step, of Adam Smith, to recognise that agriculture is merely one form of economic activity—one application of labour.

The third use of the word in the *1844 Manuscripts* again refers to mercantilism, in its crudest form, for Marx refers to "those nations which are still dazzled by the sensuous glitter of precious metals and therefore make a fetish of metal money", describing them as "not yet fully developed money-nations" (Marx 1977: 116). The passage continues with the claim that true practice is the condition for a "real and positive theory", which introduces an interesting reference to fetishism that implies that for the fetishist "reality" is, in some sense, actually different:

> The sensuous consciousness of the fetish-worshipper is different from that of the Greek, because his sensuous existence is different. The abstract enmity between sense and spirit is necessary so long as the human feeling for nature, the human sense of nature and therefore also the *natura*l sense of *man*, are not yet produced by man's own labour. (Marx 1977: 116)

The Holy Family (1844)

In the context of the present discussion, *The Holy Family* has little to contribute. Marx again castigates political economy for recognising the essential determinants of human activity "only in an estranged, alienated form" (Marx and Engels 1975: 50) and for taking private property for granted, and he commends Proudhon for making "the first resolute, ruthless, and at the same time scientific investigation" of property (Marx and Engels (1975: 32). The work is also of interest insofar as it indicates Marx's antipathy towards the excesses of Hegel (or, more accurately, his followers) apparently more concerned with ideas than real life. As Marx most succinctly puts it: "But not having is not a mere category, it is a most dismal reality" (Marx and Engels 1975: 42).

Theses on Feuerbach (1845)

The last of the Theses is perhaps the most famous—rejecting the role of the philosopher as mere "interpreter" of the world; and the emphasis throughout is on revolutionary practice. More relevant to the current discussion, however, is Marx's emphasis on the social. Feuerbach's failure to understand religion is akin to the errors of political economy:

> Feuerbach resolves the religious essence into the *human* essence. But the human essence is no abstraction inherent in each individual. In its reality it is the ensemble of the social relations. … (He) does not see that the 'religious sentiment' is itself a social product, and that the abstract individual whom he analyses belongs to a particular form of society. (Marx and Engels 1975: 122)

The German Ideology (1846)

In *The German Ideology*, also, the word "fetish" is not used, but the subject matter closely relates, in places, to the emerging concept. For example:

> The production of ideas, of conceptions, of consciousness, is at first directly interwoven with the material activity and the material intercourse of men, the language of real life. Conceiving, thinking, the mental intercourse of men, appear at this stage as the direct efflux of their material behaviour. … If in all ideology men and their circumstances appear upside-down as in a *camera obscura*, this phenomenon arises just as much from their historical life-process as the inversion of objects on the retina does from their physical life-process. (Marx and Engels 1974: 47)

In addition, the analysis of private property is further developed, and its link with the division of labour:

> Division of labour and private property are, moreover, identical expressions: in the one the same thing is affirmed with reference to activity as is affirmed in the other with reference to the product of the activity. (Marx and Engels 1974: 53)

Marx's Letter to Annenkov (December 28, 1846)

The significance of this letter is that it contains Marx's first criticisms of Proudhon, which are later to take fuller form in *The Poverty of Philosophy*. (The letter is also often cited because of its references to historical materialism.) Marx distinguishes between material reality, and the transitory social context:

> The machine is no more an economic category than the ox which draws the plough. The contemporary *use* of machinery is one of the relations of our present economic system. (Marx 1975a: 170)

And he criticises Proudhon for failing to see that the politico-economic categories are "abstract expressions of the real, transitory, historic social relations" and instead, "owing to a mystic inversion, regard(ing) real relations merely as reifications of these abstractions" (Marx 1975a: 172).

> M. Proudhon ... has not grasped that, in accordance with their productive forces, these men also produce the *social relations* amid which they manufacture cloth and linen. Still less has he understood that men ... also produce *ideas, categories*, that is to say the abstract ideal expression of these same social relations. Thus the categories are no more eternal than the relations they express. They are historical and transitory products. (Marx 1975a: 174)

As a result Proudhon sees the categories as the motive force, and erroneously believes that "one must change the categories and the consequence will be a change in the existing society" (Marx 1975a: 176).

The Poverty of Philosophy (1847)

The Poverty of Philosophy: Answer to the "Philosophy of Poverty" by M. Proudhon was, to quote from Engels' Preface to the First German Edition, "produced in the winter of 1846–1847, at a time when Marx had cleared up for himself the basic features of his new historical and economic outlook" (Marx 1975a: 9). It represents another important stage in the gradual crystallisation of Marx's ideas on the theory of value, and the methodology of economics. Indeed, it is, in McLellan's words "Marx's first comprehensive statement on economics" which, together with *The Communist Manifesto*, Marx recommended as an introduction to *Capital* (McLellan 1980: 41).

It begins with a critique of Proudhon on value, based in part on Proudhon's misguided starting point of individual man. Marx develops the labour theory of value, noting how labour is itself a commodity, and moves on to money, and thence to "the surplus left by labour". Many of the ideas in *Capital* are already evident here. The second part, "The Metaphysics of Political Economy", and particularly its first section "The Method" is more Hegelian, and is concerned with the genesis of the economic categories, and how they relate to the social relations of production. The work in general, and this section in particular, are of interest in the context of fetishism, for many of the ideas which are central to the concept are discussed here. And yet the word itself never appears.

Grundrisse (1858)

After the five-year period 1842–1847, extending from the first articles in the *Rheinische Zeitung* to *The Poverty of Philosophy*, there followed a period of ten years in which Marx's efforts were devoted mainly to political action and writing, for 1848 was the year of the *Communist Manifesto* and the revolution in Paris.

His next major work on economics was the *Grundrisse*. The ideas presented here were in many ways the same as those in *Capital*, discussed in detail in the chapters that follow, although the form of presentation was very different. To avoid undue repetition, therefore, comments on this work are here kept to a minimum.

The discussion on money is especially relevant. Marx portrays capitalist society as alienated, with individuals existing as owners of money, linked only through exchange-value:

> The reciprocal and all-sided dependence of individuals who are indifferent to one another forms their social connection. This social bond is expressed in *exchange value*. … The power which each individual exercises over the activity of others … exists in him as the owner of *exchange values* of *money*. (Marx 1973: 157)

And this relates to what Marx was later to refer to as fetishism[2]:

> The general exchange of activities and products, which has become a vital condition for each individual—their mutual interconnection—here appears as something alien to them, autonomous, as a thing. In exchange value, the social connection between persons is transformed into a social relation between things; personal capacity into objective wealth. (Marx 1973: 157)

But in this work Marx uses the word fetishism only in the context of his discussion of capital.[3] And in the passage that follows, as in his letter to Annenkov quoted above, he is concerned with the confusion between the physical properties of a thing and the social setting which determines how it is categorised in economic terms. More specifically, the issue is what determines whether or not something is fixed capital. Having noted that a house can serve for production as well as for consumption he quotes Ricardo:

> According to this, a coffee-pot would be fixed capital, but coffee circulating capital. The crude materialism of the economists who regard as the *natural properties* of things what are social relations of production among people, and qualities which things obtain because they are subsumed under these relations, is at the same time just as crude an idealism, even fetishism, since it imputes social relations to things as inherent characteristics, and thus mystifies them. (Marx 1973: 687)

---

[2] In this case he blurs the distinction between a thing and a relation between things. See Chap. 4 for discussion of this point.

[3] I exclude here a passing reference in Marx's comment on Bastiat and Carey: "The direct transition from the African's fetish to Voltaire's supreme being, or from the hunting gear of a North American savage to the capital of the Bank of England, is not so absurdly contrary to history as is the transition from Bastiat's fisherman to the wage labourer" (Marx 1973: 891).

Marx himself seems somewhat unsure whether the word fetishism is appropriate here; but it is clear that he associates it with mystification, and with attributing characteristics to things which are not in fact inherent to them.

A Contribution to the Critique of Political Economy (1859)

In this work, Marx uses the word "fetish" only once, in what may be interpreted as an example of the simple "fetishism of wealth":

> Nature no more produces money than it does bankers or a rate of exchange. But since in bourgeois production, wealth as a fetish must be crystallised in a particular substance, gold and silver are its appropriate embodiment. (Marx 1970: 155)

Despite this, the *Contribution* marks the transition to what I have classified as the third stage in the development of fetishism, for in this book (as indeed in the *Grundrisse*) we find the concept very well elaborated, for example:

> Only the conventions of our everyday life make it appear commonplace and ordinary that social relations of production should assume the shape of things,[4] so that the relations into which people enter in the course of their work appear as the relations of things to one another and of things to people. This mystification is still a very simple one in the case of a commodity. … As soon as the modern economists, who sneer at the illusions of the Monetary System, deal with the more complex economic categories, such as capital, they display the same illusions … the phenomenon they have just described as a thing reappears as a social relation and, a moment later, having been defined as a social relation, teases them once more as a thing. (Marx 1970: 34–35)

[4] See note 2 above.

This very rapid review of Marx's works up to 1859 brings us to what I have called the third stage in the development of his use of the word fetishism. The most important references here are to be found in *Capital Volume I*, on commodity fetishism, and in *Capital Volume III* and *Theories of Surplus Value Part III*—Marx's critique of bourgeois economic categories, the Trinity Formula, and especially the fetishism of interest-bearing capital.[5]

As will become apparent in the following chapters, commodity fetishism is in an important sense different from the other forms—and especially the 'highest' form, the fetishism of interest-bearing capital. Commodity fetishism is both more complex and more basic; it stands at the very starting point of the whole process—where value takes the form of exchange-value.

Bibliography

Arthur, C. (1986). *Dialectics of Labour: Marx and his Relation to Hegel*. Oxford: Blackwell.

Marx, K. (1959). *Capital* (Vol. III). Progress: Moscow.

Marx, K. (1970). *A Contribution to the Critique of Political Economy*. Moscow: Progress.

Marx, K. (1973). *Grundrisse*. Harmondsworth: Penguin.

Marx, K. (1975a). *The Poverty of Philosophy*. Moscow: Progress.

Marx, K. (1975b). *Early Writings*. Harmondsworth: Penguin.

Marx, K. (1977). *Economic and Philosophic Manuscripts of 1844*. Moscow: Progress.

Marx, K., & Engels, F. (1974). *The German Ideology* (C. J. Arthur, ed.). London: Lawrence and Wishart.

Marx, K., & Engels, F. (1975). *Collected Works* (Vol. 4). Moscow: Progress.

McLellan, D. (1973). *Karl Marx, His Life and Thought*. London: Macmillan.

McLellan, D. (1980). *The Thought of Karl Marx: An Introduction*. London: Macmillan.

Roll, E. (1973). *A History of Economic Thought*. London: Faber & Faber.

[5] There are also a few other references to fetishism where Marx reverts to his earlier, more straightforward use of the word fetish.

4

Fetishism: A Preliminary Exegesis

There (with commodities) it is a definite social relation between men, that assumes, in their eyes, the fantastic form of a relation between things. In order, therefore, to find an analogy, we must have recourse to the mist-enveloped regions of the religious world. In that world the productions of the human brain appear as independent beings endowed with life, and entering into relation both with one another and with the human race. So it is in the world of commodities with the products of men's hands. This I call the Fetishism which attaches itself to the products of labour, so soon as they are produced as commodities, and which is therefore inseparable from the production of commodities.

(Marx 1954: 77)

In this chapter, which concludes the first section of the book, I will give a preliminary exegesis of the concept of fetishism, based on the famous quotation on commodity fetishism just quoted. I begin, however, with a brief review of what others have written about fetishism. Marxian

This is a revised version of a chapter in McNeill, D (1988) *Fetishism and the Form of Value*. Unpublished thesis, University of London.

D. McNeill, *Fetishism and the Theory of Value*, Palgrave Studies in the History of Economic Thought, https://doi.org/10.1007/978-3-030-56123-9_4

economists have usually devoted rather little attention to this concept and its significance in Marx's work.[1] There are a number of reasons for this; perhaps the most important is that it is widely regarded as belonging to the realms of philosophy or sociology—not economics proper. Economists do not understand fetishism largely because they do not see it as necessary to try. As I shall seek to show, the concept of fetishism is in fact of central importance to Marx's economics—to an adequate appreciation of *Capital* and his theory of value. It deserves to be given a central place not merely in philosophy or sociology, but in economics too.

It is appropriate to begin my review of other writers with Lukács, sometimes described as the founder of Western Marxism, and his seminal essay on reification. By this he meant what Marx referred to as fetishism.[2] He argues that the commodity is the "universal structuring principle" and that the essence of commodity-structure is "that a relation between people takes on the character of a thing" (Lukács 1968: 83). Thus Lukács certainly cannot be accused of underestimating the importance of fetishism. More important, however, is the fact that he does not approach the subject as an economist, and indeed specifically excludes the economic from consideration:

> It is beyond the scope of this essay to discuss the central importance of this problem for economics itself. Nor shall we consider its implications for the economic doctrines of the vulgar Marxists which follow from their abandonment of this starting-point. (Lukács 1968: 84)[3]

Paul Sweezy, in *The Theory of Capitalist Development*, pays tribute to Lukács as one who "has developed and applied the doctrine of Fetishism

[1] I limit myself here to economists writing in—or translated into—English.

[2] The title of this essay, in the volume *History and Class Consciousness*, was "Reification and the Consciousness of the Proletariat". Lukács quotes the famous passage on commodity fetishism from Chapter 1 of *Capital*, but prefaces it with the words "Marx describes the basic phenomenon of reification as follows: …" (Lukács 1968: 86).

[3] Lukács is a rather controversial figure. His *History and Class Consciousness* is described by Stedman Jones as "the first major irruption of the romantic anti-scientific tradition of bourgeois thought into Marxist theory" but also as "brilliant and persuasive" (Stedman Jones 1971: 34). Lukács' lack of concern for economics is common to all Western Marxism, according to Merquior who portrays it as "a set of philosophical writings seldom engaging in sociological, let alone economic, issues" (Merquior 1986: 44).

probably as skilfully and successfully as any Marxist writer" (Sweezy 1968: 36). And Sweezy himself does contribute to economists' understanding of the concept through his elaboration of the "qualitative" (as opposed to the "quantitative") aspect of Marx's theory of value, which "with its corollary in the doctrine of Commodity Fetishism is the essential first step in the Marxian analysis of capitalism" (Sweezy 1968: 40).

Dobb, also, accords importance not only to the quantitative aspect of Marx's theory of value (see, e.g., his Introduction to *A Contribution to the Critique of Political Economy*, 1978: 11). But he describes fetishism as "an important element in Marx's theory of ideology" (Dobb 1972: 132), rather than an integral part of his economic analysis. Indeed, a perceptive reviewer of *Political Economy and Capitalism*, writing in 1938, criticises Dobb for his undue emphasis on the quantitative aspect of Marx's value theory (Lowe 1938).

Sweezy rightly asserted that "the doctrine of Fetishism has implications which transcend the conventional limits of economics and economic thinking" (Sweezy 1968: 40). The section of *Capital* entitled "Fetishism of Commodities and the Secret Thereof" has been justifiably described as "brilliant, and, for the uninitiated, correspondingly difficult" (Korsch 1971: 55). Perhaps it is for this reason that standard texts tend to treat it as somewhat peripheral to Marx's economics.[4]

Yet it is often recognised as a crucial element in Marx—at least by those with a wider perspective. Thus, McLellan (1980: 121) suggests that the notion "that relations between people have been replaced by relations between things" may be said to be one of *Capital*'s basic themes; and Fine (1975: 25) refers to Marx's "brilliant parallel between commodity fetishism and religious devotion". Despite this, the theory of fetishism is not integrated into Marx's theory of value in economic terms.

In treating the matter historically it is important to note that some of Marx's early works—particularly the *1844 Manuscripts* and the *Grundrisse*—came to light much later than other works, and were not

[4] Howard and King (1975) are something of an exception to this rule. Junankar (1982) discusses the issue, but does not integrate it into Marx's economic theory. Brewer goes so far as to introduce his discussion of commodity fetishism with the words "Marx next turns to a quite different question" (Brewer 1984: 26). Desai does not, in his major work, appear to regard fetishism as central (Desai 1979), but he perhaps modified this view somewhat (Desai 1986).

immediately translated into English.[5] The former resulted in numerous works on the subject of alienation. Perhaps it was some of these that influenced major Marxist commentators to reconsider their position.

Thus Colletti, for example:

> On reading and re-reading *Capital*, especially the first sections which on Marx's own admission are the most difficult (if not downright esoteric), it began to dawn on me that the theory of value was entirely at one with the theory of alienation and fetishism. (Colletti 1975: 20)

And Meek, when invited to reissue his *Studies in the Labour Theory of Value* added an Introduction in which he remarks that

> Marx's use of the concept of alienation in some of the passages which Mr. McLellan has translated from the *Grundrisse* is very interesting indeed; and in the light of these passages I would certainly wish, were I rewriting my book today, to amend and expand. (Meek 1973: xi)

He goes on to make an important distinction between different types of alienation and between different types of fetishism, indicating a more sophisticated understanding of the issues than is contained in the original version of his book. But he does not elaborate on these further; and they do not appear to have been taken up by other Marxian economists.

Other writers have noted the importance of alienation, but primarily from the perspective of sociology, for example Fromm (1961), or philosophy, for example Arthur (1986), or some combination of the two, for example Ollmann (1976) and Mészaros (1970). The treatment of alienation in such works is complex and sophisticated; but fetishism receives a far more cursory discussion. And in his major work, devoted more to Marx's economics, Rosdolsky (1980) fails to recognise any distinction between the two (as noted in Mepham 1979).

Those who do accord significance to fetishism are often those who attach importance to Hegel, and his influence on Marx. Apart from

[5] As indicated above, the present discussion is limited to works written in, or translated into, the English language. Rubin, discussed below, makes reference to a number of Russian and German writings on fetishism which are not covered in this brief summary.

Lukács and Korsch, already mentioned, another example is provided by Hook (1936), although he associates the concept of fetishism more directly with Feuerbach. One of Hegel's strongest critics has been Althusser; it is perhaps not surprising, therefore, that he does not simply pass over the theory of fetishism, but is positively critical, referring to it as "a last trace of Hegelian influence, this time a flagrant and extremely harmful one" (Althusser 1971: 91).[6]

Elster, too, from a very different perspective, has been critical, referring to it as a "strained notion, with no interesting sociological implications" (Elster 1980: 23). But he subsequently grants it some significance—albeit in psychological rather than social terms (Elster 1985: 95–99).

Neither of these last two writers, however, refers to the work of Rubin, who has surely devoted more attention than any other Marxian commentator to the concept of fetishism, and its central importance not simply to Marx's sociological analysis, but to his economics too. Although *Essays on Marx's Theory of Value* was published in Russian in 1928 (third edition) it was not published in English until 1972. Some recent writers, however, have benefitted from this important book. Sayer, for example (1983), acknowledges his debt, especially in dealing with the issue of abstract labour. And Pilling (1980) is equally complimentary about this work, particularly in relation to fetishism.

One of the most rigorous discussions of fetishism is to be found in Cohen (1978) who accords considerable significance to the concept. He, however, sees no significant difference between commodity fetishism and other forms. Before elaborating on this observation, which serves as the starting point of Section II, I will conclude this section with my own preliminary exegesis of the concept. For this purpose I return to the quotation from the first volume of *Capital* cited at the beginning of this chapter ("There [with commodities] it is a definite social relation").

[6] Althusser, of course, was also responsible for initiating the somewhat arid debate about the "young" and the "mature" Marx. It is evident—as I shall seek to show—that the concept of alienation remained of great importance in *Capital*, and indeed informs Marx's understanding of the theory of value. In this summary of works by other writers, mention should also be made of a short, but often-quoted article by Geras (1971) "Essence and Appearance: Aspects of Fetishism in Marx's *Capital*", which, inter alia, contains a good critique of Althusser.

The analogy between the commodity and the religious fetish is that in both cases the power of the thing appears to be inherent in the thing itself. A commodity has exchange-value only by virtue of the context within which it is set—just as a religious fetish does not have power autonomously, but only by virtue of the beliefs and practices of those who treat the object as a fetish.

This, in brief, is the concept of fetishism. But its meaning in Marx is, I suggest, rather more complex. To demonstrate this, I will extract the central core of the idea from the foregoing quotation, and then examine it in detail—part by part, and also as a whole. Thus I shall give a gloss on each word or phrase in turn, leaving to the last, however, the critical linking phrase "assumes the fantastic form of", which effectively integrates the parts into a whole.

The core of the definition is that commodity fetishism occurs where a "social relation between men … assumes the fantastic form of a relation between things".

Thus, in summary, my exposition is divided into five sections:

1. "social"
2. "relation"
3. "social relation between men"
4. "relation between things"
5. "assumes the fantastic form of"

1. Social

Marx's analysis differs from that of most other economists (and particularly those whom he labelled "vulgar economists") in stressing the social, in contradistinction to the natural, the material, the ahistorical:

> Individuals producing in a society … is of course the point of departure. The solitary and isolated hunter or fisherman, who serves Adam Smith and Ricardo as a starting-point, is one of the unimaginative fantasies of eighteenth-century romances *à la* Robinson Crusoe. … Man is a zoon

politikon in the most literal sense: he is not only a social animal, but an animal that can be individualised only within society. (Marx 1970a: 188)

Economics is about people in society. The individual cannot be divorced from the social context for the purposes of study. And the society can and does change over time. This is not to ignore the material in economics, or the validity of natural laws; but as Marx put it:

> Every child knows that the volume of products corresponding to the various needs calls for various and quantitatively determined amounts of social labour. … Natural laws can never be negated. Only the *form* in which those laws are applied can be altered in historically different situations. (Letter to Kugelmann. Marx and Engels 1983: 148))

Thus economics is not simply concerned with the physiological survival of man; and economics cannot be studied merely in material terms. The social is manifest most clearly in labour, which is of significance not only in its material aspect:

> From the moment that men in any way work for one another, their labour assumes a social form. (Marx 1954: 76)

It was in recognising the importance of the *social* aspect of labour that Marx most effectively distinguished his theory of value from that of Ricardo. He thus emphasised not simply the quantitative but (more importantly in the context of this book) the qualitative aspect of value.

This is not to say that the material is of no significance for Marx; quite the reverse. One of his most famous quotes, which begins by reiterating the point just established, about the relation between the economic and the social, goes on to stress the dominant importance of the material in determining the social.

> The mode of production of material life conditions the general process of social, political and intellectual life. (Marx 1970b: 20)

But economics can never exclude the social. It must be concerned with things and people set in a social context, and not comprehensible except in social terms. But the context may vary over time and space—with the capitalist mode of production only one of several possible modes. (According to Marx, of course, changes in the mode of production arise precisely from interaction between the material and the social—from contradiction between the forces and relations of production.)

Although the social is conceptually distinct from the material, the two seem to be almost inextricably intertwined. Thus, to give a purely material description of any phenomenon involving persons turns out to be extremely difficult—as Winch (1958) and numerous social scientists and philosophers have pointed out. Any attempt to provide what Ryle has called "thin" as opposed to "thick" descriptions of events proves extremely difficult:

> Consider, he says, two boys rapidly contracting the eyelids of their right eyes. In one, this is an involuntary twitch; in the other, a conspiratorial signal to a friend. The two movements are, as movements, identical. … Yet the difference, however unphotographable, between a twitch and a wink is vast. … Contracting your eyelids on purpose when there exists a public code in which so doing counts as a conspiratorial signal is winking. That's all there is to it: a speck of behaviour, a fleck of culture, and—voilà—a gesture. (Geertz 1975: 6)

In dealing with the complex phenomena of economics, we are confronted with more than "a fleck of culture", and the problem is correspondingly more intractable. Marx's intention was to concentrate on the social, and to analyse the capitalist system as a social phenomenon. His starting-point in *Capital* was the commodity—a material thing set in a social context. To understand the significance of this approach, it is helpful to consider an analogy which I take from Cohen:

> The term 'commodity' denotes use-values in virtue of a status they sometimes assume. It is thus far comparable to the term 'chairman', which denotes persons in virtue of a status persons sometimes assume. The

> application of 'chairman' presupposes that social relations of a certain type obtain. (Cohen 1978: 346)

How, and to what extent, can phenomena be described independently of their social context? Can we envisage a complete "socio-neutral" description of a society? It may be conceptually possible to distinguish the "purely" material from the social context. But it is extremely difficult, and it can be dangerously misleading.[7] The methodological problems inherent in such an exercise account, in part, for the complexity of *Capital*, and especially its first chapter. A commodity is a thing set in a definite social context. More specifically it is a use-value in a capitalist system. A coat is a use-value in any social system; under capitalism it is a commodity. There are numerous other examples, such as that cited by Marx in *Wage Labour and Capital*:

> A cotton-spinning jenny is a machine for spinning cotton. It becomes *capital* only in certain relations. Torn from these relationships it is no more capital than gold in itself is *money*. (Marx and Engels 1968)

Thus the social may be seen as a system of relations within which the material is located, and from which it cannot be torn with impunity. Indeed, this is an enlightening way of analysing social phenomena and the concept of fetishism, as may be shown by moving on to the second part of this exegesis.

---

[7] Cohen, who proposes the term "socio-neutral" categories, suggests a possible criterion according to which the social and the material might be distinguished: "A description is social if and only if it entails an ascription to persons—specified or unspecified—of rights or powers vis-à-vis other men" (Cohen 1978: 94). "Rights or powers" seem a rather narrow interpretation of the range of potential social relations between persons. This he perhaps also feels, for he goes on to suggest that we may envisage a complete "socio-neutral" description of a society in which "ownership patterns, distribution of rights and duties, social roles, will go unremarked" (Cohen 1978: 94).

Sayer, in discussing the same issue, proposes the term "transhistorical categories" (Sayer 1983), that is categories which are not dependent on a specific social context, at a given time in history, but may be applied in all modes of production. Thus, he argues, labour is a transhistorical category, but wage-labour is not, and, of course, a use-value is a transhistorical category, but exchange-value is not. This choice of terminology also has its merits, but draws attention more immediately to the ahistorical rather than the asocial nature of "bourgeois" categories.

2. Relation

As the foregoing suggests, the social is best conceptualised in terms of relations. That is, a social entity exists by virtue of the relations in which it stands to other entities. Thus, an emphasis on the social as opposed to the material necessarily also involves an emphasis on relations as opposed to entities. Indeed Marx defines society in such terms:

> For the aggregate of these relations, in which the agents of this production stand with respect to Nature and to one another, and in which they produce, is precisely society, considered from the standpoint of its economic structure. (Marx 1959: 818)

And again:

> Society does not consist of individuals, but expresses the sum of interrelations, the relations within which these individuals stand. … To be a slave, to be a citizen, are social characteristics, relations between human beings. … Human being A, as such, is not a slave. He is a slave in and through society. (Marx 1973: 265)

This emphasis on relations, in Marx's works, may justifiably be claimed as one of his major methodological strengths. Before going on to elaborate on this point, however, it should be noted that this relation/entity distinction is important to the concept of fetishism only indirectly. It might appear, from some of Marx's uses of the term, that fetishism involves, inter alia, treating a relation as if it were an entity; for example:

> The modern economists … display the same illusions … the phenomenon they have just described as a thing reappears as a social relation and, a moment later, having been defined as a social relation, teases them once more as a thing. (Marx 1970b: 4)

And

> First we have the use-value *land*, which has no value, and the exchange-value *rent*; so that a social relation conceived as a thing is made proportional to nature. (Marx 1959: 817)

There is, on the basis of such passages (and others already cited in Chap. 3), a case for arguing that the phenomenon of fetishism involves, or can involve, treating what is in fact a relation as if it were a thing. But Marx charged Samuel Bailey with fetishism, although he conceded that Bailey was very aware of the relational concept of value (Marx 1971: 147). Bailey's crime was a failure to see that value is a relation between persons (see Chap. 6).

I shall, therefore, adhere to the formulation of fetishism contained in Chapter 1 of *Capital*, that a relation between men is treated as a *relation* between things, not merely as a *thing*. This is not, of course, to belittle the importance of the relation/entity distinction, or its significance in Marx's works.

Among those who have stressed the importance of relations in Marx's work, perhaps the most notable is Ollmann who argues that Marx's whole approach is "relational":

> The relation is the irreducible minimum for all units in Marx's conception of social reality. This is really the nub of our difficulty in understanding Marxism, whose subject matter is not simply society but society conceived of 'relationally'. Capital, labour, value, commodity, etc., are all grasped as relations, containing in themselves, as integral elements of what they are, those parts with which we tend to see them externally tied. (Ollmann 1976: 14)

Ollmann distinguishes two different senses in which Marx uses the term relation. "First, to refer to the factor itself, as when I call capital a relation, and also as a synonym of 'connection', as in speaking of the relation between different factors" (Ollmann 1976: 15). Marx does indeed use the term "relation" in (at least) two different ways. But Ollmann's resolution of the problem (to use the terms "relation" and "Relation" to distinguish the two meanings) is not fully satisfactory. A better approach is that of Cohen, who rightly notes that:

> X … cannot be *both* (i) a relation between y … and z … *and* (ii) what y is in virtue of its relation to z. (Cohen 1978: 90)

To clarify the argument, he introduces the concept of a relational property:

> A husband is a man related by marriage to a woman: he is not also a relationship of marriage. Being a husband is a property of that man, one he has in virtue of that relationship, and commonly styled a *relational property*. (Cohen 1978: 90)

In summary, the sorts of entities with which economics has to deal are entities which have certain relational properties. These are properties which the entities possess, but they possess them only by virtue of the social context within which they are set. Analysing relations rather than entities involves a huge increase in complexity. But this seems to be unavoidable if an adequate critique of economics is to be achieved. As Engels put it in his introduction to Marx 1970b:

> One should not ride cart-horses if one intends to go coursing over the very rough ground of abstract reasoning. (Marx 1970b: 223)

3. Social Relation Between Men

Relations between persons could be material or social. An example of the former would be where two men are carrying a table. But where relations are social, the persons concerned are not simply individual entities—flesh and blood—but rather they are persons who occupy a particular place in a social context. In capitalist society they occupy this place by virtue of their ownership of things—their standing in a property relation to a commodity, be it land, labour-power, or capital:

> The persons exist for one another merely as representatives of, and therefore as owners of, commodities. In the course of our investigation we shall find, in general, that the characters who appear on the economic stage are

but the personification of the economic relations that exist between them. (Marx 1954: 89)

Consider, once again, the example of a chairman. In a specific social context a man takes on such a role or status. Indeed one might more accurately talk of relations between roles or between statuses, rather than between men.[8]

The social relation with which Marx is primarily concerned is the production relation. Marx discusses consumption, exchange and distribution, and their relation to production; but he is clear that production is the predominant moment. (See Chap. 11 for further discussion of this important point.)

This raises the question: Precisely which relation is being referred to in the case of commodity fetishism? It is a social relation between independent producers. But it is not a direct relation; and the relation does not become apparent until the act of exchange (Marx 1954: 78). And Marx emphasises an important elision—from "relation between producers" to "relation of producers to the sum total of their own labour"—a complex issue to be discussed in more detail in Chap. 7. In *Capital* and *Theories of Surplus Value* Marx refers to three other types of fetishism: of money, of capital and of interest-bearing capital, each involving different relations, as discussed in the following chapter.

4. Relation Between Things

The relation between things refers to exchange-value. With the fetishism of commodities, the relation between producers takes the form of the exchange-value of commodities. Clearly the relation between these things—exchange-value—cannot be material. Even in so-called

[8] Thus it might be helpful to establish a distinction between what may be called "interpersonal relations" (i.e. relations between persons by virtue of their individual characteristics) and "social relations" (relations between persons by virtue of their social standing; a standing which in capitalist society is, according to Marx, determined by their ownership or otherwise of the means of production).

bourgeois economics, it is not presented as such. But exchange-value is sometimes presented as "natural", as in Walras:

> Wheat is worth 24 francs a hectolitre. … This particular value of wheat in terms of money, that is to say this particular price of wheat, does not result either from the will of the buyer or from the will of the seller or from any agreement between the two. … Thus any value in exchange, once established, partakes of the character of a natural phenomenon, natural in its origins, natural in its manifestations and natural in essence. If wheat and silver have *any value at all*, it is because they are scarce, that is, useful and limited in quantity—both of these conditions being natural. (Walras 1954: 69)

A later, though less explicit, formulation is to be found in Allingham's book entitled simply *Value*, which owes much to Walras:

> The values of things, or their equilibrium prices, are determined by the degree to which they are considered useful and on the amounts in which they are available. (Allingham 1983: 1)

Debreu, in his famous work on value, allows rather more scope than Walras to the social, but displays a very impoverished view of it:

> The fact that the price of a commodity is positive, null, or negative is *not* an intrinsic property of that commodity; it depends on the technology, the tastes, the resources, … of the economy. (Debreu 1959: 33)

The social can hardly be captured by simply adding in "tastes" and "technology". For Marx, this is wholly inadequate. Exchange-value is not a material, nor a natural relation. It is a social relation: a relation between *persons* which assumes the form of a relation (albeit social) between things.[9]

[9] According to Elster, the nature of the relation between things differs from the nature of the relation between men. The former is one of comparison and the latter of interaction. That A has more money than B is an example of a relation of comparison; that A exploits B is an example of a relation of interaction. He therefore concludes that:

5. Assumes the Fantastic Form Of

This expression is, in many ways, the most crucial of all, for it lies at the very heart of the concept of fetishism. Yet it is one which can be interpreted in different ways. For example, one might assert that capitalism, as a system, simply "produces" these forms. Or one could take the view that fetishism is a deliberate and self-serving mystification, which capitalists engage in, served by their tame economists—or "hired prize-fighters", as Marx described them (Marx 1954: 25). Certainly, if one extends the discussion to different types of fetishism the range of possible interpretations is wide; but even if it is credible to suggest intentionality in the case of "higher" forms of fetishism, this cannot be argued with regard to commodity fetishism.

The ultimate fetishism, of interest-bearing capital, is the final stage in a long process, which Marx analysed by his "logico-historical" method.[10] Here, as Marx himself put it:

> The whole result of the capitalist production process appears as a property inherent in a thing. (Marx 1971: 456)

> The fetishism thesis can in fact be stated as follows: relations of interaction between men appear as relations of comparison between objects. Even more sharply: they appear as external relations, since the properties by which the objects are compared do not appear to have a relational component (i.e. to embody a reference to the relations between men), but to inhere in the objects as natural qualities. (Elster 1985: 96)

Elster is right to address the issue of apparent inherence; and the distinction between relations of comparison and relations of interaction might potentially be enlightening. But he concludes by proposing an even more "general and parsimonious" way of presenting the thesis of fetishism, that "In commodity-producing societies there is a tendency to overlook the implicitly relational character of certain monadic predicates" (Elster 1985: 96). This is surely going too far in pursuit of parsimony.

[10] See Engels' review of *A Contribution to the Critique of Political Economy*:

> The logical method of approach was (therefore) the only suitable one. This, however, is nothing but the historical method, only stripped of the historical form and diverting chance occurrences. (Marx 1970b)

Here the mystification is apparent. But what about the case of the fetishism of commodities? Why does "labour assume the form of value"? Is the form attributable to the social relation itself (allowing this relation causal efficacy) or is it the way in which this relation is perceived that matters? Does the relation explicitly and necessarily take this form, or is the form attributable merely to the way that members of a capitalist system perceive it? Is it, indeed, possible wholly to separate the perception from the social phenomenon perceived? Marx's expression "assumes the fantastic form of" (regarding commodity fetishism) does not in itself provide the answer. To seek one, it is instructive to examine the higher forms of fetishism. This is therefore the starting point of the next section.

Bibliography

Allingham, M. (1983). *Value*. London: Macmillan.

Althusser, L. (1971). *Lenin and Philosophy and Other Essays*. London: Verso.

Arthur, C. (1986). *Dialectics of Labour: Marx and his Relation to Hegel*. Oxford: Blackwell.

Brewer, A. (1984). *A Guide to Marx's Capital*. Cambridge: University Press.

Cohen, G. (1978). *Karl Marx's Theory of History: A Defence*. Oxford: Clarendon.

Colletti, L. (1975). Marxism and the Dialectic. *New Left Review*, No. 93.

Debreu, G. (1959). *Theory of Value: An Axiomatic Analysis of Economic Equilibrium*. Newhaven: Yale University Press.

Desai, M. (1979). *Marxian Economics*. Oxford: Blackwell.

Desai, M. (1986). Men and Things. *Economica*, Vol. 53, No. 209.

Dobb, M. (1972). *Political Economy and Capitalism: Some Essays in Economic Tradition*. London: Routledge and Kegan Paul.

Elster, J. (1980). Cohen on Marx's Theory of History. *Political Studies*, Vol. 28.

Elster, J. (1985). *Making Sense of Marx*. Cambridge: University Press.

Fine, B. (1975). *Marx's Capital*. London: Macmillan.

Fromm, E. (1961). *Marx's Concept of Man*. New York: Ungor.

Geertz, C. (1975). *The Interpretation of Cultures*. New York. Basic Books.

Geras, N. (1971). Essence and Appearance: Aspects of Fetishism in Marx's Capital. *New Left Review*, No. 65.

Hook, S. (1936). *From Hegel to Marx: Studies in the Intellectual Development of Karl Marx*. London: Reynal & Hitchcock.

Howard, M., & King, J. E. (1975). *The Political Economy of Karl Marx*. Harlow: Longman.

Junankar, P. N. (1982). *Marx's Economics*. Oxford: Philip Allan.

Korsch, K. (1971). *Three Essays on Marxism*.

Lowe, A. (1938). Mr Dobb and Marx's Theory of Value. *Modern Quarterly*, Vol. III.

Lukács, G. (1968). *History and Class Consciousness: Studies in Marxist Dialectics*. London: Merlin.

Marx, K. (1954). *Capital* (Vol. I). Moscow: Progress.

Marx, K. (1959). *Capital* (Vol. III). Moscow: Progress.

Marx, K. (1970a). *A Draft Introduction to Grundrisse*. Moscow: Progress.

Marx, K. (1970b). *A Contribution to the Critique of Political Economy*. Moscow: Progress.

Marx, K. (1971). *Theories of Surplus Value, Part III*. Moscow: Progress.

Marx, K. (1973). *Grundrisse*. Harmondsworth: Penguin.

Marx, K., & Engels, F. (1968). *Selected Works*. Moscow: Progress.

Marx, K., & Engels, F. (1983). *Letters on "Capital"*. London: New Park.

McLellan, D. (1980). *The Thought of Karl Marx: An Introduction*. London: Macmillan.

Meek, R. L. (1973). *Studies in the Labour Theory of Value*. London: Lawrence & Wishart.

Mepham, J. (1979). From the *Grundrisse* to *Capital*: the Making of Marx's Method. In J. Mepham & D.-H. Ruben (Eds.), *Issues in Marxist Philosophy, Volume Three: Epistemology, Science, Ideology*. Brighton: Harvester.

Merquior, J. C. (1986). *Western Marxism*. London: Paladin.

Mészaros, I. (1970). *Marx's Theory of Alienation*. London.

Ollmann, B. (1976). *Alienation: Marx's Conception of Man in Capitalist Society*. Cambridge: Cambridge University Press.

Pilling, G. (1980). *Marx's 'Capital': Philosophy and Political Economy*. London: Routledge Kegan Paul.

Rosdolsky, R. (1980). *The Making of Marx's 'Capital'*. London: Pluto.

Sayer, D. (1983). *Marx's Method: Ideology, Science and Critique in 'Capital'*. Brighton: Harvester.

Stedman Jones, G. (1971). The Marxism of the Early Lukacs: An Evaluation. *New Left Review, 70*, 27–66.

Sweezy, P. (1968). *The Theory of Capitalist Development: Principles of Marxian Political Economy*. New York: Modern Reader Paperbacks.

Walras, L. (1954). *Elements of Pure Economics*. London.

Winch, P. (1958). *The Idea of a Social Science and Its Relation to Philosophy*. London: Routledge & Kegan Paul.

Part II

The Ontology of Fetishism

5

Fetishism of Money, Capital, Interest-Bearing Capital and Commodities

As … interest-bearing money-capital … capital assumes its pure fetish form. … (T)he intervening process is omitted. … Capital is now a thing, but as a thing it is capital. Money is now pregnant.
(Marx 1959: 393)

In *Capital* Volume I, Marx takes the commodity as the starting point for presenting his theory of value and fundamental critique of the capitalist system. To understand what Marx calls the qualitative aspect of value theory, I have argued that it is crucial to analyse the concept of fetishism, which places an emphasis on the social relations underlying the system, and reveals how these different relations are concealed. Fetishism, however, is not a simple concept. I suggest that it may be better understood if, in addition to commodity fetishism, one studies also other forms of fetishism—of money, capital and interest-bearing capital. This is the approach adopted in the present chapter. A second approach for analysing Marx's qualitative theory of value is to examine his earlier economic

This is a revised version of a chapter in McNeill, D (1988) *Fetishism and the Form of Value*. Unpublished thesis, University of London.

D. McNeill, *Fetishism and the Theory of Value*, Palgrave Studies in the History of Economic Thought, https://doi.org/10.1007/978-3-030-56123-9_5

writings. Marx's dissatisfaction with Ricardo's theory of value is crucial, and his critique of Ricardo is therefore an appropriate starting point. This is the approach adopted in Chap. 6. In this chapter I begin by considering all the different types of fetishism that Marx describes. I start with money where the fetishism is "more complicated" and manifests itself "in a more striking manner … than it does in commodities". I then move on, through capital, to the most extreme fetishism—of interest-bearing capital—the "consummate automatic fetish", before returning to the fetishism of commodities.

Although I will cite a number of references, this is not intended to be an exhaustive textual analysis. I will be particularly concerned with what, precisely, fetishism implies in each case, and to what extent each type of fetishism may be portrayed as serving the interests of a particular group, and intentionally promoted by them.

The Fetishism of Money

> we have already pointed out the mystifying character that transforms the social relations … into properties of these things themselves (commodities) and still more pronouncedly transforms the production relation itself into a thing (money). (Marx 1959: 826)

As discussed in Chap. 3, the word 'fetish' appears here and there in several of Marx's works published before *Capital Volume I*. During this period he is also gradually developing the analysis which, in its final form, will give a central place to the concept of the 'fetishism of commodities'. As a result, he does not always use the term in a way that is consistent with his presentation of commodity fetishism in *Capital Volume I*. This applies especially with regard to money, as I shall discuss.

The fetishism of money, the subject of discussion here, needs to be distinguished from the money fetish. The latter, as noted in Chap. 3, appears in Marx's writings of the intermediate stage, in his discussion of Mercantilism, to describe what might better be called the fetishism of wealth.

Nor is the fetishism of money to be equated with the gold fetish—a term which Marx does use, once, in *Capital*: "In order that gold may be held as money, and made to form a hoard, it must be prevented from circulating, or from transforming itself into a means of enjoyment. The hoarder, therefore, makes a sacrifice of the lusts of the flesh to his gold fetish. He acts in earnest up to the Gospel of abstention" (Marx 1954: 133). This is not, I suggest, a reference to the fetishism of money in the complex sense I am here discussing[1].

Although Marx does not use the term 'fetishism of money', it is clearly this he is describing in the following passage from *A Contribution to the Critique of Political Economy*:

> All the illusions of the Monetary System arise from the failure to perceive that money, though a physical object with distinct properties, represents a social relation of production. (Marx 1970: 35)[2]

An editors' footnote in *Theories of Surplus Value Part III* makes reference to this passage:

> In *A Contribution to the Critique of Political Economy* (1859) Marx had already shown that in bourgeois society the mystification of social relations appears strikingly in money, that the crystallisation of wealth as a fetish in the form of precious metals is a characteristic of bourgeois production. (Marx 1971: 490)

I suggest that this blurs the issue. The "mystification of social relations" should be clearly distinguished from "the crystallisation of wealth in the form of precious metals" (even though, as I have described, Marx used the term money fetish to refer to both in his writings). In *A Contribution*, I suggest, he is discussing money fetishism, but without using the term.

There is a similar important passage later in the same volume:

[1] According to Elster, in Marx's personal copy of the book he replaced the word "Gold" by "Geld" (Elster 1985: 1987).

[2] One could cavil at the description of money as "a physical object with distinct properties"—certainly in contemporary society, where it may be no more than an entry in a computer.

> A social relation of production appears as something existing apart from individual human beings, and the distinctive relations in which they enter in the course of production in society appear as the specific properties of a thing. … This perverted appearance manifests itself merely in a more striking manner in money than it does in commodities. (Marx 1970: 49)

Here, Marx is making the point that money fetishism is a developed form of commodity fetishism. His understanding of money, already evident in *A Contribution to the Critique of Political Economy*, is further elaborated in *Capital*, notably in the discussion of money as a medium of circulation. By contrast with its role as a means of payment, here money not only expresses production relations among persons, it creates them—as Rubin points out

> Thus money is not only a 'symbol', a sign, of social production relations which are concealed under it. By uncovering the naiveté of the monetary system, which assigned the characteristics of money to its material or natural properties, Marx at the same time threw out the opposite view of money as a 'symbol' of social relations which exist alongside money. … Thus social production relations are not only 'symbolized' by things, but are realized through things. (Rubin 1982: 11)

When Marx writes of money in his later works he is not making a simple, indeed very obvious, point about money as a symbol; he is portraying the fetishism of money as similar to, and an extension of, the commodity fetish. Money is key to the transition from the elementary form of value to the money-form, and indeed the whole process from the commodity through to surplus value.

Rubin makes a significant point in the following quotation:

> What appears to happen is not that a particular commodity becomes money because all other commodities express their values in it, but, on the contrary, that all other commodities universally express their values in a particular commodity because it is money. The movement through which this process has been mediated vanishes in its own result, leaving no trace behind. (Rubin 1982: 187)

What Rubin is describing is an apparent reversal in direction of causality, which mystifies the process, concealing any traces of how it operates. (Marx refers to a similar phenomenon with regard to capital, as discussed below.) In the few passages in which he makes reference to the fetishism of money, Marx does not explicitly state which social relation is fetishised, but Rubin does, in a footnote to the passage quoted above:

> But it [paper money} is a thing in the sense that through it are expressed, in 'objectified' form, social production relations between buyer and seller. (Rubin 1982: 12)

Thus, the "social relation between persons" that fetishism of money refers to is the relation between buyer and seller—just as in the case of commodity fetishism.[3]

To conclude: the fetishism of commodities is the most basic type, and the others discussed in this chapter are developments from it. In *Capital*, applying his "logico-historical" method, Marx traced the route from the commodity, through money to capital and interest-bearing capital. Money is a necessary link in the chain that Marx describes—from the commodity through to capital and surplus-value.

> Marx's economic theory deals precisely with the 'differences in form' (social-economic forms, production relations) which actually develop on the basis of certain material-technical conditions. ... It is precisely this that represents the completely *new methodological formulation* of economic problems which is Marx's great service and distinguishes his work from that of his predecessors, the Classical Economists. ... Marx's methodological formulation of the problem runs approximately as follows: why does labour assume the form of value, means of production the form of capital, means of workers' subsistence the form of wages, increased productivity of labour the form of increased surplus value? (Rubin 1982: 42)

[3] But Marx notes that "it was the common expression of all values in money that alone led to the establishment of their character as values. It is, however, just this ultimate money form of the world of commodities that actually conceals, instead of disclosing, the social character of private labour, and the social relations between the individual producers" (Marx 1954).

The fetishism of money, as I have shown here, is very similar to the fetishism of commodities.[4] In both cases, the relevant social relation is that between buyer and seller. But the situation is rather different with the fetishism of capital and interest-bearing capital, to which I now turn.

The Fetishism of Capital

In the case of capital fetishism, Marx is concerned with the relation between capital and labour. Not only is this relationship one of exploitation, but the exploitation is concealed. It appears as if capital itself is productive:

> We have already pointed out the mystifying character that transforms the social relations … into properties of these things themselves (commodities). … (But) under the capitalist mode of production and in the case of capital, which forms its dominant category, its determining production relation, this enchanted and perverted world develops still more. … *Capital thus becomes a very mystic being since all of labour's social productive forces appear to be due to capital, rather than labour as such.* (Marx 1971: 826, 827; my emphasis)

And this, says Marx, is an instance of fetishism:

> Thus the productive power of social labour and its special forms now appear as productive powers and forms of capital, of *materialised* labour, of the material conditions of labour—which, having assumed this independent form, are personified by the capitalist in relation to living labour. Here we have once more the perversion of the relationship, which we have already, in dealing with money, called *fetishism*. (Marx 1963: 389)

Much of Marx's discussion of the fetishism of capital is to be found in connection with his famous Trinity Formula, in *Capital Vol III*:

---

[4] *The Devil and Commodity Fetishism* (Taussig 1980) is the title of an interesting and much-referenced study of peasants in Colombia and Bolivia as they "enter the ranks of the proletariat", but I suggest that the phenomenon he describes might be better termed fetishism of money.

> Capital—profit (profit of enterprise plus interest), land—ground-rent, labour—wages, this is the trinity formula which comprises all the secrets of the social production process. (Marx 1959: 817)

This formula constitutes a highly condensed summary of an argument that is crucial in Marx's analysis. It brings together two triads: the three classes—capital, labour and landowners—and their respective 'returns' under capitalism. Marx asserts that presenting these relations as 'returns' is meaningless: "The alleged sources of the annually available wealth belong to widely dissimilar spheres and are not at all analogous with one another. They have about the same relation to each other as lawyer's fees, red beets and music" (Marx 1959: 817).

They are also, importantly, fetishistic in the more specific sense of concealing the exploitative nature of the relation between capital and labour; the relations capital-profit and labour-wages are fetishised—appearing as if they were natural.

> The form of revenue and the sources of revenue are the *most fetishistic* expression of the relations of capitalist production. It is their form of existence as it appears on the surface, divorced from the hidden connections and the intermediate connecting links. (Marx 1971)[5]

Marx notes that the appearance serves the capitalist well—but he does not go so far as to imply intent on the part of the capitalist, or even, indeed, understanding. For example, in the discussion of the Trinity Formula:

> Vulgar economy actually does no more than interpret, systematise and defend in doctrinaire fashion the conceptions of the agents of bourgeois production who are entrapped in bourgeois production relations. ... Thus, vulgar economy has not the slightest suspicion that the trinity which it takes as its point of departure ... are *prima facie* three impossible combinations. (Marx 1959: 817)

[5] It is interesting to note that here again Marx stresses the hidden connecting links. There are several places in his writings where he uses the term "obliteration" in association with his analysis of how fetishism operates.

The price of labour may be as irrational as "a yellow logarithm", but the vulgar economist is satisfied because he has "gained the profound insight of the bourgeois, namely, that he pays money for labour".

> The contradiction between the formula and the conception of value relieves him of all obligation to understand the latter. (Marx 1959: 818)

To summarise: with regard to capital, Marx uses the term fetishism in a similar, but slightly different sense than with commodity or money fetishism. The relevant social relation is between buyer and seller of labour. What is concealed, mystified, is the appropriation of surplus-value by capital, by virtue of the apparently 'natural' relations, capital-profit and labour-wage. The accepted categories of thought, Marx indicates, may not have been constructed by the bourgeoisie, but they certainly serve their interest; and vulgar economists do not question them.

The Fetishism of Interest-Bearing Capital

Marx begins Part V of the third volume of *Capital* as follows:

> The relations of capital assume their most externalised and most fetish-like form in interest-bearing capital. We have here M—M', money creating more money, self-expanding value, without the process that effectuates these two extremes. (Marx 1959: 391)

A rather more extensive treatment is contained in the *Addenda* to *Theories of Surplus Value Part III*, "Revenue and Its Sources, Vulgar Political Economy".[6] Profit, or surplus-value, is divided into two forms: interest and industrial profit.

---

[6] In portraying interest-bearing capital as the perfect fetish, Marx draws a comparison with the other two categories of the Trinity Formula: "The *land* or *nature* as the source of *rent*, i.e., landed property, is fetishistic enough. *Labour* as the source of wages … this is pretty enough" (Marx 1973: 454). But he does not, in fact, employ the terms that are thus implied: 'fetishism of rent' and 'fetishism of wages'.

> (Thus) the nature of surplus-value, the essence of capital and the character of capitalist production are not only completely obliterated in these two forms of surplus-value, they are turned into their opposites. But even insofar as the character and form of capital are complete [it is] nonsensical [if] presented without any intermediate links and expressed as the subjectification of objects, the objectification of subjects, as the reversal of cause and effect, the religious *quid pro quo*, the pure form of capital expressed in the formula M-M'. The ossification of relations, their presentation as the relations of men to things having a definite social character is here likewise brought out in quite a different manner from that of the simple mystification of commodities and the more complicated mystification of money. The transubstantiation, the fetishism, is complete. (Marx 1971: 493–494)

This, then, is presented by Marx as the ultimate form of fetishism, "a manifestation of the mystification of capital in its most extreme form" (Marx 1971: 494). Here again we encounter the obliteration of the intermediate links in a complex process, resulting in the relation between capitalist and worker being entirely concealed: "Moneyed (capitalist) A does not confront the worker at all, but only another capitalist—capitalist B" (Marx 1971: 460).

Although, as Marx says, interest and interest-bearing capital actually express the contradiction of materialised wealth as against labour, "this position is turned upside down in the consciousness of men because, prima facie, the *moneyed capitalist* does not appear to have any relations with the wage-worker, but only with other capitalists" (Marx 1971: 477).

> Interest, insofar as it presents surplus-value as something deriving from money, commodities etc., as their natural fruit, is therefore merely a mystification of capital in its most extreme form; insofar as it at all represents a social relation *as such*, it expresses merely relations between capitalists, and by no means relations between capital and labour. (Marx 1971: 494)

With the fetishism of interest-bearing capital, the focus shifts from the relation between capital and labour to the relation between capitalists; interest appears as the 'natural' return to the moneyed capitalist, and the exploitative nature of the capital-labour relation is concealed even more.

> To the vulgar economist who desires to represent capital as an independent source of value, a source which creates value, this form is of course a godsend, a form in which the source of profit is no longer recognisable. … In M-M' we have the incomprehensible form of capital, the most extreme inversion and materialisation of production relations. (Marx 1971: 462)

Classical economy succeeded in destroying the "false appearance and illusion" of this "enchanted, perverted, topsy-turvy world"; and yet "even the best spokesmen of classical economy remain more or less in the grip of the world of illusion which their criticism had dissolved". These illusions serve the capitalists well: "It is just as natural for the actual agents of production to feel completely at home in these estranged and irrational forms. … This formula simultaneously corresponds to the interests of the ruling classes" (Marx 1959: 830).

In *Capital*, Marx traces a long and complex route: from his starting-point in the commodity; through different forms of value to money; from money to capital and surplus-value; and from there to the different forms of surplus-value. Interest-bearing capital is the end of the road:

> Interest-bearing capital is the consummate *automatic fetish*, the self-expanding value, the money-making money, and in this form it no longer bears any trace of its origin. The social relation is consummated as a relation of things (money, commodities) to themselves. (Marx 1971: 455)

This, then, is the most extreme form of fetishism. To illustrate its power (and its irrationality) Marx again employs a religious metaphor, recalling the Moloch of his Doctoral Thesis:

> The complete *objectification, inversion,* and *derangement* of capital as interest-bearing capital … is capital which yields 'compound interest'. It appears as a Moloch demanding the whole world as a sacrifice belonging to it of right. (Marx 1971: 456)

Before turning to commodity fetishism itself, I will briefly summarise my findings. All the three manifestations of fetishism here discussed—as with commodity fetishism—involve the mystification of social relations.

They make something appear natural which is in fact social—in the sense of being dependent on the shared beliefs and practices of members of society. The fetishism of money is more complicated than the fetishism of commodities, but is very similar in ontological terms, as discussed below. The fetishism of capital refers to the relation between capital and labour relation and allows the capitalist's profit to appear to be 'natural'. Thus the exploitative nature of the relation is concealed. The fetishism of interest-bearing capital refers to the relation between the moneyed capitalist and other capitalists; here the role of the wage-worker is completely concealed.

The higher forms of fetishism are at the very least a godsend to the capitalist. They may even be a mystification of which the capitalist is actually aware; but this is certainly not the case with commodity fetishism. The capitalist, and indeed the "vulgar economist", not only do not understand the fetishism of commodities—they are entirely unaware of it. And this is not merely because it is well hidden;

> It is this perverted appearance, *this prosaically real, and by no means imaginary, mystification* that is characteristic of all social forms of labour positing exchange-value. (Marx 1970: 49) (My stress)

This could be interpreted to mean that commodity fetishism is, in a sense, a real illusion. Certainly the ontological status of these different types of fetishism merits further discussion. This is the challenge taken up in the remainder of this chapter, and the next.

Commodity Fetishism

I return to commodity fetishism itself in order to compare this with the other forms of fetishism just discussed. I find it helpful to begin with a discussion of Cohen's views. He, along with Elster, Roemer and others, belongs to a group commonly referred to as 'Analytical Marxists'. Although Cohen's interpretation differs in important respects from my own, it is set out with great clarity, so that such differences of interpretation as do exist should be made very evident.

I begin with the doctrine of capital fetishism, which Cohen summarises as follows:

1. The productivity of men operating with physical facilities takes the form of the productivity of capital.
2. Capital is productive.
3. It is not autonomously productive.
4. It appears to be autonomously productive.
5. Capital, and the illusion accompanying it, are not permanent, but peculiar to a determinate form of society. (Cohen 1978: 116)

According to Cohen, therefore, the key to the fetishism of capital is that something appears to be so, but is not in fact so. Capital appears to be inherently, or autonomously productive; but it is not. This is, I believe, an accurate interpretation of Marx's position, most eloquently expressed, perhaps, in his discussion of the Trinity Formula. Fetishism is here akin to mystification. Capital appears to have inherent powers, but in reality these powers derive from the shared beliefs and practices associated with the capitalist system.

Where I disagree with Cohen, however, is in his interpretation of the doctrine of commodity fetishism which he summarises as follows:

1. The labour of persons takes the form of the exchange-value of things.
2. Things do have exchange-value.
3. They do not have it autonomously.
4. They appear to have it autonomously.
5. Exchange-value, and the illusion accompanying it, are not permanent, but peculiar to a determinate form of society. (Cohen 1978: 116)

As is immediately evident, Cohen is at pains to portray these two types of fetishism in the most similar possible way. Thus, he presents commodity fetishism as structurally identical to capital fetishism. Although I certainly agree that there are very strong similarities, there are also, I suggest, important differences.

I have already noted that commodity fetishism is the most basic form of fetishism, in the sense that it is only by virtue of commodity fetishism that other forms of fetishism are possible. But there is a more crucial difference between my own interpretation and that of Cohen, which requires more detailed elaboration and which is perhaps most evident in his interpretation of the expression "takes the form of" in his summaries of the two types of fetishism. To the first of these, he adds a footnote that:

> Statements 2, 3 and 4 explicate 'takes the form of' as it is used in statement 1 (Cohen 1978: 116)

This may be adequate for the fetishism of capital and interest-bearing capital. But it does not fully capture the meaning of the term as it relates to commodity fetishism, as I shall seek to show. This crucial ontological issue can be more precisely posed in terms of the question: whence does the fetish derive its power?

Cohen begins as follows:

> Since thinking does not make things so, the religious fetish does not really acquire the power mentally referred to it. But if a culture makes a fetish of an object, its members come to perceive it as endowed with the power. What is mistakenly attributed to it is experienced as inhering in it. The fetish then manifests itself as endowed with a power which in truth it lacks. (Cohen 1978: 115)

This is not quite right. Certainly the fetish lacks any *inherent* power, but it has power nonetheless. Indeed Cohen discusses what he calls a special case, which is very relevant to this point:

> Where worshippers believe of an idolized object that if it fell off its pedestal, they would be stricken with frenzy. It is possible that they would, therefore, suffer a frenzy if it fell. (Cohen 1978: 115, footnote)

But this is surely quite a common case. A fetish cannot cause the rain to fall; but it might be able to cause sickness, and could certainly confer authority on its possessor—if others in the same society shared the appropriate belief. A chairman is a chairman because people believe him to be so. In this and such cases thinking does indeed make it so—provided the thinking is common to the group and not merely confined to a single individual.

This point may not be of central importance to Cohen's argument since he seems prepared to concede power to the economic if not the religious fetish.[7] However, his explanation of the source of this power indicates a deeper problem:

> The appearance of power in the economic fetish does not result from a thought process, but from a process of production. (Cohen 1978: 115)

This is of crucial importance, for it concerns the very source of the fetishism itself. But how, precisely, is this sentence to be understood? If the dichotomy that Cohen presents is between the mental (a thought process) and the material (process of production), then this is surely incorrect. The source of the power is to be found in neither the mental nor the material but in the social—for the beliefs are not idiosyncratic, but *shared*.

Yet, as I noted in an earlier chapter, Cohen lays great stress on the social, and indeed analyses very perceptively the distinction between the social and the material, devoting much of his book to clarifying the place of each in a given mode of production. Perhaps, then, the process of production is, for Cohen, precisely social. But this is far from clear in what follows. For example, Cohen states that the economic fetish does not have the power inherently; rather: "it is in fact delegated by material production" (Cohen 1978: 116). The term "delegated" is open to differing interpretations, while the stress on "material" production seems to de-emphasise the social correspondingly.

Cohen's interpretation of Marx is undoubtedly right insofar as he attributes the central role to the production process. Two questions arise, however: first, whether the power of the economic fetish is real or apparent; and second, whether the process of production is to be seen simply in material terms. I would suggest that his sentence could be better worded, by omitting "the appearance" and stressing the social; thus:

[7] It is not entirely clear where he stands. He states, in a footnote that the economic fetish "*has* the power, but not inherently" (Cohen 1978: 115, my stress) but then goes on (as noted above) to talk of "the *appearance* of power" in the economic fetish.

> The power of the economic fetish does not result from a thought process, but from a *social* process of production.

Even if Cohen accepted this version, it seems that the detail of his interpretation of fetishism still differs from my own, for he goes on:

> The time taken to produce a commodity takes the form of the exchange-value of the commodity. (Cohen 1978: 116)

This is surely an inaccurate reading of Marx. Labour-time is only a *measure* of value. Labour, not labour-time, takes the form of exchange-value. (I elaborate on this point in Chap. 6.)

Cohen later states that the fetish character of commodities does not "result from the fact that commodities are products of a certain amount and a certain kind of labour: all products are" (Cohen 1978: 119). But Marx's argument is that in capitalism there is indeed a special kind of labour.[8] Cohen is certainly aware of the significance of the social:

> All production proceeds within a social form. Mystery arises not because there *is* a social form, but because of the particular social form it is. The enigma 'comes clearly from this form itself'. (Cohen 1978: 119)

Thus, the difference between Cohen and Marx is largely in the way in which the idea is expressed. Marx speaks of labour taking the form of value; he emphasises the *type* of labour. For Marx, the fetish character of commodities results from their being commodities—not mere products. All products are the result of labour; but under one specific form of society—capitalism—such products are commodities, products of a very specific kind of labour. Cohen seems to prefer discussing the issue in terms of the social form within which production takes place, placing the emphasis rather less on labour and rather more on the social.[9]

---

[8] And Ricardo was criticised by Engels, in his Preface to (Marx 1956), for failing to analyse "*what* labour it was that produced value" (Marx 1956: 16). Again, see Chap. 6.

[9] Some would regard this as a very minor difference. Cohen himself does not consider there to be a significant contrast between the two formulations (personal communication).

Cohen's interpretation of fetishism may be better understood in the light of his analysis of exploitation. In an appendix in which he investigates further the distinction between appearance and reality, Cohen asks "why class societies present themselves in a guise which differs from the shape correct social theory attributes to them". He responds:

> Part of the answer is that they rest on the exploitation of man by man. If the exploited were to see that they are exploited, they would resent their subjection and threaten social stability. (Cohen 1978: 330)

This may be a part of the answer—but he never gives the rest, which, I suggest, lies deeper.[10] Even if one accepted an intentionalist (or at least functional) explanation of capital fetishism, this would surely not be adequate for commodity fetishism.

At the heart of Cohen's argument with regard to commodity fetishism is a misrepresentation of Marx's labour theory of value. Elsewhere, he reveals that he does not, indeed, accept this theory:

> I have long thought the labour theory of value false, and I was not wishing to commit myself to it in expounding Marx's theory of fetishism, which does, indeed, presuppose it. (Cohen 1980: 135)

Thus he attempts to provide an analysis of fetishism without Marx's labour theory of value. In his own words:

---

[10] Elster, also an 'analytical marxist', claims, on the basis of arguments "from Marx and others", "that there is a natural tendency for the exploited to believe in the inevitability of exploitation" (Elster 1985: 487).

It is surely inadequate to resort to "natural" tendencies in seeking to explain such a very social phenomenon. Yet Elster also states "that the exploiting classes can be victims of similar illusions" (Elster 1985: 487). And his understanding of fetishism seems in some respects quite similar to my own:

> We are dealing here with a generalized form of fetishism, that is structurally induced illusions about how the economy works. … The—systematically distorted—beliefs about the structure (1) are to be explained by the structure and (2) enter into the explanation of its persistence. (Elster 1985: 127)

> Our exposition will not distinguish between a generally material and a specifically labour-theoretical account of value. (Cohen 1978: 116, footnote)

This, I suggest, is why his explanation of commodity fetishism is inadequate—unlike that of capital fetishism. Indeed he himself would perhaps agree with such a view, for the quotation just cited continues:

> My own view is that the doctrine of *commodity fetishism* is largely false, but that there is a deep truth in the idea of the fetishism of *capital*. (Cohen 1980: 135)

It is impossible, I believe, to give an adequate exposition of Marx's concept of commodity fetishism without being very sympathetic towards Marx's labour theory of value—at least in its qualitative aspect. Under capitalism, Marx says, relations between producers appear "as what they *really* are, material relations between persons and social relations between things" (Marx 1954: 78) (my stress). In some sense he regards commodity fetishism as "more real" than the higher forms. But what does this mean? To attempt to address this question, it is helpful to establish a better understanding of the challenge that Marx faced in seeking to advance on the work of his predecessors. This is the subject of the next chapter.

Bibliography

Cohen, G. (1978). *Karl Marx's Theory of History: A Defence*. Oxford: Clarendon.
Cohen, G. (1980). Reply to Elster. *Political Studies*, Vol. 28.
Elster, J. (1985). *Making Sense of Marx*. Cambridge: University Press.
Marx, K. (1954). *Capital* (Vol. I). Moscow: Progress.
Marx, K. (1956). *Capital* (Vol. II). Moscow: Progress.
Marx, K. (1959). *Capital* (Vol. III). Moscow: Progress.
Marx, K. (1963). *Theories of Surplus Value, Part I*. Moscow: Progress.
Marx, K. (1970). *A Contribution to the Critique of Political Economy*. Moscow: Progress.
Marx, K. (1971). *Theories of Surplus Value, Part III*. Moscow: Progress.
Marx, K. (1973). *Grundrisse*. Harmondsworth: Penguin.
Rubin, I. I. (1982). *Essays on Marx's Theory of Value*. Montreal: Black Rose Books.

6

The Form of Value: The Scylla of Bailey and the Charybdis of Hegel

The whole mystery of the form of value lies hidden in this elementary form (20 yards of linen = 1 coat). Its analysis, therefore, is our real difficulty.
(Marx 1954: 55)

Having discussed fetishism in the previous chapter, I now turn to the theory of value—to trace Marx's route beyond Ricardo to the value-form. As Engels notes in his Preface to the second volume of *Capital*:

> The *existence* of that part of the value of products which we now call surplus-value had been ascertained long before Marx. … Some—the classical bourgeois economists—investigated at most the proportion in which the product of labour was divided between the labourer and the owner of the means of production. Others—the Socialists—found that this division was unjust and looked for utopian means of abolishing this injustice. They all remained prisoners of the economic categories as they had come down to them. (Marx 1956: 16)

This is a revised version of a chapter in McNeill, D (1988), *Fetishism and the Form of Value.* Unpublished thesis, University of London.

D. McNeill, *Fetishism and the Theory of Value*, Palgrave Studies in the History of Economic Thought, https://doi.org/10.1007/978-3-030-56123-9_6

Marx's greatness lay in his ability to question, and even to break out of these traditional economic categories. But this meant starting from the very foundations, as Engels noted.

> In order to understand what surplus-value was, Marx had to find out what value was. He had to criticise above all the Ricardian theory of value. Hence he analysed labour's value-producing property and was the first to ascertain *what* labour it was that produced value, and why and how it did so. He found that value was nothing but congealed labour of *this* kind. (Marx 1956: 16)

The theory of surplus-value could only be reached through a new theory of value. And central to this theory is the issue of *what* labour it is that produces value, and why and how it does so. Key to this great discovery was his radical break from the Ricardian theory of value. The classics had a labour theory of value, which identified the *substance* and *measure* of value. Marx, however, went much further—by investigating the *form* of value; by establishing that labour takes a certain form under capitalism. This view was both informed by, and also gave further clarity to, his understanding that the categories of economic thought are not eternal and natural, but transitory and social. It is this which marks his great break from Ricardo.

But this break was a gradual one which emerged over many years of Marx's work.[1] Indeed, Marx initially rejected the labour theory of value, despite asserting that labour was the substance of private property (Morishima and Catephores 1978: 14). Next, in *The Poverty of Philosophy*, when he breaks with Proudhon, he clearly asserts a labour theory of the Ricardian type. His own very different version is not yet apparent:

> 'The Poverty of Philosophy' still lacks the fundamental definition of value which distinguishes Marx's theory of labour-value from Ricardo's labour-value theory … the concept of abstract labour as labour which creates value is still missing. (Vygoskdi 1973: 28)

[1] I shall not attempt to trace this development in any detail. What follows here is merely an outline, based on other commentators.

Vygodski identifies the *Grundrisse* as the work in which Marx clearly sets himself apart; for here we find "the doctrine of the two-fold character of labour" which "marks the point at which Marx's theory differs from the labour-value theory of the classics" (Vygoskdi 1973: 54).

But even as late as *A Contribution to the Critique of Political Economy*, according to Rubin, Marx did not effectively distinguish between abstract labour and socially necessary labour (Rubin 1982: 128) nor between exchange-value and value (Rubin 1982: 107).

By the time of *Capital* not only was the break total, but Marx's alternative theory of value had developed into its final form. Criticisms of Ricardo are certainly to be found in the *Grundrisse* and in *A Contribution to the Critique of Political Economy*, but they are perhaps most clearly spelled out in *Theories of Surplus Value*, especially in Part III, "The Disintegration of the Ricardian School". Here Marx draws attention to Ricardo's failure to analyse the form of value:

> All commodities can be reduced to labour as their common element. What Ricardo does not investigate is the *specific* form in which labour manifests itself as the common element of commodities. (Marx 1971: 138)

He had made a similar point in Part II, that Ricardo examined only the magnitudes of value, but did not examine "this abstract, general, and in this form social labour, which engenders differences in the *magnitudes of value* of commodities" (Marx 1968: 172).

Ricardo's labour theory of value is simply of the embodied labour type, with the emphasis on the substance and measure of value. Thus:

> He (Ricardo) says, however: only because labour is the common factor of commodities, only because they are all mere manifestations of the same common element, of labour, is labour their measure. It is their measure only because it forms their *substance* as values. (Marx 1971: 138)

The important part played by the form of value in Marx's break with the Ricardian school and the classics in general is reiterated in *Capital* Volume I:

> Even Adam Smith and Ricardo, the best representatives of the (classical) school, treat the form of value as a thing of no importance. (Marx 1954: 85)

This is not only because their attention was focussed solely on the magnitude of value. The other reason, as Marx noted, was that they treated it as eternally fixed by nature; they remained prisoners of the traditional categories.

Despite the fact that Marx so clearly distanced himself from his predecessors in this way, some commentators have tended to underestimate the significance of what Marx was trying to say about value, and the form of value.[2] This is not entirely surprising; for not only does Marx express his ideas in complex ways, his position also seems to vary somewhat, even within a single sentence. For example, he criticises Ricardo whose "attention is concentrated on the *relative quantities of labour* which the different commodities represent, or which the commodities as values embody" (Marx 1971: 131).

It would appear that Marx attaches no significance to the two alternative wordings. But the distinction between "embodying" labour and "representing" labour is surely very important.[3]

It is by no means easy to understand what Marx means in such extracts. The value of commodities is not simply the quantity of labour-time, a measure of the amount of a substance which they contain. This is clear. But elsewhere Marx says that this substance is "manifested"; or, again, that commodities are not merely materialised labour-time, but they have an "aspect" as materialised labour-time.

Here, I suggest, Marx is searching for, but not yet finding, an alternative to Ricardo. His search is perhaps most frantic in the section on Bailey[4] in "The Disintegration of the Ricardian School" in *Theories of Surplus Value* Part III. Marx uses expressions like "representing quantities

---

[2] Rubin makes this point in relation to economists of his era; it could also be applied to many subsequent commentators, and perhaps most especially to Neo-Ricardians.

[3] Of course, the difficulties of translation greatly complicate the issue. These are not limited to English. See, for example, Rubin's discussion of the Russian translation of "darstellen" (Rubin 1982: 111).

[4] Samuel Bailey (1791–1870), British economist.

of a substance", "expressing the same element", "manifesting a substance" and "embodying a substance". Thus:

> As such, they (commodities) are *qualitatively* the same, and differ only *quantitatively* according to whether they represent smaller or larger quantities of the *same* substance, i.e., labour-time ....
>
> It is as manifestations of this substance that these different things constitute *values* and are related to one another as values. ...
>
> (Hence) the *individual commodity* as *value*, as the *embodiment of this substance*, is different from itself as use-value, as an object, quite apart from the expression of its value in other commodities. (Marx 1971: 127)

Even so, he concludes with a statement which appears to situate him dangerously close to a simple theory of embodied labour time:

> As the embodiment of labour-time, it is *value* in general, as the embodiment of a definite quantity of labour-time, it is a definite *magnitude of value*. (Marx 1971: 128)

But he veers away from this absolutism once again. Commodities ("heterogeneous things") must be considered as "proportionate representations, expressions of the *same common unity*, (of) an element quite different from their natural existence or appearance" (Marx 1971: 128). And a commodity, as value,

> appears as something ... merely determined by its relation to socially necessary, equal, simple, labour-time. (Marx 1971: 129)

Note that Marx again stresses the relational character of value. Indeed, he uses the rather curious phrase "relation to socially necessary ... labour-time". But the crucial distinction between labour and labour-time is here blurred, for he goes on:

> As values, commodities are *social* magnitudes, that is to say, something absolutely different from their 'properties' as 'things'. As values they constitute only relations of men in their productive activity. (Marx 1971: 129)

Then he speaks of a relation to social labour:

> Thus he (Bailey), the wiseacre, transforms value into something absolute, 'a property of things', instead of seeing in it only something relative, the relation of things to social labour, social labour based on private exchange, in which things are defined not as independent entities, but as mere expressions of social production. (Marx 1971: 130)

It may be inappropriate to subject this section of Marx's writing to such detailed scrutiny, since there are major problems of translation. But, I suggest, there is evidence not simply of confusion, but of a conceptual shift—from substance/magnitude, through social substance/magnitude, to a relation to productive activity/social labour. What is missing is the concept of abstract labour. Marx's finely balanced position at this stage is perhaps best captured by a quotation from *Theories of Surplus Value Part II*:

> The relativity of the concept of value is by no means negated by the fact that all commodities, in so far as they are exchange-values, are only *relative* expressions of social labour-time and their relativity consists by no means solely of the ratio in which they exchange for one another, but of the ratio of all of them to this social labour which is their substance. (Marx 1968: 172)

This is Marx's formulation of the answer. But it is one which demands further elaboration. What is meant by "relative expressions of social labour-time"? And how is the concept of a "ratio of commodities to their substance" to be distinguished from their measure in that substance?

Certainly Marx's meaning in such passages is far from simple. But what is abundantly clear is that he regarded his own position as distinct, in important respects, from that of the classics. Their view had the advantage of being rather easier to state. Marx accepted that the value of commodities is expressed in their relative exchange-values, and even that it does not have any independent existence. But he did not accept that value was simply a natural property of things. His difficulty lay in describing what it was that lay beneath value, without committing himself to the Ricardian view that this was merely embodied labour.

The way forward is indicated, but not clearly expressed, in *Theories of Surplus Value* Part III:

> It (relative value) means, secondly,[5] the value of one commodity expressed in the use-value of another commodity. This is *only* a *relative* expression of its value, namely in relation to the commodity in which it is expressed. The value of a pound of coffee is only relatively expressed in tea; to express it absolutely—even in a relative way, that is to say, not in regard to labour-time, but to other commodities—it ought to be expressed in an infinite series of equations *with all other commodities*. This would be an *absolute* expression of its relative value; its absolute expression would be its expression *in terms of labour-time* and this absolute expression would express it as something relative, but in the absolute relation, by which it *is* value. (Marx 1971: 132)

This appears at first sight rather confusing. But it represents both Marx's resolution of the absolute/relative value debate, as well as the basis for much of his analysis of the forms of value. In summary, Marx distinguishes the following:

1. **Relative value**. This is what Marx refers to in *Capital* as exchange-value—and more particularly the Elementary Form; it is expressed in the use-value of another commodity (and hence, in this sense, is "relative").
2. **Absolute expression of relative value**. This is the totality of all exchange-values of a given commodity (cf. the Total or Expanded Form). A comparison with set theory is instructive here. A relation (or more precisely a binary relation) may be defined as a set of ordered pairs which stand in that relation to each other. For example, the relation "marriage" is defined simply as the set of all

[5] The first meaning is "*magnitude of value* in contradistinction to having *value* at all. For this reason the latter is not something absolute."

> ordered pairs (x,y) ... for which x is a man, y is a woman, and x is married to y. (Halmos 1974: 26)

Similarly, the exchange-value of a commodity may be defined in "absolute" terms as the set of all other use-values for which it is exchangeable.

3. **Absolute expression of value.** This is the expression of value in terms of labour-time. But note that Marx adds a final twist:

> this ... would express it (value) as something relative, but in the absolute relation, by which it *is* value.

Marx seems here to delight in complexity; and if there were no further elaboration of the argument it would be extremely unsatisfactory. Indeed, it might even suggest, quite erroneously, that value is no more than labour-time. But any such conclusion is clearly ruled out by Marx's equating, two pages later, "labour-time" with "social labour, as it presents itself specifically in commodity production" (Marx 1971: 135). He goes on:

> A quantity of labour has no value, is not a commodity, but is that which transforms commodities into values, it is their *common substance*. (Marx 1971: 135)[6]

Thus the qualitative aspect of the question needs to be distinguished from the quantitative, which is concerned merely with the magnitude of labour-time. Under capitalism, says Marx, labour is *social* labour. For this reason it has the power to transform "commodities into values". Precisely what this means is not very clearly expressed. But this is the crucial distinction between Marx and Ricardo; the starting point of Marx's alternative approach.

It was from this point that Marx reached the position that he took up in the first volume of *Capital.* In order to gain a clearer understanding of

[6] Marx here calls it "a social substance" but retracts even this in his *Marginal Notes on Wagner*.

how he did so, it is helpful to set Marx in context: to take account of other ideas which were current at the time and which exerted influence, whether positive or negative, on his own. In this regard, I will discuss two particularly important elements in his argument: an emphasis on the relational and a recognition of the crucial role of money.

Marx's emphasis on value as relational is something which he shares with Bailey; although he says that Bailey, "the fetishist" (Marx 1971: 147), sees this only as a relation between things. With regard to the crucial role of money, it is Hegel who provides the key to the exposition of the process. But these two figures were, if anything, an inhibiting influence on Marx's theory of social labour. Bailey (like the neo-Classical economists that followed) was certainly no help, being quite unaware of the importance of the social. Hegel, on the other hand, was dangerously mystical.

Marx's route beyond Ricardo can, I suggest, be traced by reference to these two, very different, figures. My aim in the rest of this chapter is to discuss some of the failings of the Ricardian School in more detail, in the light of this point. This will demonstrate more clearly how Marx's theory differed from that of Ricardo, and hence allow a better understanding of his theory of value.

In his Preface to Marx 1956 Engels argues that:

> The Ricardian school suffered shipwreck ... on the rock of surplus-value. (Marx 1956: 18)

The basic issue related to the theory of value, but it was in relation to the theory of surplus-value that the weaknesses of the argument became most evident. Just as commodity fetishism is both the most basic type of fetishism and also the most difficult to comprehend (in contrast to the higher forms) so too is the concept of value less accessible than its developed form, surplus-value.

I shall argue that in seeking a passage beyond Ricardo, Marx had to steer clear of two very different hazards. On one side lay the Scylla of

Samuel Bailey; a solid rock which spelt the end of any further debate on the meaning of value; for with Bailey, as with neo-classical economists today, value is no more than price: "Here we have it. *Value* equals *price*. There is no difference between them" (Marx 1971: 147). On the other side, however, lay an equally treacherous hazard, the Charybdis of Hegel—an almost irresistible whirlpool of mystification, where "the real world is only the external, phenomenal form of 'the Idea'" (Marx 1954: 29).

It is not customary to accord great importance to Samuel Bailey as an influence on Marx's economic writings.[7] The more usual account presents Ricardo as the central figure. My interest, however, is in how Marx went beyond Ricardo; and in this context, Bailey is of considerable interest, for several of his criticisms were very similar to those which Marx himself made. In particular he, like Marx, insisted that value is not an absolute but a relational concept. He did not reach the same conclusions as Marx with regard to the concept of value; and in some cases "instead of the problem being resolved, it is only emphasised (here) that a problem remains unresolved" (Marx 1971: 110). Nevertheless, it is helpful to observe the extent to which Marx and Bailey followed the same passage beyond Ricardo, for then the point of divergence between them becomes all the more evident.

Engels himself identifies two specific errors in the Ricardian school which caused its "shipwreck": a failure to distinguish between labour and labour-power, and what has come to be known as the transformation problem. The latter is not my concern here. It is worth noting, however, that Bailey at least came close to identifying this failing in the Ricardian School, although he was not the first to do so:

> Like his predecessors, Bailey catches hold of Ricardo's confusion of values and cost-prices in order to prove that value is not determined by labour, because cost-prices are deviations from values. (Marx 1971: 164)

[7] Although Rubin does credit him with influencing Marx's reformulation of the opening chapter of *Capital* (Rubin 1982: 108).

According to Marx, Bailey was not always aware of what he was saying. Thus, when Bailey observes, in his comments on Ricardo, that "this *difference in value of the two commodities* ... would be inconsistent with *the acknowledged equality of profits*, which Mr *Ricardo maintains*". Marx concedes only that he "stumbles unconsciously on a real objection to Ricardo" (Marx 1971: 159).

It is Ricardo's other errors that are of more significance for my purpose. And indeed Marx maintains that the objection just stated "does not refer to the theory of value, but to a blunder of Ricardo's in applying this theory" (Marx 1971: 159). Ricardo's first error is his failure to distinguish labour and labour-power. Marx quotes Bailey's comment on Ricardo:[8]

> There is an obvious difficulty in supposing that *labour* is what we mentally allude to, when we talk of value or of real price, as opposed to nominal price; for we often want to speak of the *value or price of labour itself*. (Marx 1971: 110)

And as Marx concedes:

> As far as labour is concerned, the objection to Ricardo is correct insofar as he ... speaks directly of the value of labour, while what is bought and sold is the temporary use of labour-power, itself a product. (Marx 1971: 110)

The distinction between labour and labour-power is, of course, no minor point. The worker does not sell his labour, but his labour-power. Failure to recognise this fact, as Marx noted in an earlier passage (on Mill), leads to the difficulty in the Ricardian system that the law of value,

[8] In this instance, Marx was unaware that Bailey was the object of his comments, for the *Observations on Certain Verbal Disputes in Political Economy*, from which this extract is taken, was published anonymously—and only later identified as Bailey's work.

> does not hold good in the greatest of all exchanges, which forms the foundation of capitalist production, the exchange between capitalist and labourer. (Marx 1971: 89)

As a result, this most crucial transaction is transformed:

> into a common transaction between commodity owners, owners of materialised labour … the worker is a seller of commodities like any other. … He does not sell a particular commodity differing from all other commodities. He sells labour embodied in a product, that is, a commodity which as such is not specifically different from any other commodity. (Marx 1971: 89)

Thus, for Marx, the distinction between labour and labour-power provides the key to understanding how surplus-value is extracted; how the apparently fair exchange between labourer and capitalist masks the exploitation of one by the other. Ricardo failed to see this. Bailey certainly did not see it either, but, according to Marx, he was at least aware of the weakness in Ricardo's analysis in this regard.

Another major limitation of the Ricardian School was the failure to distinguish use-value and exchange-value. Here too the critique by Bailey (at that time anonymous) comes close to the same point.

> The author of the *Observations* accuses Ricardo of having transformed *value* from a relative attribute of commodities in their relation to one another, into something absolute.
>
> The only thing that Ricardo can be accused of in this context is that, in elaborating the concept of value, he does not clearly distinguish between the various aspects, between the exchange-value of the commodity, as it *manifests itself, appears* in the process of commodity exchange, and the existence of the commodity as value as distinct from its existence as an object, product, use-value. (Marx 1971: 125)

Certainly this too is a very basic error; indeed its discovery was identified by Marx himself as one of the best points about *Capital*. But again it is not clear just how far Bailey's understanding went. Did he recognise the crucial distinction between the use-value and exchange-value aspects of the commodity, which Ricardo failed adequately to develop?

In any event, Bailey was surely right to criticise Ricardo's absolutism. Indeed, it is some similarity between their perceptions of this issue that renders so instructive Marx's comments on Bailey's work on value. Although reaching very different conclusions, they both recognise similar errors in Ricardo, and appreciate that there is a need to come to grips with the relational aspect of value, rather than treating it simply as an absolute.[9]

Indeed, despite his strong antagonism, Marx does give grudging recognition to the validity of some of Bailey's criticisms, which touch on some of the most important aspects of the theory of value. He does, for example, allow that this book "has rendered a good service insofar as the objections he raises help to clear up the confusion between 'measure of value' expressed in money as a commodity along with other commodities, and the immanent measure and substance of value" (Marx 1971: 137).

Further evidence of the influence of Bailey on Marx emerges from a detailed comparison of the first chapters in the First and Second editions of *Capital* (see Annex to this chapter). Although most of the changes were, according to Marx, minor ones, they did include the addition of five references to Bailey in the space of some 30 pages—one in the text itself, the remainder in footnotes. For example: "The few economists, amongst whom is S. Bailey, who have occupied themselves with the analysis of the form of value" (Marx 1954: 56) and "However narrow his own views ... he laid his finger on some serious defects in the Ricardian theory" (Marx 1954: 68).

[9] Here Marx is surely inaccurate in accusing Bailey too of absolutism, when he writes:

> Thus he, the wiseacre, transforms value into something absolute, 'a property of things', instead of seeing in it only something relative. (Marx 1973: 130)

Indeed he concedes as much, even when describing Bailey as a fetishist. (See below.)

My purpose, however, is not to raise Bailey to the status of a major economist, or claim that he and Marx were in complete agreement. In a sense, I am arguing the opposite. For although much of Bailey's critique of Ricardo was correct, and similar to that of Marx himself, yet they came to diametrically opposite conclusions. The important point to stress is the shared perception of Marx and Bailey, contra Ricardo, that value is a relational concept. An appropriate place to start is Marx's discussion in *Theories of Surplus Value* Part III, where he quotes Ricardo as follows:

> A franc is not a measure of value for any thing … unless francs, and the thing to be measured, can be referred to *some other measure which is common to both*. This, I think, they can be, for they are both the *result of labour*; and, therefore, … labour is a *common measure*, by which their *real* as well as their *relative value* may be estimated. (Ricardo, quoted in Marx 1971: 138)

Marx then offers a gloss on real and relative value:

> By *real value*, Ricardo, in the passage cited above, understands the commodity as the embodiment of a definite amount of labour-time. By *relative value*, he understands the labour-time the commodity contains expressed in the use-values of other commodities. (Marx 1971: 139)

It is this distinction between real and relative value that provides a clue to Ricardo's error, and also to Marx's progression beyond him. It is elaborated on more fully in *Theories of Surplus Value* Part II:

> First of all, Ricardo speaks of *'value in exchange'* and, like Adam Smith, defines it as *'the power of purchasing other goods'*. This is exchange-value as it appears at first. Then, however, he proceeds to the real determination of value:
>
> 'it is the comparative quantity of commodities which labour will produce, that determines the present or past *relative value*'.
>
> 'Relative value' here means nothing other than the exchangeable value as determined by labour-time. (Marx 1968: 170)

As Marx notes, Ricardo's terminology is somewhat confusing. He uses the term "absolute value", "real value" or simply "value" to denote "relative value" in this sense, that is exchangeable value as determined by embodied labour-time.

> But *relative value* can also have another meaning, namely, if I express the exchange-value of a commodity in terms of the use-value of another, for instance the exchange-value of sugar in terms of the use-value of coffee. ... In the first sense, the relative value of sugar is determined by the quantity of sugar which can be produced by a certain amount of labour-time. In the second case, the relative value of sugar (and coffee) expresses the ratio in which they are exchanged for one another and changes in this ratio can be the result of a change in the 'relative value' in the first sense, in coffee or in sugar. ... (Hence) whether the values of two commodities are expressed in their own reciprocal use-values or in their money price—representing both commodities in the form of the use-value of a third commodity—these *relative* or *comparative* values or prices are the same. (Marx 1968: 170)

This suggests a resolution of the problem, which Marx later develops more fully. It is a problem which can be traced back to Adam Smith's confusion between labour embodied and labour commanded, as determinants of value. Indeed the resolution could even be stated in such terms: labour embodied is *expressed* in labour commanded.

Just how great is the difference between Ricardo's position and that of Marx emerges very clearly from a letter which Ricardo wrote to Trower shortly after the appearance of the third edition of the *Principles*:

> I do not, I think, say that the labour expended on a commodity is a measure of its exchangeable value, but of its positive value. I then add that exchangeable value is regulated by positive value, and therefore is regulated by the quantity of labour expended.
>
> You say that if there were no exchange of commodities they could have no value, and I agree with you, if you mean exchangeable value, but if I am obliged to devote one month's labour to make me a coat, and only one

> week's labour to make a hat, although I should never exchange either of them, the coat would be four times the value of the hat. (Ricardo, quoted in Meek 1973: 113)

To Ricardo, then, value seems to be something which Robinson Crusoe would have recognised—alone on his island. The *social* is eliminated—or at least restricted to exchangeable value, which itself is regulated by labour embodied. Not only does Ricardo tend to absolutism, but he also underplays the social.[10] Bailey made the latter error but not the former.

As Meek notes:

> The tendency to identify absolute value with embodied labour became more and more apparent (in late Ricardo). No doubt it was always present to some extent: one can scarcely talk about embodied labour as the 'source' and 'foundation' of value, and as being 'realised' in commodities without at the same time tending to regard value as virtually *consisting* of embodied labour. (Meek 1973: 117)

But this was rather similar to what Marx was seeking to do; and it indicates both how narrow is the passage which Marx was trying to follow, and also how easy it is for commentators to see no difference between this and the Ricardian route.

One way past this particular hazard (the route favoured by Bailey and the "vulgar economists") leads only to the solid rock of tautology:

> 'Value denotes … nothing but the *relation* in which two objects stand to each other as exchangeable objects.'
>
> Nobody will contest this tautology. What follows from it is that the 'value' of an object 'denotes *nothing*'. For example, 1 lb. of coffee = 4 lbs. of cotton. What then is the value of 1 lb. of coffee? 4 lbs. of cotton. And of 4lbs. of cotton? 1 lb. of coffee. (Marx 1971: 141)

[10] This despite the fact that,

> Like all economists worth naming, … Ricardo emphasises that labour as *human activity*, even more, as socially determined *human activity*, is the sole source of value. (Marx 1973: 181)

Here we have the clear distinction between Marx and Bailey. In summary:

> Bailey is a fetishist in that he conceives value, though not a property of the individual object (considered in isolation), but as a *relation of objects to one another*, while it is only a representation in objects, an objective expression, of a relation between men, a social relation, the relationship of men to their reciprocal productive activity. (Marx 1971: 147)

Bailey's tautological formulation was clearly inadequate. According to Marx, he was right to emphasise the relational aspect of value but wrong to conclude that there was nothing underneath. What Marx revealed below was not material, substantial—but no less "real" for that. He concluded that exchange-value is the manifestation of value, the form of value.

Bailey certainly failed to see this. And this marks the point of divergence between them. As Marx said, Ricardo and others of the classical school "treat the form of value as a thing of no importance". Bailey may have been one of the few economists "who have occupied themselves with analysis of the form of value" but they too failed to resolve the issue:

> first, because they confuse the form of value with value itself; and second, ... because they exclusively give their attention to the quantitative aspect of the question. (Marx 1954: 56)

The way forward, then, is to be found by concentrating on the qualitative, the form of value. This makes it possible for Marx to stand outside the capitalist system, to criticise the very categories themselves, and, in particular, to understand the role of labour in this system.

Marx's primary concern is with capitalism, and with the form that labour takes under capitalism. Ricardo sees labour as the measure of commodities "only because labour is the common factor of commodities ... only because it forms their *substance* as values. Ricardo does not sufficiently differentiate between labour insofar as it is represented in use-values or in exchange-value. Labour as the foundation of value is not any particular labour, with particular qualities" (Marx 1971: 138). Thus, Ricardo does not grasp the crucial concept of abstract labour.

> (Ricardo) does not even examine the form of value—the particular form which labour assumes as the substance of value. He only examines the magnitudes of value, the quantities of this abstract, general, and in this form social labour, which engenders differences in the **magnitudes of value** of commodities. (Marx 1968: 172)

Both Ricardo and Bailey might have understood value if they had better understood money—for money is the key to the process, from value-form to surplus-value. Money is both the ultimate form of value, as well as the first stage in its development. Ricardo failed to understand, or even fully investigate, the role played by money:

> This circumstance—the necessity of *presenting* the labour contained in commodities as *uniform social labour*, i.e. as money—is overlooked by Ricardo. (Marx 1971: 131)

Bailey recognised the importance of money to only a limited extent. Thus, he tried to understand value through simple exchange, not the elementary form. Marx argues that if Bailey had analysed money "not only as a quantitative measure but as a qualitative transformation of commodities, he would have arrived at a correct analysis of value" (Marx 1971: 137). The failure is traced to the lack of a qualitative dimension, the key to which is money.

Thus Marx comments on Bailey:

> But what is this unity of objects exchanged against each other? This exchange is not a relation which exists between them as natural things. It is likewise not a relation which they bear as natural things to human needs. … What is therefore their identity? … As what do they become *exchangeable*? (Marx 1971: 144)

It arises through their existence as "social things", that is commodities (Marx 1954: 77). Bailey tries to understand exchange by looking at only two products, plus money. But, as Marx says, "if only two products existed, the products would never become commodities, and consequently the exchange-value of commodities would never evolve either" (Marx 1971: 144). And only through this evolution does the exchange economy and money itself evolve: "The determination of the product as value (which) leads to the establishment of money".

> It is this development of the labour embodied in them (commodities) as social labour, it is the development of their *value*, which determines the formation of money. (Marx 1971: 145)

The direction in which Marx was heading is now indicated. But it was not an easy route to chart. Marx regards the form of value as one of the most difficult points to comprehend, for it exists only in relational terms. Thus, he notes in the First German Edition of *Capital*:

> It is relatively easy to distinguish the value of a commodity from its use-value, or the labour which forms the use-value from that same labour insofar as it is merely reckoned as the expenditure of human labour-power in the commodity value. If one considers commodity or labour in the one form, then one fails to consider it in the other, and vice versa. These abstract opposites fall apart on their own. ... It is different with the *value-form* which exists only in the relationship of commodity to commodity. (Marx 1976: 21)

The value-form finds its expression in money:

> All products as *values* are compelled to assume a form of existence distinct from their existence as use-values. And it is this development of the labour embodied in them as social labour, it is the development of their *value*, which determines the formation of money ... thereby directly transforming the labour embodied in this exclusive commodity into *general, social* labour. (Marx 1971: 144)

But this is a two-way process; it is by virtue of money that the development can take place. "This necessity to express individual labour as general labour is equivalent to the necessity of expressing a commodity as money" (Marx 1971: 136). The importance of money, for Marx, lay not only in its explanatory power, but also because it provided the key to his exposition. Thus the first chapter of *Capital* traces through a complex process from the commodity to money; a process which mirrors, albeit imprecisely, a historical process. Here, Hegel was a most useful guide—as Marx himself declares. The dialectic provided Marx with a most appropriate way of expressing the complex process of transformation which is the subject not merely of Chapter 1 of *Capital*, but of the work as a whole. Yet in another respect Hegel was a constraining influence. It is for this reason that I refer to the Charybdis of Hegel. Marx, I suggest, was seeking an adequate means of conceptualising the social, and more specifically the form of value. Hegel offered an alluring, but dangerously mystical solution which Marx was anxious to avoid. Certainly Hegel was a very positive influence on the way in which Marx portrayed the process—from the form of value onwards. But, I suggest, he was a negative influence on Marx's exposition of the form of value itself.

The extent and nature of Hegel's influence on Marx, especially in the first chapter of *Capital*, is of course a subject which has been much discussed—not least by Marx himself. It is therefore enlightening to examine the changes that Marx made when he revised the First German Edition of *Capital*. I have already referred to these in respect of Samuel Bailey, where they are very minor, and certainly do not affect the argument. The more notable differences between the First and Second Editions relate to the treatment of Hegel. Marx reacted sharply to early criticisms that *Capital* was "metaphysical" by distancing himself firmly from the excesses of Hegel, claiming that his "dialectic method is not only different from the Hegelian, but is its direct opposite" (Marx 1954: 29). He goes on:

> With him it is standing on its head. It must be turned right side up again, if you would discover the rational kernel within the mystical shell. (Marx 1954: 29)

Thus even where he is most inclined to be critical of Hegel, he admits the existence of a "rational kernel". And indeed it is clear from a comparison of the first two editions of *Capital* Volume I that he did not modify the dialectical method of presentation of the argument in any way. The changes he did make were less crucial, but of interest nevertheless. For he was seeking a passage beyond Ricardo's version of value—as merely embodied labour-time—which nevertheless avoided any suggestion that it was a mere phantasm of the mind. Marx did not have any cause to abandon the dialectical method (which gave him the key to money). But he did wish to avoid the Charybdis of Hegel—the tempting, but wholly unsatisfactory philosophy, in which "the life-process of the human brain, i.e. the process of thinking, ... under the name of 'the Idea'" is transformed "into an independent object" (Marx 1954: 29).

In the Afterword to the Second German Edition of *Capital*, Marx describes the various changes he has made. (See Annex for details.) The major change is the incorporation of "The Form of Value" (previously an Appendix) into the main text. This involved considerable rewriting of Chapter I, Section 3, "The Form of Value or Exchange-Value"; and some alterations to Chapter I, Section 4, "The Fetishism of Commodities and the Secret Thereof", and to Chapter III, Section 1. Marx also refers to additional footnotes, and numerous "partial textual changes, which were often purely stylistic".

Apart from these, Marx himself draws attention to only two "important" changes. The first is his revision of the argument regarding the derivation of value. In the First Edition he merely asserts his position, while in the Second Edition he makes more effort to justify it ("with greater scientific strictness", in his own words). This "greater scientific strictness" in his derivation of value consists mainly in the additional argument that there must be a "common something" which cannot be any natural property of commodities". Leaving use-value out of consideration, this leaves only "one common property left, that of being products of labour". This is the type of argument by residual which Marx quite commonly employs (e.g. Marx 1954: 164) It is now often portrayed as his main argument in support of the labour theory of value, and has been the target of much criticism—starting with the classic critique by Bohm-Bawerk, who refers to the "processes of distillation by means of which Marx obtains the sought-for 'common factor' in labor" and describes these as "the most vulnerable point in the Marxian theory" (von Bohm-Bawerk 1984: 69).

The second "important" change is that "the connexion between the substance of value and the determination of the magnitude of value by socially necessary labour-time … is now expressly emphasised" (Marx 1954: 22). This refers to the addition of some ten lines of text, in which the concept of "labour-power of society" (not stressed in the First Edition) is given great prominence.

But there are other changes, not explicitly referred to by Marx in his Afterword, which are of interest too. Though each is in itself quite minor, taken together with the two changes just described, they add up to a significant modification to the content of the first chapter. In Section 3 of the Second Edition, Marx notes various "peculiarities" of the equivalent form of value, of which the second is "that concrete labour becomes the form under which its opposite, abstract human labour, manifests itself". Thus, "Just as the coat in bodily form became a direct expression of value, so now does tailoring, a concrete form of labour, appear as the direct and palpable embodiment of human labour generally". There is, in Marx's words, "a complete turning of the tables … weaving creates the value of linen not by virtue of being weaving, as such, but by reason of its general property of being human labour" (Marx 1954: 64).

In the First German Edition this point was rather more obscurely stated; and Marx elaborated somewhat on the "turning of the tables", or "inversion":

> This *inversion* whereby the sensibly concrete counts only as appearance-form of the abstractly-universal, and it is not to the contrary that the abstractly-universal counts as property of the concrete—this inversion characterizes the value-expression. At the same time it renders difficult its comprehension. If I say: Roman Law and German Law are both law, that is obvious. But if I say, on the other hand, *the* law, (this abstract entity) *realizes itself* in Roman Law and German Law (these concrete laws), then the connection becomes mystical. (Marx 1976: 57)

The analogy with forms of law, which Marx uses here, is abandoned in the Second German Edition. It is, however, enlightening; and the reason that it is abandoned, I suggest, is not so much because it is invalid but rather because it reveals just how thin is the line which distinguishes Marx's own position from the "mysticism" of Hegel. Marx roundly condemned the speculative philosophy of Hegel's followers in the following passage from *The Holy Family*:

> If from real apples. pears, strawberries and almonds I form the general idea "*Fruit*", if I go further and *imagine* that my abstract idea "*Fruit*", derived from real fruit, is an entity existing outside me, is indeed the *true* essence of the pear, the apple, etc., then—in the *language of speculative* philosophy—I am declaring that "*Fruit*" is the "*Substance*" of the pear, the apple, the almond, etc. I am saying that … what is essential to these things is not their real existence, perceptible to the senses, but the essence that I have abstracted from them, and then foisted on them, the essence of my idea—"*Fruit*". The speculative philosopher argues somewhat as follows … "*the* fruit" is not dead, undifferentiated, motionless, but a living, self-differentiating, moving essence. … The different ordinary fruits are different manifestations of the life of the "*one* Fruit"; they are crystallisations of "*the* Fruit" itself. … (Thus,) "*the* Fruit" presents itself as a pear, "*the* Fruit" presents itself as an apple, "*the* Fruit" presents itself as an almond; and the differences which distinguish apples, pears and almonds from one another are the self-differentiations of "*the Fruit*" and make the particular fruits different members of the life-process of "*the* Fruit". Thus "*the* Fruit" is no longer an empty undifferentiated unity; it is oneness as *allness*, as "totality" of fruits, which constitute an *organically linked series of members*. (Marx and Engels 1975: 57–59)

This surely describes what Marx, in his Afterword to the Second German edition of *Capital*, referred to as the mystifying side of Hegel, to whom "the real world is only the external, phenomenal form of 'the Idea'" (Marx 1954: 29). Yet the following, very similar, extract is contained in the First German Edition of *Capital*:

> In Form III … the linen appears on the other hand as the *general form* of the Equivalent for all other commodities. (1 coat = 20 yards of linen, u coffee = 20 yards of linen etc.) It is as if alongside and external to lions,

> tigers, rabbits and all other actual animals, which form when grouped together the various kinds, species, subspecies, families etc. of the animal kingdom, there existed also in addition *the animal*, the individual incarnation of the entire animal kingdom. Such a particular … is a *universal.* … (L)inen becomes—as the form of appearance of value common to all commodities—the *universal Equivalent universal value-body, universal materialization of abstract human labour*. The *specific* human labour materialized in it now thereby counts as *universal form of realization* of human labour, as *universal labour*. (Marx 1976: 27)

It might appear that Marx is here indulging in precisely the sort of speculative philosophy that he had so savagely criticised nearly thirty years before. And it seems likely that he was responding to such an impression in the minds of his readers when he amended this passage for the Second Edition, and, more specifically, excised the "animal" analogy. But my interpretation is different. The concept of the form of value is indeed a difficult one to grasp. Marx rejects the Hegelian view, that value "realises itself" in linen, just as he rejects the view that the law realises itself as Roman Law, or fruit as apples, or animals as rabbits. But rather than draw attention to this rather fine distinction, he chooses simply to omit the two analogies from the text.[11]

Taking account also of the two changes explicitly referred to by Marx, it is fair to conclude that his revised version is somewhat "de-Hegelianised"; not, as I have stressed, with regard to the unfolding of the argument, which remains dialectical, but with regard to the meaning of the form of value. Marx does indeed discuss the process, from the commodity to money—and beyond. But he is less forthcoming in saying what value *is*; better on the forms of value than the form of value. We may applaud Marx's desire not to appear "mystifying". But the mystery, like the mystery of fetishism, is not in men's heads but in reality. It is, in this sense, a real mystery. The mystification is not a product of the mind (Marx's, Hegel's, or with a capital M) but of men acting together in society. It

[11] Arthur (1978) notes the similarity between these two texts, but his interpretation of Marx's position is rather different from my own.

deserves to be discussed, even at the risk of sailing perilously close to the Charybdis of Hegel.

It is appropriate, then, to subject Marx's argument to close scrutiny. Certainly he does not hold that value is merely embodied labour-time (as Ricardo generally seems to suggest). Nor does he agree with "the fetishist" Bailey that value is nothing more than a relation between things. Hegel provides a guide to the process from value through to surplus-value, and the role of money in that process. But what, more precisely, is the starting point? It is to this that I now turn.

Annex: A Comparison Between the First and Second German Editions of *Capital*[12]

Marx draws attention to the textual changes he has made in *Capital Volume* I in his Afterword to the Second German Edition; as follows:

Modification 1

> In Chapter 1, Section 1, the derivation of value from an analysis of the equations by which every exchange-value is expressed has been carried out with greater scientific strictness. (Marx 1954: 22)

This refers to the argument concerning the equation of wheat (or corn) and iron. Marx asks what such an equation means, and concludes that the two must have something in common. In the First Edition he makes little attempt at proof, being confident to assert that:

> Commodities as objects of use or goods are corporeally different things. Their reality as *values* forms, on the other hand, their *unity*. This unity does not arise out of nature but out of society. The common social substance which merely manifests itself differently in different use-values, is *labour*. (Marx 1954: 9)

[12] Based on the English translation by A. Dragstedt, 1976. (Referred to in this book as Marx 1976.)

In later editions he seeks to justify this assertion more fully:

> This common 'something' cannot be … any … natural property of commodities. … If then we leave out of consideration the use-values of commodities, they have only one common property left, that of being products of labour. (Marx 1954: 45)

Further, this is not concrete labour but,

> what is common to them all … human labour in the abstract. … All that these things now tell us is, that human labour-power has been expended in their production, that human labour-power is embodied in them. When looked at as crystals of this social substance, common to them all, they are—Values. (Marx 1954: 46)

This is therefore another example of the sort of argument by residual which is to be found elsewhere in Marx's writings (e.g. Marx 1954: 164).

Modification 2

> Likewise the connexion between the substance of value and the determination of the magnitude of value by socially necessary labour-time, which was only alluded to in the first edition, is now expressly emphasised. (Marx 1954: 22)

In this instance, Marx has added (before the words "But only the *socially* necessary labour-time" in the First Edition):

> The labour, however, that forms the substance of value, is homogeneous human labour, expenditure of one human labour-power. The total labour-power of society, which is embodied in the sum total of all the values of all commodities produced by that society, counts here as one homogeneous mass of human labour-power, composed though it be of innumerable individual units. (Marx 1954: 46)

Modification 3

> Chapter 1, Section 3 (the Form of Value), has been completely revised, a task which was made necessary by the double exposition in the first edition, if nothing else. (Marx 1954: 22)

There are a number of changes here which have to be described in detail. These will be dealt with in the order of the final and more familiar version, of the Second German Edition. (Note: In the First Edition, the first chapter was titled "The Commodity", while the Appendix was titled "The Form of Value". In the following summary, the abbreviation C will refer to the former, and F to the latter.) In summary, the chapter from the First German Edition titled "The Commodity" (C) lacks "The Money-form" but provides the basis for sections 1, 2 and 4 of the Second Edition (and a little of 3); while the Appendix "The Form of Value" (F) provides the basis for section 3.

Introduction

As F, with two additional paragraphs, of which the central points are:

> If, however, we bear in mind that the value of commodities has a purely social reality, and that they acquire this reality only in so far as they are expressions or embodiments of one identical social substance, viz., human labour, it follows as a matter of course, that value can only manifest itself in the social relation of commodity to commodity. (Marx 1954: 54)

> the task of tracing the genesis of this money-form, of developing the expression of value implied in the value-relation of commodities, from its simplest almost imperceptible outline to the dazzling money-form. (Marx 1954: 54)

A. Elementary or Accidental form of value.
20 yards linen = 1 coat
(In C this is titled "First or Simple Form"; in F, "Simple Value Form").

1. The two poles of the expression of value. Relative form and Equivalent form.
   As F, somewhat reduced; nothing substantial lost.

2. The Relative form of value.
   (a) The nature and import of this form
       Much modified mixture of F and C.
   (b) Quantitative determination of Relative value
       As C, with minor additions.

3. The Equivalent form of value.
   Largely as F, but much modified and with additions.

4. The Elementary form of value considered as a whole
   Very much modified—but based mainly on F.

B. Total or Expanded Form of Value

20 yards linen = 1 coat or = 10 lbs. tea

(In C titled "Second or developed form of relative value"; in F, "Total or expanded value-form").

Almost identical to F, with a few excerpts from C. For example "It becomes plain that it is not the exchange of commodities which regulates the magnitude of their value; but, on the contrary".

C. The General Form of Value

1 coat, 10 lbs. tea, … = 20 yards of linen"

(In C titled "Third, reversed or reciprocal second form of relative value"; in F "Universal value-form").

Modified version of F, with additions.

> The first form … occurs practically only in the first beginning. … The second form … comes into actual existence for the first time so soon as a particular product of labour, such as cattle, is no longer exceptionally, but habitually, exchanged for various commodities. (Marx 1954: 71)

D. The Money-Form

20 yards of linen, 1 coat, 10 lbs. of tea, … = 2 ounces of gold.

(In C there is no "Money Form". There is a Form IV—untitled—but this is different, that is 20 yards of linen = one coat or = u coffee or = v tea ….; In F there is "Money-form").

As F.

In addition to the foregoing, the following may be noted (whether classified by Marx as part of this "complete revision" or as "partial textual changes, which were often purely stylistic").

- changes in, or additions to, the analogies used (especially regarding the Elementary Form of Value), for example

> to borrow an illustration from chemistry. (Marx 1954: 56)

> A, for instance, cannot be 'your majesty' to B, unless at the same time majesty in B's eyes assumes the bodily form of A. (Marx 1954: 58)

> The fact that it is value, is made manifest by its equality with the coat, just as the sheep's nature of a Christian is shown in his resemblance to the Lamb of God. (Marx 1954: 58)

> the linen itself, so soon as it comes into communication with another commodity, the coat. Only it betrays its thoughts in that language with which alone it is familiar, the language of commodities. (Marx 1954: 58)

> In a sort of way, it is with man as with commodities. … Peter only establishes his own identity as a man by comparing himself with Paul as being of like kind. And thereby Paul, just as he stands in his Pauline personality, becomes to Peter the type of the genus homo. (Marx 1954: 59 footnote)

- Omissions of analogies used in the first version (although this earlier version had fewer analogies); notably two, both discussed in this chapter:

> "it is as if alongside … animals …." (C) (Marx 1976: 27)

"If I say: Roman Law and German Law …." (F) (Marx 1976: 57)

- addition of footnotes; frequently referring to Bailey (in addition to one reference in the main text):

> The few economists, amongst whom is S. Bailey, who have occupied themselves with the analysis of the form of value, have been unable to arrive at any result. (Marx 1954: 56)

> A superficial observation of this fact, namely, that in the equation of value, the equivalent figures exclusively as a simple quantity of some article, of some use-value, has misled Bailey, … into seeing, in the expression of value, merely a quantitative relation. (Marx 1954: 62)

> S. Bailey … fancied that … he had proved the impossibility of any determination of the concept of value. However narrow his own views … he laid his finger on some serious defects in the Ricardian theory. (Marx 1954: 68)

> The insufficiency of Ricardo's analysis of the magnitude of value, and his analysis is by far the best. (Marx 1954: 84)

> It is one of the chief failings of classical political economy that it has never succeeded … in discovering that form under which value becomes exchange-value. (Marx 1954: 85)

> S. Bailey accuse(s) Ricardo of converting exchange-value from something relative into something absolute. (Marx 1954: 87)

Modification 5

> The last section of the first chapter, 'The Fetishism of Commodities, etc.', has largely been altered. (Marx 1954: 22)

Section 4. The fetishism of commodities and the secret thereof.
Generally as C, but:

- The order is somewhat changed.
- Some from F is incorporated.
- There are some additions, notably that in discussing systems other than capitalism, paragraphs on the European Middle Ages and the peasantry are added to those on Robinson Crusoe and communal production.

Note: Marx also points out that:

> Chapter III, Section 1 (The Measure of Value), has been carefully revised. (Marx 1954: 22)

This, however, is of less significance for the purposes of this book.

Bibliography

Arthur, C. (1978). Labour: Marx's Concrete Universal. *Inquiry*, Vol. 21.
von Bohm-Bawerk, E. (1984/1896). *Karl Marx and the Close of His System.* Porcupine Press
Halmos, P. (1974). *Naive Set Theory*. New York. Springer.
Marx, K. (1954). *Capital* (Vol. I). Moscow: Progress.
Marx, K. (1956). *Capital* (Vol. II). Moscow: Progress.
Marx, K. (1968). *Theories of Surplus Value, Part II*. Moscow: Progress.
Marx, K. (1971). *Theories of Surplus Value, Part III*. Moscow: Progress.
Marx, K. (1973). *Grundrisse*. Harmondsworth: Penguin.
Marx, K. (1976). *Value: Studies by Marx* (Translation of the First German Edition by A. Dragstedt). London: New Park.
Marx, K., & Engels, F. (1975). *Collected Works* (Vol. 4). Moscow: Progress.
Meek, R. L. (1973). *Studies in the Labour Theory of Value*. London: Lawrence & Wishart.
Morishima, M., & Catephores, G. (1978). *Value, Exploitation and Growth: Marx in the Light of Modern Economic Theory*. London: McGraw-Hill.
Rubin, I. I. (1982). *Essays on Marx's Theory of Value*. Montreal: Black Rose Books.
Vygoskdi, V. S. (1973). *The Story of a Great Discovery: How Karl Marx Wrote "Capital"*. Berlin: Verlag Die Wirtschaft.

7

Appearance and Reality: Some Ontological Issues

(T)he relations connecting the labour of one individual with that of the rest appear … as what they really are, material relations between persons and social relations between things.
(Marx 1954: 78)

I will begin this chapter, which concludes the first two sections of the book, by drawing together the argument so far. In summary, the concept of fetishism informs and enriches Marx's theory of value, manifested in the complex concept of the value-form. The form of value, or value-form, is the starting point of the complex process which Marx seeks to describe in *Capital*. And here the quantitative and qualitative aspects of Marx's theory of value are integrated.

The analysis of the quantitative aspect of value raises what has come to be known as the Transformation Problem. This is not my concern, but I am inclined to accept that it is of no significance for Marx's argument. Baumol has argued this point that since Marx demonstrates that "the

This is a revised version of a chapter in McNeill, D (1988) *Fetishism and the Form of Value*. Unpublished thesis, University of London.

D. McNeill, *Fetishism and the Theory of Value*, Palgrave Studies in the History of Economic Thought, https://doi.org/10.1007/978-3-030-56123-9_7

relevant **social** source of production is labour", "Profits, interest, and rent must also be attributed to labour, and their total is equal (tautologically) to the total value produced by labour minus the amount consumed by labour itself" (Baumol 1974: 59).

Marx's theory of value was not intended to show how *prices* are determined, so that his failure adequately to do so does not invalidate his major contribution.

> Value theory was never intended as a theory of price, which, as a superficial manifestation of the bourgeois economy, Marx considered worth very little attention, but was instead designed to explain something to him far more fundamental: the process of production, i.e. the extraction of surplus values in the various sectors of the economy. (Baumol 1974: 54)

> To Marx, indeed, it (the determination of competitive prices) was worth discussing only to reveal its irrelevance and to tear away the curtain it formed before our eyes. (Baumol 1974: 57)

Marx began with the commodity and value, not because this was the way to understand price formation, but because this was the way to understand the reality behind the appearance of the capitalist economic system. In *Capital*, and *Theories of Surplus Value*, Marx traced a route from the commodity (and value) through money and capital to interest (and other forms of surplus value). This is why commodity fetishism is to be found at the very starting-point of Marx's voyage.

Running parallel with the development—commodity, money, capital, interest-bearing capital—is an intimately linked development—commodity fetishism, money fetishism, capital fetishism, fetishism of interest-bearing capital. And one can trace the earliest stages in the development of the fetishised forms in parallel with the development of the different "forms of value" that Marx discusses in detail in Chapter 1 of *Capital* Vol I. It is evident that even within this first stage the extent to which fetishism is "visible" increases as the process unfolds, for, as Marx noted in the First Edition of *Capital*: "The fetishism of the commodity-form is more striking in the equivalent-form than in the relative value-form" (1st ed. Capital: 59).

The case of commodity fetishism, at the very base of the system, is different from that of interest-bearing capital, where Marx did little more than point out the mystification of the phenomenon—by reference to the Trinity Formula. For commodity fetishism the analogy with religion is inadequate if it merely indicates a gap between appearance and reality. And commodity fetishism is certainly not brought about by the intentional acts of those involved in the system. How, then, is it to be understood?

Insofar as Marx provides the answer it is to be found at the very beginning of *Capital*, which is where he gives his most final and coherent account of his views on value and the concept of the value-form.[1] Indeed, the importance of the theory of value for Marx's whole enterprise is surely indicated by its place at the very beginning of his major work on political economy. This is a section which Marx himself recognises as difficult to comprehend—a problem which, as I have argued (contrary to many other commentators), is exacerbated by his desire to distance himself from the excesses of Hegel. But it merits detailed study. In Section 3 of Chapter 1, Marx identifies very clearly where the key to the problem is to be found:

> The whole mystery of the form of value lies hidden in this elementary form (20 yards of linen = 1 coat). Its analysis, therefore, is our real difficulty. (Marx 1954: 55)

In the pages that follow, Marx traces a path from the elementary form, through the expanded form and the general form, to the money-form. The clue to the mystery of the form of value, however, lies in the particular character of labour under capitalism: its power to create value. This Marx reveals with respect to the elementary form—although it becomes most readily apparent only in the money-form.

> By making the coat the equivalent of the linen, we equate the labour embodied in the former to that in the latter. … It is the expression of

[1] It is, I suggest, remarkable that commentators have not made more attempt to study the origin of this process, although the role played by money in the process, and the influence of Hegel on the way that it is understood, have both been much discussed.

> equivalence between different sorts of commodities that alone brings into relief the specific character of value-creating labour, and this it does by actually reducing the different varieties of labour embodied in the different kinds of commodities to their common quality of human labour in the abstract. (Marx 1954: 57)

Labour has the capacity to create value (which is manifested as exchange-value) by reducing concrete labour to abstract labour. But labour is not to be *equated* with value (as many supporters of Marx, as well as critics, have sought to do):

> Human labour creates value, but is not itself value. It becomes value only in its congealed state, when embodied in the form of some object. (Marx 1954: 57)

And even when value is embodied in a specific object, it is value only **in relation to** another object. It is a relational phenomenon.

> In order to express the value of the linen as a congelation of human labour, that value must be expressed as having objective existence, as being a something materially different from the linen itself, and yet a something common to the linen and all other commodities. The problem is already solved. (Marx 1954: 57)

Again, Marx makes it clear that value is not the same as labour—it is "expressed" as human labour.

> When occupying the position of equivalent in the equation of value, the coat ranks qualitatively as the equal of the linen, as something of the same kind, because it is value. In this position it is a thing in which we see nothing but value. … And as equivalent of the linen in the value equation, it exists under this aspect alone, counts therefore as embodied value, as a body that is value. … Hence in the value equation, in which the coat is the equivalent of the linen, the coat officiates as the form of value. (Marx 1954: 58)

Note, again, the careful choice of terms. Value's existence is social; it becomes apparent only in certain relations. To return to an earlier analogy, a man is a man under all circumstances, but a chairman only in a specific social context. Similarly, here, the coat "officiates" as the form of value.

In almost his last recorded writings, the *Marginal Notes on Wagner,* Marx reiterates and further clarifies this same position.

> (Therefore) I do not say that 'the common social substance of exchange-value' is 'labour'; and since I deal extensively in that particular section with the *value-form*, i.e. the development of exchange-value, it would be strange to reduce that 'form' to 'a common social substance', labour. … Commodities, so far as they are values, only represent a *social* something, labour. (Marx 1975: 183, 184)

In Marx's theory, then, commodities do not embody but "represent" labour; and he does not describe labour as a substance, or even a social substance, but a "social something"; something which has the capacity to create value. This is the special quality of labour under capitalism. The labour embodied in commodities is represented as "*social* labour, as alienated individual labour" (Marx 1971: 131).

This equation of social labour with alienated labour is crucial. It emphasises that alienation lies at the root of the form of value. It is important to stress this equation between alienated and social labour under capitalism, not least because Marx's use of the word "labour" has been often misrepresented by commentators. To quote Arthur (who deals with this issue at length), in the *1844 Manuscripts*: "Marx restricts the term to *productive activity carried on under the rule of private property*. It is not the term he uses when he wishes to thematize that activity which is the universal ontological ground of social life" (Arthur 1986: 13).

The term "labour" changes its meaning in the course of Marx's writings. In the *1844 Manuscripts* it means alienated labour. By the time of *Capital*, however, it "settled its meaning as one of his fundamental ahistorical categories" (Arthur 1986: 13). In *Capital*, therefore, the term "labour" is used in a broad sense. But the crucial point that Marx makes is that under capitalism, labour (in this broad sense) becomes alienated.

This is the special feature of capitalism which lies at the heart of Marx's analysis. It is a result of this that the aggregate of individual concrete labours becomes a mass of homogeneous abstract labour.

This indicates the relationship between alienation and fetishism, for we may distinguish two points: one, individual labour is alienated, leading to abstract labour; two (and as a result), people relate not as independent commodity producers but via the mass of abstract labour. The relation between persons is not direct, but indirect, and it takes the form of a relation between things.

This also indicates how the qualitative and the quantitative are synthesised. Individual, non-homogeneous labour is alienated, resulting in homogeneous abstract labour: this is the qualitative aspect. The mass of abstract labour has a measure, namely socially necessary labour time: this is the quantitative aspect, which is expressed in terms of exchange-value, money.[2]

Thus, in a sense, money allows the qualitative aspect of value to be transformed into quantitative terms. And, as Marx puts it, in the same paragraph from which derives the more famous quotation on commodity fetishism:

> The relation of the producers to the sum total of their own labour is presented to them as a social relation, existing not between themselves, but between the products of their labour. (Marx 1954: 77)

Thus value is transformed into exchange-value; a social relation between persons takes the form of a relation between things. Under capitalism, private labour becomes social labour and takes the form of value. This is a "form of exchangeability", the starting-point of the long

[2] It is clear that I disagree with the Althusserian view that alienation is a concept of the young Marx which plays no part in his mature works. My own view is quite the opposite: the concept of alienated labour is of great importance in *Capital*. It may perhaps be used in his earlier works as a sociological concept only, but in *Capital* it is integrated with the economic, in the concept of the value-form. A great deal has been written about alienation (at least in its sociological sense) so that the use and development of the term in Marx's writings is better established than is the case with fetishism. I would suggest that there are some clear parallels between the two: each becoming both more rigorously defined and more allied with the economic as Marx's theory developed into its final form.

process, in which money plays a crucial role, which Marx traces in *Capital*. The process concerns both the categories of bourgeois economics and capitalism itself; it leads to the higher fetishised categories (of capital and interest-bearing capital) and the complex unfolding of the capitalist system. It is the first stage in this process that is so difficult to grasp. The substance and measure of value are, as Marx says, more straightforward. "What remains" is the problem: "the form of value which transforms value into exchange-value" (Rubin 1982: 112).

With regard to the two points distinguished above (concerning alienated labour) it should be noted that although point two follows logically from point one, I am not claiming a corresponding gradual historical development—although Marx himself is perhaps trying to do something similar in the following extract:

> What … practically concerns producers when they make an exchange, is the question, how much of some other product they get for their own? … When these proportions have, by custom, attained a certain stability, they appear to result from the nature of the products. … It requires a fully developed production of commodities before … the scientific conviction springs up, that all the different kinds of private labour … are continually being reduced to the quantitative proportions in which society requires them. (Marx 1954: 79)

But why does this occur? Why is labour alienated? Why are commodities fetishised? The quotation continues with the following answer:

> Because … the labour-time socially necessary for their production forcibly asserts itself like an over-riding law of Nature. (Marx 1954: 80)

Yet it is not a law of Nature. What, then, is it? Marx's critique is not only of economic theory but of capitalism itself: not just of the appearances, as described by economists, but of the reality. The relationship between these two is complex. To portray interest as the return on capital is fetishistic, mystifying and self-serving. But commodity fetishism is not so simply dealt with. It is, in a sense "more real". But in what sense? What is the relationship between the phenomenon of capitalism and the categories used to describe it? To what extent is the reality separable from the categories? How far do the categories themselves not merely reinforce but even create this reality? These are very basic ontological issues, not readily resolved within a few pages. I shall conclude this chapter by at least opening up discussion of the subject.

Marx's critique of bourgeois economists is not that they deliberately—or even unknowingly—falsify the realities of the capitalist system.[3] His diagnosis of commodity fetishism is not that reality is misperceived, but that reality "presents itself" in precisely this way. Under capitalism, "the relations connecting the labour of one individual with that of the rest appear … *as what they really are*, material relations between persons and social relations between things" (Marx 1954: 78) (my stress). Marx refers to commodities as "social things" (Marx 1954: 77). The commodity is not merely a thing, a use-value, with natural properties, but also a value, hence a social thing. Certainly the ontological status of use-value differs from that of value (and indeed of exchange-value, the form or manifestation of value). We are quite accustomed to dealing with (or at least taking for granted) the ontological status of material things. But what about value—what is its ontological status?

Bourgeois economists treat economic categories as natural and eternal. This is incorrect. But nor are such categories mere phantasms of the mind. These are "real abstractions", as Marx himself put it. In the remainder of this chapter I will elaborate further on this important claim. It is appropriate to begin with a brief statement of Marx's views on the role of science in "lifting the mystical veil". Marx regarded his own endeavours as scientific, in the sense that he sought to reveal the true reality beneath the, often illusory, appearance:

> Vulgar economy feels particularly at home in the estranged outward appearances of economic relations in which these *prima facie* absurd and perfect contradictions appear. … But all science would be superfluous if the outward appearance and the essence of things directly coincided. (Marx 1959: 817)

[3] As discussed in Chap. 5, he sometimes seems tempted by such an argument; but he certainly does not apply this to *commodity* fetishism.

On numerous occasions, he draws comparisons between his work and that of natural science, where also the task is to reveal the reality behind the appearance. But there is surely a crucial distinction between the two which Marx did not sufficiently investigate. Material reality is independent of the beliefs of persons, social reality is not. This raises the very basic issue of the relationship between the individual and society, and it may be helpful, by way of introduction, to distinguish a variety of alternative views on this question. For ease of presentation, I suggest that these may be ranged along a continuum. At one extreme is the view that individuals have clear intentions and take decisions in the furtherance of these intentions; and that social phenomena can be explained as the (intentional) outcome of individual decisions. At the other extreme, society is a "thing" with independent existence, which determines the actions of individuals within it.

As thus expressed, these views are somewhat caricatured, and may not be held in such unqualified form by any serious theorist. But what is important is the dichotomy between methodological individualism and methodological holism. I suggest the more extreme versions of each be referred to as "strong" and the more qualified versions "weak". Thus I would classify Elster (and others, such as Hayek and Popper) as advocating weak methodological individualism.[4]

One of the shortcomings of my classification is that it does not distinguish between small-scale and large-scale phenomena—between a wink and a world war. Strong holism becomes more credible at the macro scale, and strong individualism at the micro. On the weak methodological individualist account, then, social phenomena may be explained by the intentional actions of individuals. But these actions may not have the intended result. This, according to Elster, is the position that Marx adopts:

[4] Elster (1985), Hayek (1942) and Popper (1961, 1966). One could go further back—to Durkheim, Comte, Vico and Hobbes—for this is a huge topic, basic to the philosophy of social science. Lukes' "Methodological Individualism Reconsidered" remains a most authoritative source. He describes methodological individualism as the doctrine that "facts about society and social phenomena are to be explained solely in terms of facts about individuals" (Lukes 1968: 120). My interpretation puts rather more stress on actions, and even intentional actions, of individuals, in defining methodological individualism. For its opposite, I have preferred the term "methodological holism" to either "sociological holism" or merely "holism", mainly on grounds of symmetry.

> Marx's most original contribution to the theory of belief formation was, in my opinion, his idea that the economic agents tend to generalize locally valid views into invalid global statements. … This is perhaps the most powerful part of the Marxist methodology: the demonstration that in a decentralized economy there spontaneously arises a *fallacy of composition* with consequences for theory as well as practice. (Elster 1985: 19)

This is an unorthodox (some would even say perverse) interpretation of Marx's views.[5] This alone, however, is not sufficient grounds for rejection; especially since Elster argues rigorously and to considerable effect. The fallacy of composition is indeed important in some of Marx's arguments, but I do not think this can be elevated to such a central position.[6] Marx certainly argues that many social phenomena occur "behind the backs" of the persons involved, but this does not allow of only an individualist interpretation.

Most commentators (contra Elster) would surely place Marx on the "holist" side of the divide. Thus they would argue that social phenomena (if not "society" as a "thing") have effective causal power. The whole is more than the sum of the parts, not simply in a game-theoretical sense of individuals interacting, but in the sense that individuals are influenced in their actions not only by the actions of other individuals.

Where, more precisely, does Marx stand, if the "weak individualist" position is ruled out? (And certainly he does not adhere to the strong individualist position). There are a few passages in his writings where, if the word "history" were replaced by "society" one might be tempted to place him at the extreme "holist" end of the spectrum. But I would suggest that, in terms of my crude classification, he should best be termed a weak methodological holist, that is he takes the view that social relations exist and are causally effective.[7]

---

[5] Farr cites Oppenheim and Putnam as portraying Marxist sociology as "micro-reductionist" (Ball and Farr 1984: 225) but vigorously rejects such a view.

[6] According to Roemer (1986: 192) Elster equates it to dialectics itself; but this may be a slight exaggeration.

[7] Precisely how they are causally effective is extremely difficult to describe, and I shall not attempt to do so in a few words. This, indeed, is the subject of much of this book. It is perhaps enough, at this point, to affirm that the behaviour of persons is influenced by a "totality" which cannot be fully captured by the sum of individual actions. For further discussion of holism see Lukes (1968). His

I now turn to the question of how social reality is perceived; and how the categories that describe this social reality are produced. Again, a simple dichotomy may initially be considered: either the concepts are "man-made" or they are spontaneously "thrown up" by the social reality itself.[8]

In the first case, there is the extreme possibility that the concepts are created by sections of the society to further their own interest—what might be called a "conspiracy theory" of concept formation. In places, it seems that Marx is tempted by this view. For example, he quotes, with approval, the analogy that Luther draws with the monster Cacus in his discussion of usury:

> An excellent picture, it fits the capitalist in general, who pretends that what he has taken from others and brought into his den, *emanates from him*, and by causing it to go *backwards* he gives it the semblance of having *come from his den*. (Marx 1971: 536)

Generally, however, he seems to adopt the position that though the concepts serve the interests of the bourgeoisie, they are at most promulgated by them and their "hired prize-fighters" (i.e. economists). As Marx put it in a passage quoted in an earlier chapter:

> To the vulgar economist who desires to represent capital as an independent source of value … this form (interest) is a godsend. (Marx 1971: 462)

But, as I have noted, the situation is not necessarily the same in the case of all types of fetishism. Even if interest-bearing capital is manifestly fetishistic, this is not true of the commodity. Indeed, in some of Marx's writings, it is evident that far from being intentionally mystified, the form is described as being necessarily, and autonomously, "produced" by

---

quotations from Watkins are relevant here; indeed they roughly indicate the range I am describing: from weak holism ("social systems constitute 'wholes' at least in the sense that some of their large-scale behaviour is governed by macro-laws … that … are *sui generis* and not to be explained as mere regularities or tendencies resulting from the behaviour of interacting individuals") to strong holism ("some superhuman agents or factors are supposed to be at work in history") (Lukes 1968: 121).

[8] The latter alternative is, roughly, what is commonly assumed for material reality. But even here there is scope for variations in perception—heavily influenced by the social.

the social phenomena themselves. Thus, in introducing the concept of commodity fetishism for the first time, Marx writes:

> Whence, then, arises the enigmatical character of the product of labour, so soon as it assumes the form of commodities? Clearly from this form itself. (Marx 1954: 76)

According to Rubin, this formulation did not occur to Marx until he wrote *A Contribution to the Critique of Political Economy*. Before then (in *Poverty of Philosophy*) Marx "did not yet ask why production relations among people necessarily receive this material form in a commodity economy" (Rubin 1982: 58).[9]

As Rubin puts it: "Of course the cause of this reification of production relations lies in the spontaneous character of the commodity economy" (Rubin 1982: 47).

> The materialisation of production relations does not arise from 'habits' but from the internal structure of the commodity economy. Fetishism is not only a phenomenon of social consciousness but of social being. (Rubin 1982: 59)

How does this fetishism come about? Marx does not, in his writings as a whole, elaborate much on this crucial point. The major source for further enlightenment is again Chapter 1 of *Capital*, and especially the section on commodity fetishism. Here Marx notes that:

> The Fetishism of commodities has its origin … in the peculiar social character of the labour that produces them. … The two-fold social character of the labour of the individual appears to him, when reflected in his brain, only under those forms which are impressed upon that labour in every-day practice by the exchange of products. (Marx 1954: 77)

---

[9] Other commentators have stressed the same point; for example Sayer (1983); also Pilling:

> Fetishism is not mere illusion. … Matters appear *necessarily* this way. The inverted form taken by man's consciousness is a *necessary* inversion. (Pilling 1980: 160, 164)

Value "converts every product into a social hieroglyphic" (Marx 1954: 79). This is not by intent; we are not even aware of it. But it is so. This appears as a "reality" to us:

> The fact that in … the production of commodities, the specific social character of private labour carried on independently … assumes in the product the form of value—this fact appears to the producers … to be just as real and final, as the fact that, after the discovery by science of the component gases of air, the atmosphere itself remained unaltered. (Marx 1954: 79)

And in a sense it is indeed so. It is by no means evident that there is here a "gulf between appearance and reality". This occurs, according to Cohen, "when and only when the explanation of a state of affairs falsifies the description it is natural to give of it if one lacks the explanation" (Cohen 1978: 329). But commodities do indeed, in the capitalist system, have value—just as the atmosphere is indeed not divided into component gases. Even within the capitalist system, however, the Trinity Formula can be revealed as a mystification. There is thus an important distinction between fetishism of commodities and other varieties, which may be better understood in the light of more modern theories of the philosophy of science. Marx perhaps had some inkling of this, although his own understanding was, as Cohen notes, necessarily "Victorian".

Thus far, I have formulated the discussion in terms which imply that social reality and the categories through which this reality is perceived are distinct. But the situation is not, of course, as simple as this. One of the interesting features of social phenomena is that they owe their existence to the beliefs and actions of persons. Material reality does not. This crucial point is well expressed in the following passage describing Marx's position:

> People are, it is clear, dominated in important ways by the structure of social relations. However, such relations do not have an existence in a society apart from the human activity that produced and continues to produce them. Social phenomena are thus irreducibly made by humans. But for any single person such relations have an existence apart from his or her activity. Individually, people correctly perceive the powerless nature of their

> situations. The form that social relations take is unintended by any single individual, but results from the interdependent activities of the past and present members of that and related societies. These social relations are not material things but they are real. They have ontological status, but not that of a person. Such relations are causally effective but they do not fully determine the course of individual behaviour. (Keat and Urry 1982: 193)

Social phenomena can be said to exist, and indeed to be causally effective. But they are peculiar in that they are constituted by, and also constitutive of, beliefs. What people believe determines (in part at least) social phenomena; and social phenomena influence (and can even determine) what people believe. This greatly complicates the matter. Social phenomena are different from material phenomena in this important sense: not only do we perceive social phenomena through concepts which are socially constructed; the very phenomena themselves exist by virtue of these concepts. It would certainly be impossible to describe any economic phenomenon in terms which did not refer to the beliefs of the society in which the phenomenon is manifested. (An example of one of the most basic of these concepts, in capitalist society, is private property.) But more than this, the beliefs themselves are constitutive of the economic phenomena. The categories through which we perceive the economic system are themselves part of that system. Our understanding of the system can itself change the system. There is a complex reciprocal relationship between the phenomena and the way in which those phenomena are perceived.

Something of this complexity is revealed in Marx's draft Introduction to *Grundrisse*—what has sometimes been called his "discourse on method". More specifically, he discussed the relationship between the evolution of concepts and the evolution of their referents. Take, for example, the term "labour". This is in one sense "the simplest and most ancient relation in which human beings act as producers—irrespective of the type of society which they live in". Yet it was an "immense advance" by Adam Smith to recognise "labour as such" rather than manufacturing, commercial or agricultural labour. Abstract labour, not tied to a particular individual or activity, was, according to Marx, most evident in the United States, "the most modern form of bourgeois society". Thus, "the simplest abstraction, which plays a decisive role in modern political economy, an abstraction which expresses an ancient relation existing in all social formations, nevertheless appears to be actually true in this abstract form only as a category of the most modern form of society" (Marx 1970: 210).

Here, then, is a curious paradox. Labour existed for centuries before the category "labour" was discovered. An investigation of "the simplest economic category, e.g., exchange-value" is equally revealing, for this, as a category,

> leads an antediluvian existence. Thus to consciousness—and this comprises philosophical consciousness—which regards the comprehending mind as the real man, and hence the comprehended world as such as the only real world; to consciousness, therefore, the evolution of categories appears as the actual process of production—which unfortunately is given an impulse from outside—whose result is the world. (Marx 1970: 206)

Thus far, Marx seems to be presenting a Hegelian interpretation which he himself would not favour. But he goes on:

> And this (which is however again a tautological expression) is true in so far as the concrete totality regarded as a conceptual totality, as a mental fact, is indeed a product of thinking, of comprehension; but it is by no means a product of the idea which evolves spontaneously and whose thinking proceeds outside and above perception and imagination, but is the result of the assimilation and transformation of perceptions and images into concepts. The totality as a conceptual entity seen by the intellect is a product of the thinking intellect which assimilates the world in the only way open to it, a way which differs from the artistic, religious and practically intelligent assimilation of this world. (Marx 1970: 207)

There is no other way open to the intellect. The world presents itself this way—and is so perceived. Value is not an abstraction in the sense that it is the product of the intellect; but rather because that is the social reality under capitalism:

> Although it (value) is an abstraction, it is an historical abstraction which can only be assumed on the basis of a particular economic development of society. (Marx and Engels 1983:

> The equalisation of the most different kinds of labour can be the result only of an abstraction from their inequalities. ... Hence when we bring the products of labour into relation with each other as values, it is not because we see in these articles the material receptacles of homogeneous labour. Quite the contrary. (Marx 1954: 78)

This is very different from the extreme Hegelian view that the world "out there" is a product of the mind. But it is equally opposed to the view that there is a world of social phenomena which is autonomous. Social reality is not the construct of the individual mind (or the "Mind") but it is, for reasons elaborated upon above, constituted by the concepts of the members of society. Social phenomena, and I include here commodities, are not mere illusions, even if their ontological status may be less privileged than that of material objects. In his doctoral thesis (quoted at the head of this chapter) Marx confronted a similar question: "Did not the ancient Moloch reign?"[10] In his subsequent work on the mysteries of economics he investigated more complex, more "real" abstractions, and found them to be necessary products of the commodity economy. As Rubin puts it:

> The central insight of commodity fetishism is not that political economy discloses production relations among people behind material categories, but that in a commodity-capitalist economy, these production relations among people necessarily acquire a material form and can be realized only in this form. (Rubin 1982: 62)

[10] The quotation continues: "*That which a particular country is for particular alien gods, the country of reason is for god in general, a region in which he ceases to exist*". Marx's critique of capitalism owed its power to the fact that he departed the country—but only in thought. The question still remains whether the country of reason is doomed to remain only a country of thought. (It should perhaps be added, to set the passage in context, that Marx is here offering a critique of the "ontological proof" of the existence of God—not a defence of it.)

Commodity fetishism is also necessary for the commodity economy, for exchange-value exists only by virtue of alienation and fetishism. It is "real" at the very minimum in this sense—that it is causally effective. Marx must surely be claiming at least as much as this when he asserts that:

> The relations connecting the labour of one individual with that of the rest appear, not as direct social relations between individuals at work, but *as what they really are* (my stress) material relations between persons and social relations between things. (Marx 1954: 78)

But Marx does not state his position very precisely with regard to the ontological status of commodity fetishism, or of value itself. As Lukács comments: "We find in Marx no independent treatment of ontological problems" (Lukács 1978: 1). Insofar as Marx does deal with these issues his analysis is rather obscure. I suggest that this weakness can be largely attributed to Marx's lack of a coherent ontology of social being. No other thinkers of his time had adequately addressed the issue, so Marx was reliant on his own resources. And here he was inhibited by the influence of Hegel, being determined to avoid an idealist position. Marx chose a physical, material model for conceptualising value which, I argue, is inappropriate. A better model for understanding social reality is one based on analogy with language. This is the issue that I take up in the section that follows.

Bibliography

Arthur, C. (1986). *Dialectics of Labour: Marx and His Relation to Hegel.* Oxford: Blackwell.

Ball, T., & Farr, J. (1984). *After Marx.* Cambridge: University Press.

Baumol, W. (1974). The Transformation of Values: What Marx Really Meant (An Interpretation). *Journal of Economic Literature, 12*, 51–62.

Cohen, G. (1978). *Karl Marx's Theory of History: A Defence.* Oxford: Clarendon.

Elster, J. (1985). *Making Sense of Marx.* Cambridge: University Press.

von Hayek, F.A. (1942). *Scientism and the Study of Society.* Economica.

Keat, R., & Urry, J. (1982). *Social Theory as Science.* London: Routledge & Kegan Paul.

Lukács, G. (1978). *The Ontology of Social Being. Vol. 2, Marx's Basic Ontological Principles*. London: Merlin.
Lukes, S. (1968). Methodological Individualism Reconsidered. *British Journal of Sociology, 19*, 119–129.
Marx, K. (1954). *Capital* (Vol. I). Moscow: Progress.
Marx, K. (1959). *Capital* (Vol. III). Moscow: Progress.
Marx, K. (1970). *A Contribution to the Critique of Political Economy*. Moscow: Progress.
Marx, K. (1971). *Theories of Surplus Value, Part III*. Moscow: Progress.
Marx, K. (1975). *Karl Marx: Texts on Method* (Translated and edited by Terrell Carver). Oxford: Blackwell.
Marx, K., & Engels, F. (1983). *Letters on "Capital"*. London: New Park.
Pilling, G. (1980). *Marx's 'Capital': Philosophy and Political Economy*. London: Routledge & Kegan Paul.
Popper, K. (1961). *The Poverty of Historicism*. London: Routledge & Kegan Paul.
Popper, K. (1966). *The Open Society and its Enemies. Vol. 2, Hegel & Marx*. London: Routledge & Kegan Paul.
Roemer, J. (Ed.). (1986). *Analytical Marxism*. Cambridge: University Press.
Rubin, I. I. (1982). *Essays on Marx's Theory of Value*. Montreal: Black Rose Books.
Sayer, D. (1983). *Marx's Method: Ideology, Science and Critique in 'Capital'*. Brighton: Harvester Press.

Part III

On Value and Meaning

8

What Is Value? Marx's Use of Analogy

Do not forbid me use of metaphor;
I could not else express my thoughts at all.
(Goethe. Quoted by Mehring in his study of Marx's style [Korsch 1938])

In the previous section, I discussed the enormity of Marx's break with his predecessors which, following Kuhn (1970), one might justifiably call a paradigm shift. As Marx himself stressed, it was necessary to break out of the traditional categories of economics. But this introduces major problems of communication. Marx's own theory of value was so different from that of his predecessors that it was difficult for him to express it in the vocabulary available to him. How is it possible to break out of the categories if you are still restricted to the same words?

Engels, in his Preface to Volume II of *Capital*, likened Marx's achievement to the discovery of oxygen. Following this similar paradigm shift in chemistry, the word "phlogiston" (or, more accurately, "dephlogisticated

This is a revised version of a chapter in McNeill, D (1988) *Fetishism and the Form of Value.* Unpublished thesis, University of London.

D. McNeill, *Fetishism and the Theory of Value*, Palgrave Studies in the History of Economic Thought, https://doi.org/10.1007/978-3-030-56123-9_8

air") was replaced by the new word "oxygen". And this, of course, is one solution—to introduce new words. Marx did not choose to do so. As a result, some of his most important advances are masked by an apparent similarity in terminology. For example the distinction between labour and labour-power is of extreme importance, but it might, from the terminology, seem slight. It may be justifiably argued that the term "labour-power" is a neologism and should be recognised as such. But the term "labour" then becomes a new term also, but without this being so readily apparent.

In Marx's writings, the term value itself—my major concern in this section—undergoes a substantial change in meaning. But again the changes in terminology are slight; for example Marx's concept of the "form" of value. Like any innovative thinker, Marx is faced with the difficulty of discussing what is in many ways a new concept. In his case, however, the problem of replacing existing categories is exacerbated by his apparent desire to use existing words, as far as this is possible. He has somehow to shape these categories anew, but using the same vocabulary.

As has already been noted, a most effective means of both thinking and communicating new ideas is by analogy, and Marx makes considerable use of this throughout many of his writings. In this chapter, I shall examine how he uses analogy to elucidate the concept of value and I shall also propose an alternative analogy—with language—which I suggest is better suited to the purpose. The analysis of language, after Marx's time, gave rise to structuralism and semiotics, which have been applied also to the social sciences. In the remainder of Part III, I shall re-examine their application to economics, arguing that they can provide useful insights into the meaning of value—and indeed into the fundamental categories of economics.

As became evident in the previous section, it is difficult to describe precisely what it was that Marx was trying to grasp in his analysis of value. A central issue, however, is the problem of commensurability. How is it that different things are capable of being compared? Marx makes innumerable references to this problem, but states it most clearly, perhaps, in *Theories of Surplus Value:*

A = 4B. Then the value of A is *expressed* in 4B, and the value of 4B in A, so that both sides express the same. They are equivalents. They are both *equal* expressions of value. It would be the same if they were unequal ones or A greater than 4B, A smaller than 4B. In all these cases they are, insofar as they are values, only different or equal in quantity, but they are always quantities of the same quality: *The difficulty is to find this quality* (my stress). (Marx 1971: 160)

Similarly, at the very beginning of *Capital*, he discusses the equation 1 quarter of corn = x cwt. iron.

A simple geometrical expression will make this clear. In order to calculate and compare the areas of rectilinear figures, we decompose them into triangles. But the area of the triangle itself is expressed by something totally different from its visible figure, namely, by half the product of the base multiplied by the altitude. In the same way the exchange-values of commodities must be capable of being expressed in terms of something common to them all, of which they represent a greater or less quantity.

This common 'something' cannot be either a geometrical, a chemical, or any other natural property of commodities. (Marx 1954: 45)

The common something is not a natural but what might be called a social property. As Marx says, it cannot be a geometrical or chemical property; yet to try and explain what he means by value, he uses analogies relating to precisely such properties (and others of a natural or physical kind). The merits, and more importantly the limitations, of such analogies deserve detailed discussion.

The chemical analogy is one of the less successful ones. He employs it in Chapter 1 of *Capital*, in the discussion of the relative form of value (20 yards of linen = 1 coat).

To borrow an illustration from chemistry, butyric acid is a different substance from propyl formate. Yet both are made up of the same chemical substances … in like proportions, namely $C_4H_80_2$. If now we equate butyric acid to propyl formate, then, in the first place, propyl formate would be, in this relation, merely a form of existence of $C_4H_8O_2$; and in the second place, we should be stating that butyric acid also consists of $C_4H_8O_2$.

Therefore, by thus equating the two substances, expression would be given to their chemical composition, while their different physical forms would be neglected. (Marx 1954: 57)

This is not an adequate analogy for expressing the complex point which Marx is making in the relevant paragraph—that in the relative form of value "the two commodities whose identity of quality is (thus) assumed do not play the same part". The analogy would have been adequate for a more simple purpose, merely illustrating how the same content can take more than one form. And indeed Marx does this elsewhere, using oxygen to represent labour:

> Let us suppose that one ounce of gold, one ton of iron, one quarter of wheat and twenty yards of silk are exchange values of the same magnitude. As exchange-values in which the qualitative difference between their use-values is eliminated, they represent equal amounts of the same kind of labour. The labour which is materialised in them must be uniform, homogeneous, simple labour; it matters as little whether this is embodied in gold, iron, wheat or silk, as it matters to oxygen whether it is found in rusty iron, in the atmosphere, in the juice of grapes or in human blood. … As exchange-values … they represent larger or smaller portions, larger or smaller amounts, of simple, homogeneous, abstract general labour, which is the substance of exchange-value. (Marx 1970: 29)

It should be noted that this passage is from an earlier work, in which Marx was not yet fully consistent in his distinction between labour, labour-power and labour-time. Later in the same work he introduces the analogy of weight—here referring to labour-time:

> Just as a pound of iron and a pound of gold have the *same* weight despite their different physical and chemical properties, so two commodities which have different use-values but contain the same amount of labour-time have the same *exchange-value*. (Marx 1970: 34)

This analogy is further developed in *Capital*, in the context of the equivalent form of value, and proves to be quite instructive:

> A sugar-loaf being a body, is heavy, and therefore has weight: but we can neither see nor touch this weight. We then take various pieces of iron, whose weight has been determined beforehand. The iron, as iron, is no more the form of manifestation of weight than is the sugar-loaf. Nevertheless, in order to express the sugar-loaf as so much weight, we put it into a weight-relation with the iron. In this relation, the iron officiates as a body representing nothing but weight. A certain quantity of iron therefore serves as the measure of the weight of the sugar, and represents, in relation to the sugar-loaf, weight embodied, the form of manifestation of weight. … Were they not both heavy, they could not enter into this relation. … When we throw both into the scales, we see in reality, that as weight they are both the same, and that, therefore, when taken in proper proportions, they have the same weight. Just as the substance iron, as a measure of weight, represents in relation to the sugar-loaf weight alone, so, in our expression of value, the material object, coat, in relation to linen, represents value alone. (Marx 1954: 62)

But as Marx rightly notes, the analogy then ceases, for:

> The iron, in the expression of the weight of the sugar-loaf, represents a natural property common to both bodies, namely their weight; but the coat, in the expression of value of the linen, represents a non-natural property of both, something purely social, namely, their value. (Marx 1954: 63)

The weight analogy is a great improvement on those from chemistry, for the commensurability of exchange-values is here portrayed as attributable not to a common substance but to a common property. Weight, of course, is a rather complex phenomenon, in which the notion of relation between entities is central, a fact which makes it potentially very fruitful as an analogy. Something of this potential is indicated in Marx's discussion of the concept of "power of attraction". This is in response to Bailey's assertions about the power of commodities to purchase each other, where Marx notes the need to distinguish between:

> An object's 'power' of exchanging, etc. … and the *'relation in which'* an object exchanges with others. If 'power' is to be regarded as something different from 'relation', then one ought not to say that 'power of exchanging'

> is '*merely the relation*', etc. … The *relation* of a thing to another is a relation of the two things and cannot be said to belong to either. *Power of a thing*, on the contrary, is something intrinsic to the thing, although this its intrinsic quality, may only manifest itself in its relation to other things. For instance, power of attraction is a power of the thing itself although that power is 'latent' so long as there are no things to attract. (Marx 1971: 141)

This is a revealing analogy; perhaps most importantly it focuses attention on the question: where is the power to attract (analogous to the power to exchange) "located"?[1] Marx notes that the power of the thing is a relational power, manifested only in the presence of another thing (cf. the "two poles" of the expression of value in Chapter 1 of *Capital*). But he asserts, nevertheless, that it is "a power of the thing itself". It would surely have been a more valid analogy (and also, as it happens, better physics) if he had instead observed that the power of attraction derives from the location of the thing in a "field"—a gravitational field somewhat similar to the "social field" in which commodities are to be found.

By comparison with the chemical analogies (if not those of weight and power of attraction) the geometrical analogies are more instructive. Consider, first, one which was initially introduced by Bailey, and taken up by Marx in his commentary. Although clearly of the opinion that Bailey mishandles the analogy, he appears to find it a useful one nevertheless. Indeed, it has some of the same virtues of the weight analogy just discussed:

> He (Bailey) reveals his philosophical profundity in the following passage: 'As we cannot speak of the *distance of any object without* implying some other object, *between which and the former this relation exists*, so we cannot speak of the value of a commodity but in reference to *another commodity compared with it*'.

Marx comments:

[1] Marx's observations here, and in some of the quotations that follow, relate closely to Cohen's remarks about relational properties referred to in Chap. 4.

> "If we speak of the distance as a relation between two things, we presuppose something 'intrinsic' some 'property' of the things themselves, which enables them to be distant from each other. What is the distance between the syllable A and a table? The question would be nonsensical. In speaking of the distance of two things we speak of their difference in space. Thus we suppose both of them to be contained in space, to be points of space. *Thus we equalise them as being both existences of space* (my stress) and only after having them equalised *sub specie spatii* we distinguish them as different points of space. *To belong to space is their unity* (my stress). (Marx 1971: 143)

Things which can be compared as values are, in Marx's words, of like kind, "homogeneous", of the same species. What is the nature of this common unity? Marx employs another variant of the space analogy, this time referring not to distance but to area. The first time is in a footnote to the above quotation:

> If I say that the area of a triangle A is equal to that of the parallelogram B, this means not only that the area of the triangle is expressed in the parallelogram and that of the parallelogram in the triangle, but it means that if the height of the triangle is equal to h and the base equal to b, then A = hxb/2, a property which belongs to it itself just as it is a property of the parallelogram that it is likewise equal to hxb/2. As areas, the triangle and the parallelogram are here declared to be equal, to be equivalents, although as a triangle and a parallelogram they are different. In order to equate these different things with one another, each must represent *the same common element* regardless of the other. (Marx 1971: 143)

He returns later to the same analogy, but uses it in a way which differs most importantly:

> (for example, in order to compare a triangle with any of the other polygons it is only necessary to transform this latter into triangles, to express them in triangles. But to do this the triangle and the polygon are in fact supposed to be something *identical*, different figures of the same thing—space). (Marx 1971: 160)

The crucial distinction between these two passages is that in the first Marx equates the two unlike things by virtue of their containing a common element—area. In the second passage he equates them by virtue of their both being figures of space. Although two things might be considered to "share a common unity" by virtue either of both being composed of the same elements, or both being elements of the same whole, there is surely an important difference between these two types of unity. And this is of significance for an understanding of value. Thus, two things may "share a common unity" because they both contain labour, or because they are both part of some whole—of social labour. This distinction does not seem to be noted by Marx here.[2]

We know, of course, that a figure of space (or, more accurately, two-dimensional space) must have an area. But area and space are surely very distinct concepts. And, I would argue, the latter is ontologically prior. The distinction with which we are concerned seems to be very similar to that which underlies Bailey's error, to which Marx draws attention in the passage which immediately follows. Having quoted the relevant passage from Bailey, Marx goes on:

> We have the fellow here. We find the values measured, expressed in the *prices*. We can therefore (asserts Bailey) content ourselves with *not* knowing what value is. He confuses the development of the measure of value into money and further the development of money as the standard of price with the discovery of the *concept of value* itself in its development as the immanent measure of commodities in exchange. (Marx 1971: 161)

But this passage is not entirely satisfactory. To refer to value as "the immanent measure of commodities in exchange" might be taken to imply that value is more akin to area than to space. Would it not be more accurate to observe that money is the measure of value, as area is the measure of space? Is value a measure of commodities in exchange, or some common quality by virtue of which they can be compared? It is by virtue

[2] These alternative types of "common unity" are less applicable, if at all, to the other analogies already discussed. Different substances contain oxygen, but are not also part of a greater whole. Different things have weight; they are not thereby parts of a "whole"—but they are members of a system of mutually attracting things, somewhat akin to having "a common unity".

of the common unity of both being in two-dimensional space that a triangle and a parallelogram are commensurable. But that which is measured, in respect of each, is their area.

Just as space "allows" area, so too does heat "allow" temperature and gravity "allow" weight. The former, in each case, is ontologically prior. Much confusion has arisen in the interpretation of Marx's labour theory of value by the failure to understand this crucial ontological distinction (ultimately expressed as the distinction between labour and labour-power). As Engels put it:

> It is not labour which has a value. As an activity which creates value it can no more have any special value than gravity can have any special weight, heat any special temperature, electricity any special strength of current. It is not labour which is bought and sold as a commodity, but labour-*power*. (Engels in Marx 1956: 18)

Perhaps Engels' comparison of Marx with Lavoisier is too modest a claim. For Lavoisier merely discovered a new element, whereas with value we may be confronted by a category as basic as space.

These ideas were, I suggest, not fully worked out at the time of writing *Theories of Surplus Value*, which may account for some of the weaknesses noted above. Even in *Capital* Marx sometimes seems to be inconsistent in his formulation. This is most notable in his discussion of Aristotle on value (see also Chap. 12).

> Aristotle therefore, himself, tells us what barred the way to his further analysis; it was the absence of any concept of value. What is that equal something, that common substance, which admits of the value of the beds being expressed by a house? Such a thing, in truth, cannot exist, says Aristotle. And why not? Compared with the beds, the house does represent something equal to them, in so far as it represents what is really equal, both in the beds and the house. And that is—human labour. (Marx 1954, 65)[3]

[3] This passage *could* be interpreted as consistent with the view that labour is not a substance. The more common reading would be that labour is indeed a substance and that Aristotle's error lay not in looking for such a substance but in failing to find it.

Marx rightly identifies a conceptual void—the absence of any "concept of value". There must be something which allows things to be compared. Commensurability requires some form of common unity. But it is necessary to stop a moment and ask what sort of thing value has to be in order to fill this conceptual void. It need not, I suggest, be a common substance. Marx sometimes, but not always, appears to take the same view.[4]

Although some of the analogies here discussed—notably weight and space—have considerable merit, they have the limitation of referring to natural phenomena. This is true of all the analogies that Marx employs for value. Yet it is perfectly clear that value is a social phenomenon *par excellence*; as Marx was very much aware. Also, these physical analogies give no scope for investigating the process, the way in which value comes to be and, most important of all, for investigating the starting point itself.

It is surely strange that Marx on the one hand stressed that value was not a natural phenomenon (and that indeed many of the errors of his predecessors could be traced to their failure to recognise this) while on the other hand he was apparently content to use analogies of an entirely natural, asocial kind in order to try and understand or explain the concept.

Marx was impressed by, and well acquainted with, the work of contemporary natural scientists. And he saw his own enterprise as scientific, in a similar way. But the object of his analysis—value—was clearly not a natural phenomenon. And the discipline of economics had, in his view, been severely hampered by its asocial approach. This creates something of a paradox. He uses religious metaphors (such as fetishism, the Trinity

---

[4] Here Rubin's discussion of the "Content and Form of Value" is of interest. He asks "what is that 'form of value' which as opposed to exchange value is included in the concept of value?" His answer is as follows:

> I will mention only one of the clearest definitions of the form of value in the first edition of Capital: 'The *social form* of commodities and the *form of value*, or *form of exchangeability* are, thus, one and the same'. As we can see, the form of value is called a form of exchangeability, or a social form of the product of labour which resides in the fact that it can be exchanged for any other commodity, *if this exchangeability is determined by the quantity of labour necessary for the production of the given commodity* (my stress). (Rubin 1982: 115)

This last sentence of Rubin's unfortunately fails to clarify—indeed even evades—the issue of the (quantitative and qualitative) relation between labour and value.

Formula) to refer to some of the phenomena which he critically analysed. But, as he discovered, such phenomena cannot readily be dismissed; commodities enjoy a rather more privileged ontological status than the ancient Moloch. In this sense, neither of the two types of analogy—the material or the religious—was adequate to his purpose.

An analogy of a very different sort was available to him—namely that of language. Marx more than once referred to language, as the epitome of the social:

> For to stamp an object of utility as a value is just as much a social product as language. (Marx 1954: 79)

> Language as the product of an individual is an impossibility. But the same holds for property. (Marx 1973, 490)

Yet he did not see fit to use language as an analogy. One passage in his writing (Marx 1973: 163) indicates that he considered, but rejected, such an idea. But the grounds for this rejection are inadequate. This I shall argue in Chap. 10 whose purpose is precisely to examine the parallels between value and meaning. Before doing so, however, I must first take account of the work of other Marxian commentators in this field.

Bibliography

Korsch, K. (1938). *Introduction to Das Kapital*. Berlin.

Kuhn, T. S. (1970). *The Structure of Scientific Revolutions*. Chicago: University Press.

Marx, K. (1954). *Capital* (Vol. I). Moscow: Progress.

Marx, K. (1956). *Capital* (Vol. II). Moscow: Progress.

Marx, K. (1970). *A Contribution to the Critique of Political Economy*. Moscow: Progress.

Marx, K. (1971). *Theories of Surplus Value, Part III*. Moscow: Progress.

Marx, K. (1973). *Grundrisse*. Moscow: Progress.

Rubin, I. I. (1982). *Essays on Marx's Theory of Value*. Montreal: Black Rose Books.

9

The Limitations of Structural Marxism

Introduction

The material world is only indirectly perceived, mediated as it is by the senses, but also by the categories of thought which we acquire from others—embodied, typically, in the language we learn. In the case of social phenomena, the power of these categories of thought is immense; for the beliefs themselves are constitutive of the social reality. Not only do our categories influence the way in which we perceive social reality, they actually contribute to that reality.

Marx was aware of the power of such categories over people. Indeed one could almost say that he was himself a very rare counter-example against his own assertions; for he was able, at least to a remarkable extent, to transcend these categories and see the world in a different light. But in this enterprise he was severely hampered, for even if he could himself perceive the faults in the categories of his time, how was he to communicate them to others? It is hard enough to think new ideas with old words;

This is a revised version of a chapter in McNeill, D (1988) *Fetishism and the Form of Value*. Unpublished thesis, University of London.

D. McNeill, *Fetishism and the Theory of Value*, Palgrave Studies in the History of Economic Thought, https://doi.org/10.1007/978-3-030-56123-9_9

but to communicate them is even harder. As discussed in the previous chapter, it is here that analogy and metaphor come into their own, But Marx tended to favour mechanical, material analogies—based on a nineteenth century, almost Newtonian world view. A more fruitful approach for describing social phenomena would have been a comparison with language—as I shall argue at greater length in Chap. 10.

Unfortunately, linguistics was, in Marx's day, a rather limited field of study, concerned largely with tracing historical origins. It was after his time that linguistics really developed, so successfully indeed that it exerted a considerable influence over the social sciences, notably through structuralism. My claim, therefore, is that Marx could have benefitted considerably from a knowledge of twentieth-century linguistics, or more specifically from structuralism, in communicating his theories—and even, perhaps, in deepening his understanding; for if a lack of words is a constraint to communication, it can also be a constraint to thought. Marxian economics, I suggest, could learn something from structuralism.

But this, it would seem, is by no means an original idea. Structural Marxism is a well-established field. Or rather, it would appear to have already come and gone—to judge by the title of Benton's *The Rise and Fall of Structural Marxism* (1984). I agree that structural Marxism has been largely ineffectual, but I maintain that this is not the end of the matter; structuralism has indeed much to offer to Marxian economics.

The main aim of the present chapter is to substantiate this view, by giving a critique of structural Marxism. I begin with Althusser, who is certainly regarded as the major figure in this field. I argue that although he had the merit of recognising the enormity of what he called "Marx's Immense Theoretical Revolution", and tried to come to grips with some of the very new concepts which Marx, implicitly or explicitly, introduced (notably what Althusser calls "structural causality"), he in fact benefitted rather little from structuralism. In part, perhaps, this was because his interests extended beyond those in which structuralism has most to offer. Perhaps, also, the way he used structuralism was inappropriate.

The latter is not a charge which could be levelled at the second person whose work I consider—Lévi-Strauss. It is he who is generally credited with extending structuralism beyond the domain of linguistics and into anthropology and the social sciences in general. It is apparent, however, that Lévi-Strauss was not very well acquainted with the detail of Marxian economics; in his writings, especially on economics, important insights are often obscured and major issues confused. It is possible, also, that Lévi-Strauss has been somewhat misrepresented by other commentators, who have sought to interpret him too literally. Certainly he is the victim as well as the beneficiary of his own eclecticism. And it emerges that he has rather little to offer in showing how Marxian economics can learn from structuralism.

The third major figure discussed in this chapter is Godelier, who has merits which both the other two lack. His knowledge of economics is superior to that of Lévi-Strauss; and he appears to avoid many of the traps into which Althusser fell. But he too, I argue, makes effective use of structuralism to only a limited extent.

In the chapter that follows this, I examine some aspects of Marxian economics—and particularly the concepts of value and the commodity—where, I believe, structuralism (or rather semiotics, or the study of signs) has more to offer. I begin both chapters, however, with de Saussure, the founder of modern linguistics, a central figure with whose work any review of structuralism should properly begin. In his *Cours de Linguistique Générale* (Course in General Linguistics), he laid the foundations of the structuralist method, introducing the key distinctions between "signifier" and "signified", between "langue" and "parole", and between "synchrony" and "diachrony".

Structural Marxism, as presented by Althusser, and as criticised by numerous commentators, typically makes reference only to the third of these distinctions. Yet for a better understanding of economics, this is perhaps the least enlightening. What is more, and what is widely ignored, is that this was pointed out by de Saussure himself. For, in the *Cours*, de Saussure makes two separate references to economics, and its possible analogy with linguistics. I shall discuss the first here, and defer discussion of the other to my next chapter.

I begin, then, with the synchrony/diachrony distinction. This is broadly similar to the distinction between cross-sectional and longitudinal analysis, and de Saussure argues that linguistics had, in his time, become unduly concerned with the diachronic at the expense of the synchronic. Whereas the "traditional grammarians" tried to describe language-states, the modern approach, which he referred to as evolutionary linguistics, dealt with changes over time. Indeed: "ever since modern linguistics came into existence, it has been completely absorbed in diachrony" (de Saussure 1974a: 82).

To illustrate the synchronic/diachronic distinction, de Saussure makes a comparison between the functioning of language and a game of chess:

> In both instances we are confronted with a system of values and their observable modifications. … First, a set of chessmen corresponds closely to a state of language. The respective value of the pieces depends on their position on the chessboard just as each linguistic term derives its value from its opposition to all the other terms. In the second place, the system is always momentary; it varies from one position to the next. … Finally, … to pass from one synchrony to the next, only one chesspiece has to be moved; there is no general rummage. … In a game of chess any particular position has the unique characteristic of being freed from all antecedent positions; the route used in arriving there makes absolutely no difference. (de Saussure 1974a: 88)[1]

de Saussure argues that very few linguists are aware of this "radical duality", which does not affect most other sciences. Astronomy, geology, law and political history of states are all cited by him as examples. But he notes an important exception—the economic sciences.

> Here, in contrast to the other sciences, political economy and economic history constitute two clearly separated disciplines within a single science; the works that have recently appeared on these subjects point up the distinction. Proceeding as they have, economists are—without being well aware of it—obeying an inner necessity. A similar necessity obliges us to divide linguistics into two parts, each with its own principle. (de Saussure 1974a: 79)

[1] De Saussure goes on to note that the comparison is weak in one respect—as discussed below, in relation to Lévi-Strauss.

For an interpretation of this passage it is helpful to enlist the assistance of other commentators. Tullio de Mauro provides a useful gloss on the "inner duality" common to linguistics and political economy in his comments on de Saussure 1974b:

> The passage is interesting because it shows that de Saussure was not only aware of the debate in sociology between Durkheim and Tarde, but also (and we say this with a certainty based on his own explicit personal testimony) of the debate between the 'Historical School' and the 'Theoretical School' in political economy in his era. (de Saussure 1974b: 451) (My translation)

The Historical School was, in the words of Roll, "for nearly forty years the most influential school of economic thought in German-speaking countries. Its reign dates from 1843, when Roscher's *Grundrisse* appeared. It was not successfully attacked until 1883, when Carl Menger published his *Untersuchungen*" (Roll 1973: 303). It was this latter work which initiated the famous *Methodenstreit*, the debate on method in the social sciences. The details of this debate cannot be spelled out here. I should merely note that although the similarity which de Saussure apparently observed between linguistics and economics had some validity, the extent and nature of this similarity (like de Saussure's own views) may have been misrepresented; for the *Methodenstreit* was not simply an attempt to replace a diachronic by a synchronic approach. Indeed, Menger is credited by Roll with drawing attention to an important difference between the physical and the social sciences, and noting that economic laws are "essentially relative and variable" (Roll 1973: 308).[2] This is a point of some significance, for the application of the structuralist method to economics has been particularly criticised for its emphasis on the synchronic (especially in relation to Althusser, as discussed below). Two points should, however, be noted. First, de Saussure does not, as some commentators imply, advocate a purely synchronic approach to linguistics, but rather an appropriate balance. Thus: "The more complex and rigorously

[2] Piaget (another famous writer on structuralism, in this case a child psychologist) suggests that "Saussure ... drew his inspiration partly from economics, which in his day chiefly stressed the former (laws of equilibrium rather than laws of development)" (Piaget 1971: 77). It would be interesting if it were indeed the case that it was economics which inspired linguistics and not the other way round; but there seems to be no textual support for this assertion in the passages quoted.

ordered a system of values is, the more it is necessary, because of its very complexity, to study it according to both coordinates (the synchronic and the diachronic)" (de Saussure 1974a: 81). Second, there is a further analogy between economics and linguistics which, according to de Saussure, also holds, and which has been given less attention in the literature; as discussed in the next chapter.

Althusser

After this brief introduction, I now turn to the work of Althusser. This may seem perverse, since he himself has denied being a structuralist and I do not believe that he uses structuralist method to much effect. Nevertheless, it is his name which is most closely linked with what has been called "structural Marxism". As Benton notes, despite Althusser's denials, and although when he "employs structuralist terminology he simultaneously distances himself from what he calls 'structuralist ideology'", he nevertheless makes no attempt at defence against "the structuralist critique. On the contrary, arguments, sometimes with a clear structuralist ancestry … are given a specific focus in the refutation of humanist and historicist Marxisms" (Benton 1984: 14).

It is certainly appropriate, then, that I should begin with Althusser's ideas. But it is not my intention to attempt a full-scale assessment of his contribution as a Marxist commentator. My interest is in structuralism, so that I shall mainly be concerned with how he makes use of it, and to what extent criticisms of Althusser are criticisms of the application of structuralism to economics.

Althusser's theoretical position may be clarified by identifying two of his main claims. First, that "Marxism is not a humanism". In terms of my earlier, and rather crude, classification, this implies that he rejects a methodological individualist interpretation of Marx. The danger inherent in such a position is that it can lead to the so-called death of the subject. In other words, human agency may be excluded, with serious implications not only for understanding but also for political action.

Second, Althusser also claims that "Marxism is not a historicism". Again referring to my earlier classification, I take this to mean that he also rejects what I have called strong methodological holism. In other words (at the risk of caricature) phenomena are not to be explained in teleological terms, by the relentless drive of history achieving its own realisation. Here, the danger is adherence to a wholly static view, denying, or at best ignoring, process. These, in brief, are two of Althusser's main claims, and the causes of much of the criticism levelled against him—and, indeed, against structuralism. But before considering these in more detail, I will first elaborate on how he "reads" Marx.

Althusser claimed that "with Marx we are at the site of a historical break of the first importance" (Althusser and Balibar 1979: 154); that Marx had a new "vision" which enabled him to see what Smith and even Ricardo had failed to see—and was thus able to "read" Smith in a new way, a way in which Althusser enjoins us to "read" *Capital*. Marx was able to identify Smith's oversights, "to see this invisible".[3] Althusser urges his readers to do the same, to which end "we need something quite different from an acute or attentive gaze; we need an *informed* gaze,[4] a new gaze, itself produced by a reflection of the 'change of terrain' on their exercise of vision, in which Marx pictures the transformation of the problematic" (Althusser and Balibar 1979: 27).[5]

Althusser identifies Political Economy with the "empiricist problematic"—in contrast with Marx's theory with which it is "in rupture". "At the economic level, strictly speaking, the *structure* constituting and determining economic objects is the following: the unity of the productive forces and the relations of production" (Althusser and Balibar 1979: 182). Three results follow from this rupture between Marx and his predecessors:

---

[3] Althusser says that political economy is necessarily blind to what it produces (Althusser and Balibar 1979: 24)—but he nevertheless refers to it as "a *psychological* weakness of 'vision'" (Althusser and Balibar 1979: 19) (my stress).

[4] cf. Schumpeter's "vision" referred to in Chap. 1 (Schumpeter 1954).

[5] Although I shall minimise the use of Althusser's neologisms, a few will inevitably creep in—such as "the problematic" which relates to the important concept of structural causality. Here we may quote Althusser directly:

> I put this term forward ... because it is the concept that gives the best grasp of the facts without falling into the Hegelian ambiguities of '*totality*'... (t) o think the unity of a determinate ideological unity ... by means of the concept of its *problematic* is to allow the *typical systematic structure* unifying all the elements of the thought to be brought to light, and therefore to discover in this unity a *determinate content.* (Althusser 1977: 66)

> *first*: the economic cannot have the qualities of a *given*. … The concept of the economic must be constructed *for each mode of production*. … *Second*: if the 'field' of economic phenomena no longer has the *homogeneity* of an infinite plane, its objects are no longer *de jure* homogeneous at all points with one another: they are therefore no longer uniformly susceptible to comparison and *measurement*. … Mathematical formalization must be subordinate to conceptual formalization. *Third*: … the concept of linear causality can no longer be applied to them as it has been hitherto. A different concept is required in order to account for the new form of causality required by the new definition of the object of Political Economy, by its 'complexity', i.e., by its peculiar determination: *the determination by a structure*. (Althusser and Balibar 1979: 183)

Althusser particularly stresses the importance of this last point, and the need to create new concepts in order to break with the empiricist ideology, and he suggests that "the birth of every new science inevitably poses theoretical (philosophical) problems of this kind". He refers to Engels' Preface to Volume II of *Capital* (discussed in Chap. 8) and concludes that:

> The epistemological problem posed by Marx's radical modification of Political Economy can be expressed as follows: …. how is it possible to define the concept of a structural causality? (Althusser and Balibar 1979: 186)

This is the "simple question" which was contained in Marx's work, which "contained enough to smash all the classical theories of causality—or enough to ensure that it would be unrecognized, that it would pass unperceived and be buried even before it was born". This, surely, was the task that Althusser believed he had achieved to disinter and shed light on this crucial question.

Althusser goes on to describe the only two theories of causality available to Marx. The first is the Cartesian, mechanistic system, "which reduced causality to a *transitive* and analytical effectivity: it could not be made to think the effectivity of a whole on its elements, except at the cost of extraordinary distortions (such as those in Descartes' 'psychology' and biology)" (Althusser and Balibar 1979: 187).

> But a second system was available, one conceived precisely in order to deal with the effectivity of a whole on its elements: the Leibnizian concept of

> *expression*. This is the model that dominates all Hegel's thought. … Here was a model which made it possible to think the effectivity of the whole on each of its elements, but … *it presupposed that the whole had a certain nature, precisely the nature of a 'spiritual' whole in which each element was expressive of the entire totality as a* 'pars totalis'. In other words, Leibniz and Hegel did have a category for the effectivity of the whole on its elements or parts, but on the absolute condition that the whole was not a structure. (Althusser and Balibar 1979: 187)

It is this last point that is crucial, and which Althusser claims Marx did not pose as a problem, although he did "set out to solve it practically in the absence of its concept, with extraordinary ingenuity. … It is on this problem that Marx is attempting to focus in the tentative sentences we can read in the *Introduction*"[6] (Althusser and Balibar 1979: 187).

In Marx's writing, the crucial word, Althusser believes, is "'*Darstellung*', the key epistemological concept of the whole Marxist theory of value, the concept whose object is precisely to designate the mode of presence *of the structure in its effects, and therefore to designate structural causality itself*" (Althusser and Balibar 1979: 188).[7]

Althusser devotes much discussion to this concept of "structural causality" but to rather little effect. This is a topic on which structuralist theory (and especially linguistics) might have something to offer. But Althusser never satisfactorily explicates this important phenomenon. Indeed his summary exposition of Spinoza—who, alone among philosophers, he credits with an understanding of this type of causality—is simply:

> In short (that) the structure, which is merely a specific combination of its peculiar elements, is nothing outside its effects. (Althusser and Balibar 1979: 189)

[6] "In all forms of society it is a determinate production and its relations which assign every other production and its relations their rank and influence. It is a general illumination in which all the other colours are plunged and which modifies their special tonalities. It is a special ether which defines the specific weight of every existence arising in it" (the contents of the brackets by Marx 1973 to *Grundrisse*).

[7] A relatively simple but clear example of structural causality has already been referred to in an earlier chapter: how is it that a spinning-jenny "is" capital?

As Benton says, in discussing this part of Althusser's work: "It is hard to see in his attempt to resolve it any more than a restatement of the question" (Benton 1984: 64). I would go further. It is not merely inadequate, but incorrect, to conclude that the structure is "nothing outside its effects". Certainly there are severe difficulties in trying to conceptualise this type of causality. There are also enormous difficulties in trying to conceptualise linear causality, as Hume has demonstrated; but this has not prevented it becoming central to our way of perceiving the world. This may help to indicate the severity of the task which Althusser had set himself; but equally it suggests that the task is an important one. Althusser rightly observes that "by other paths contemporary theory in psycho-analysis, linguistics, other disciplines such as biology, and perhaps even physics, has had to confront it" (Althusser and Balibar 1979: 187). Contemporary theory has surely achieved more, in this confrontation, than the conclusion that "the structure is nothing outside its effects"? Yet Althusser does not say so. He seems to have the worst of both worlds; accused of being a "structuralist" yet not even using structuralist method to good effect.[8]

The problem, I suggest, derives largely from Althusser's failure to distinguish adequately between two different issues. He seeks to employ the concept of structural causality not only to explicate the capitalist system of economic categories, but also to account for a wholly diachronic phenomenon: historical change. In some cases he is simply seeking to understand structural causality—to describe the effectivity of a structure—while there are other occasions when he moves on, by almost imperceptible steps, to the related but distinct concept of "overdetermination".

The term "overdetermination" is taken from the psychoanalyst Lacan (another structuralist, who in turn derived it from Freud). The word is used in mathematics to describe a situation in which there are more equations than unknowns. Althusser's usage shares something in common with this, and is explained (or at least introduced) in *For Marx* (Althusser 1977)

[8] Althusser's followers Hindess and Hirst opened themselves to damaging criticism by their attempts to describe this "effectivity" in mechanical or quasi-mechanical terms—although, as Althusser himself indicated, these are inappropriate for the analysis of this type of causality. I am thinking here particularly of the powerful polemic against Althusser and his followers in which Thompson caricatures the "Marxist Orrery" (Thompson 1978: 100).

> We must admit that contradiction can no longer be univocal. … (But) … it has not for all that become 'equivocal' … at the mercy of circumstances and chance … it reveals itself as determined by the structured complexity that assigns it to its role, as—if you will forgive me the astonishing expression—completely-structurally-unevenly-determined. I must admit I preferred a shorter term: overdetermined. (Althusser 1977: 209)

From this and some similar passages it would appear that an overdetermined contradiction is simply one which is located within a structure which is "causally effective". As in the case of "structural causality", Althusser argues the need to replace Hegel's simple view with a more complex one. But the concept of overdetermined contradictions here seems to mean no more than contradictions located within a causally effective structure.

A more extensive elaboration of the term "overdetermination" occurs, however, where Althusser explains that the revolution occurred in Russia because "It (Russia) had accumulated the largest sum of historical contradictions then possible" (Althusser 1977: 97). Here Althusser seeks to use overdetermination to explain historical phenomena. There are (at least) two problems with this. First, the practical implications of Althusser's theory of revolution seem to be nil, since he argues that "an '*overdetermined contradiction*' may either be *overdetermined* in the direction of a *historical inhibition* … or in the direction of *revolutionary rupture*" (Althusser 1977: 106), that is either something will change as a result or it will not. Second, his extension of the analysis of overdetermined contradictions to non-revolutionary situations may be invalid—as he himself concedes in a footnote: "What has been said for a revolutionary situation can therefore be referred cautiously to the social formation in a situation prior to the revolutionary crisis" (Althusser 1977: 100).

My purpose here, however, is not to criticise the concept of overdetermination as such. My concern is to point out a blurring of concepts which, I suggest, has contributed to the unsatisfactory nature of the extensive debate that raged around Althusser, and the associated vocabulary of "domination", "determination in the last instance" and so on. What is relevant here is that the distinction between structural causality and overdetermination mirrors an important distinction between what might be called the (economistic) synchrony of *Capital*[9] and the diachrony of historical materialism. Althusser is ill served by structuralism insofar as he tries to apply it to Marx's historical materialism. It has far more to offer for an understanding of *Capital* as a work of economics.

This major question—of the relevance of structuralism to historical change—relates closely to the two issues introduced above, of process and agency. Althusser has been accused of excluding both, most notably, perhaps, by Thompson, who asserted that historical materialism has come under sustained and ferocious assault from a number of positions "within orthodox 'bourgeois' academic disciplines … from enclaves within the historical profession itself … and from a 'Marxist' structuralism".

> All (including Althusser) commence by questioning the knowability of process, as a total logic of change of sets of inter-related activities, and end up by tilting the vocabularies of knowledge very heavily (even absolutely) towards synchronic rather than diachronic procedures. The diachronic is waived (sic) away as mere unstructured 'narrative', an unintelligible flow of one thing from another. Only the stasis of structural analysis can disclose knowledge. The flow of events ('historicist time') is an empiricist fable. The logic of process is disallowed. (Thompson 1978: 70)

On this charge, Althusser at first sight seems to condemn himself very clearly, for, in discussing the categories of economics he specifically attributes primacy to synchrony. But he then elaborates the point:

> When I say that 'synchrony' thus understood is primary and governs everything I mean two things:
>
> 1. that the system of hierarchy of concepts in their combination determines the definition of each concept …
>
> 2. that the system of the hierarchy of concepts determines the 'diachronic' order of their appearance in the discourse of the proof. It is in this sense that Marx speaks of the '*development of the forms*' (of the concept) of value, surplus value, etc.: this '*development of the forms*' is the manifestation, in the discourse of the scientific proof, of the systematic *dependence*

[9] And to a greater extent *Grundrisse*—see the remarks of Thompson below.

which links the concepts together in the system of the thought-totality. (Althusser and Balibar 1979: 68)

He made a similar point a few pages earlier:

The object of Marx's study is therefore contemporary bourgeois society, which is thought as a historical *result*: but the understanding of this society, far from being obtained from the theory of the genesis of this result, is, on the contrary, obtained exclusively from the theory of the '*body*', i.e., of the *contemporary structure of society*, without its genesis intervening in any way whatsoever. (Althusser and Balibar 1979: 65)

In the first extract he is saying, first, that there is a structured totality of concepts which determines the meaning of every individual concept; and second, that in *Capital* and the *Grundrisse* it is the synchronic relation between the concepts that determines their order of presentation, that is it is necessary to start with the "basic" categories, such as value. This seems entirely compatible with Marx's position, provided it is taken as a guide to the method of presentation of the material.[10]

There are two very distinct problems: to explain the genesis of existing society, its transformation from earlier forms; and to explain the structure of existing society. In *Capital*, it is the second which is primarily confronted:

In this perspective, *Capital* must be regarded as the theory of the mechanism of production of the *society effect* in the capitalist mode of production. (Althusser and Balibar 1979: 66)

And indeed Thompson seems to concede as much:

We must commence, at once, by agreeing that *Capital* is not a work of 'history'. … The work which was completed was that described (to Lassalle in 1858) as 'a critique of the economic categories or the system of bourgeois economy, critically presented'. … By the time that Marx confronted it, this

[10] It is less adequate, however, if it is intended as an explanation of the phenomena, as the second extract perhaps implies.

> (bourgeois) Political Economy had become … a very sophisticated structure indeed. … Marx identified this structure as his major antagonist, and he bent the whole energies of his mind to confounding it. (Thompson 1978: 57, 59)

Thompson marvels at Marx's endeavours, revealed in the *Grundrisse*, but he also fears that Marx is himself "sucked into a theoretical whirlpool" in which he "slowly revolves around a vortex which threatens to engulf him. Value, capital, labour, money, value, reappear again and again."[11] "There is an important sense in which the movement of Marx's thought, in the *Grundrisse*, is locked inside *a static, anti-historical structure*" (Thompson 1978: 61). He argues that in *Capital* the situation is to some extent redeemed; a historical dimension is added; but:

> in some part … the structure of *Capital* remains that of *Grundrisse*. It remains a study of the logic of capital, not of capitalism, and the social and political dimensions of the history, the wrath, and the understanding of the class struggle arise from a region independent of the closed system of economic logic. (Thompson 1978: 65)

Despite his criticisms of Althusser, then, Thompson appears to agree that, certainly in the *Grundrisse* and to a lesser extent in *Capital*, Marx is concerned more with economic logic than with history; more with a structure than a process. This same criticism has been made of structuralism. But that surely does not imply that structuralism has nothing to offer for an understanding of Marx's *Capital*; if anything the reverse would be the case. At most, it may imply that structuralism is ill-suited for certain other purposes—notably an appreciation of historical materialism. Thompson would certainly appear to believe so; for him structuralism is not only static, it also excludes agency: "The subject (or agent) of history disappears once again. Process for the nth time is re-ified" (Thompson 1978: 107).

This "disappearance" is closely linked to the structuralist approach:

---

[11] What we have at the end of this endeavour, he writes, is "not the overthrow of 'Political Economy' but another 'Political Economy'". Marx replaced the accepted categories with "anti-categories", but did not escape the notion of "the economic" (see Chap. 11 for further discussion of this point).

> We can say that a 'worker' is the bearer of productive relations. … (But) we do not go on to say that the capitalist is *being capitaled.* This is what Althusser, and, also, some structural anthropologists and sociologists would wish us to say. … The difference between 'playing' a game and being gamed illustrates the difference between rule-governed structuration of historical eventuation (within which men and women remain as subjects of their own history) and structural*ism*. … Today, … we are *structured* by social relations, *spoken* by given linguistic structures, *thought* by ideologies. (Thompson 1978: 152)

It may be asked whether Thompson is better able to account for the role of the individual agent in history. As Benton notes: "since human agency is, for Thompson, the immediate source of all historical change, it follows that he, no less than Althusser, is incapable of explaining historical change" (Benton 1984: 213). The relationship between the individual and society is undeniably complex, but neither society nor the individual need be seen as wholly "autonomous". Only an extreme version of structuralism would assign no place whatever to the individual.

In his discussion of this issue, Benton identifies three methodological principles which may provide "the beginnings of a way out of this impasse". The third of these, which I would particularly like to note, is that:

> explanation in terms of structures is not the same thing as explanation in terms of *immutable* structures. Any more or less enduring pattern of relationships between agents … or between agents and objects may be thought of as constituting a 'structure'. Relationships may confer causal powers on the agents which they relate and they may effect constraints on their behaviour in various ways. The susceptibility of relationships to deliberate dissolution or transformation by agents is similarly immensely variable—from the delicacy of the bonds constituting a friendship to the immense resilience of the relations constituting a mode of economic production. (Benton 1984: 214)

The issue need not be resolved here; for my purpose is not to defend structuralism against all criticism. I simply wish to note that it is not, of necessity, incapable either of accommodating change, or of allowing some role for the individual.

To summarise there is certainly some validity in the critique of structuralism by Thompson and others. It does tend to emphasise the synchronic rather than the diachronic, and the whole rather than the individual. But it is not incapable (as Benton notes) of accommodating process and agency; and it has important merits which other approaches lack. But perhaps the most compelling argument in its favour, in seeking to understand Marx's ideas, is that insofar as the criticisms of structuralism are valid, they are equally applicable to the argument as Marx presented it. Althusser and Thompson are in agreement with regard to the limitations of *Capital* in this respect (although Althusser did not present it as a criticism).

In closing the discussion on Althusser I would like to consider briefly what he himself said about the structuralist method. For this, we must refer to the cringing apologetics of one of his "Essays in Self-Criticism" where he tries to establish at what unfortunate point in his career "the young pup of structuralism, slipped between my legs" (Althusser 1976: 125). The "deviation" of structuralism in fact buried "the main deviation, theoreticism" in Althusser's words. In 1965, "we had not yet appreciated the exceptional importance of the role of the class struggle". "It is a fact", he goes on, "we did finally treat it as a 'science like the others', thus falling into the dangers of theoreticism. But we were never structuralists" (Althusser 1976: 131).

"It must be admitted", he says,

> that it thus became tempting to flirt not with the structure and its elements etc., (because all these concepts are in Marx) but for example with the notion of the 'effectivity of an absent cause'—which is, it must be said, much more Spinozist than structuralist!—in order to account at one and the same time for Classical Political Economy's 'mistakes' … and to herald, by the term 'structural causality' (cf. Spinoza), something which is in fact an 'immense theoretical discovery' of Marx but which can also, in the Marxist tradition, be termed dialectical *materialist* causality … we were not always able to restrain ourselves, in certain pages of *Reading Capital*, in that spring of 1965, and our 'flirt' with structuralist terminology obviously went beyond acceptable limits. (Althusser 1976: 126)

To his credit, he does refer to de Saussure and his school as "important thinkers" and concedes that there are "certain good 'structuralist' (anti-psychological, anti-historicist) reflexes". But he cannot seem to decide whether to abandon the concept of "structural causality" or to assert that it is fully compatible with historical materialism. He also ties himself in knots in his discussion of process—undecided whether or not to claim that future theory would vindicate his apparent error:

> There are those who have said, or will one day say, that Marxism is distinguished from structuralism by the *primacy of the process over the structure*. Formally, this is not false … (but) it is possible to conceive of a *formalism of the process* … therefore a structuralism … of the process!. (Althusser 1976: 125)

Although critical of both his language and his ideas, I must concede that I have benefitted from some of the insights in Althusser's writings, and I believe that his analysis of Marx is potentially enlightening. In summary, I take the view that although Althusser focussed attention on a very important issue in his discussion of the concept of structural causality, his work is seriously marred. First, and perhaps most important, it is not rigorous. Structuralism has its limitations, as I have conceded above. But Althusser not only fails to confront these failings, he does not even present his case to the best advantage. Second, and closely related to this, he blurs two conceptually distinct issues ("structural causality" and "overdetermination"); thus he introduces, but fails to resolve, problems to which a structuralist approach is less suited.

Lévi-Strauss: Communication and Exchange

If Althusser gained little from structuralism, the same cannot be said for the anthropologist Lévi-Strauss. Although not strictly a "structural Marxist", he certainly claimed Marx as a major influence on his work[12]

[12] He went so far as to describe Marxism as one of his "three mistresses"—along with geology and psychoanalysis (Freud).

and, after de Saussure, is probably the most important figure in the development of the structuralist method, for it was he who widened its application from linguistics to anthropology, and recommended its extension to other social sciences.[13] In *Structural Anthropology* (1972), he argues that linguistics is the social science in which "by far the greatest progress has been made" and notes the "close methodological analogy" which exists between sociology and linguistics. Indeed, he suggests that "it is not only permissible for, but required of, representatives of related disciplines immediately to examine its (structural linguistics') consequences and its possible application to phenomena of another order" (Lévi-Strauss 1972: 33). His recommendation has not gone unheeded, for the structuralist method has since been applied in many different fields.[14]

In support of his claim, Lévi-Strauss indicates how the structuralist method made it possible to explain the more general features of marriage rules and kinship systems:

> Though such customs had been unintelligible to anthropologists, they were perfectly clear when regarded as illustrating different modalities of the laws of exchange. ... Now, these results can be achieved only by treating marriage regulations and kinship systems as a kind of language, a set of processes permitting the establishment between individuals and groups, of a certain type of communication. That the mediating factor, in this case, should be the *women of the group*, who are *circulated* between clans, lineages, or families, in place of the *words of the group*, which are *circulated* between individuals, does not at all change the fact that the essential aspect of the phenomenon is identical in both cases. (Lévi-Strauss 1972: 60)

Lévi-Strauss also applied the structuralist method to the analysis of myth—again with very fruitful results.[15] What is of more relevance here is that he suggested extending his approach to economics, by exploring the analogy with the exchange of goods and services, and indeed seeing

[13] He acknowledges a debt, however, not to de Saussure but to a later writer, Troubetzkoy.

[14] For example, by Lacan in psychoanalysis, Barthes in literature, Derrida in philosophy, Foucault in his studies of power.

[15] His work in both these areas of study has been severely criticised. It is not my purpose to evaluate his contribution to anthropology but it cannot be doubted that he had a profound influence within and beyond this discipline.

the whole of society in terms of types of "exchange" in a wide sense of the term:

> Without reducing society or culture to language, we can initiate this 'Copernican revolution' … which will consist of interpreting society as a whole in terms of a theory of communication. This endeavour is possible on three levels, since the rules of kinship and marriage serve to insure the circulation of women between groups, just as economic rules serve to insure the circulation of goods and services, and linguistic rules the circulation of messages. (Lévi-Strauss 1972: 83)

But he did not elaborate substantially on the economic analogy in any of his major works.[16] And indeed, even in this instance, he argues that the comparison between the fields of kinship, economics and linguistics is limited by "the fact that they refer to forms of communication which are on a different scale".

> Thus, from marriage to language one passes from low- to high-speed communication; this arises from the fact that what is communicated in marriage is almost of the same nature as those who communicate (women on the one hand, men, on the other), while speakers of language are not of the same nature as their utterances. This opposition is thus one of *person* to *symbol*, or of *value* to *sign*. This helps to clarify the somewhat intermediate position of economics between these two extremes—goods and services are not persons, but they still are values. And, though neither symbols nor signs, they require symbols or signs in order to be successfully exchanged when the exchange system reaches a certain degree of complexity. (Lévi-Strauss 1972: 296)

[16] In *Structural Anthropology*, his only further comments tended to confuse the issue by noting direct interconnections rather than developing the analogy:

> These three forms of communication are also forms of exchange which are obviously interrelated (because marriage relations are associated with economic prestations, and language comes into play at all levels). (Lévi-Strauss 1972: 83)

Certainly, marriage is directly linked with exchange of goods (through dowries etc.), and language is involved in both—but this, in itself, adds little to our understanding of any of the three phenomena.

This last point, though rather obscure, recalls the signifier/signified distinction, which will be taken up later. Apart from this, however, the contribution of Lévi-Strauss to economics remains unfulfilled promise.[17] The limited use of the analogies that Lévi-Strauss draws with economics is attributable largely to the scanty, and even inconsistent, view that he has of economics as a social science, as revealed in his discussion, in *Structural Anthropology*, of the contribution which mathematics could make to the social sciences. He begins with the important distinction between *measure* and *structure*, noting how "modern developments in mathematics have given increasing importance to the qualitative point of view in contradistinction to the quantitative" (Lévi-Strauss 1972: 283). But his list of "outstanding achievements in this connection—which offer themselves as springboards not yet utilized by social scientists" is so undiscriminating as to suggest that he does not himself recognise the contribution that structuralism might make. For the list not only includes mathematical logic, set theory, group theory, topology and cybernetics, but it begins with J. von Neumann and O. Morgenstern, *Theory of Games and Economic Behaviour*. Certainly, this book has made a very major contribution to economic science; but the methodology adopted (and indeed the implicit model of society on which it is based) is surely quite incompatible with the structuralist approach. Yet it is this work which Lévi-Strauss refers to a second time, claiming that its publication "ushers in an era of close cooperation between the economist and the anthropologist" (Lévi-Strauss 1972: 297).[18]

A more complete statement of the argument is contained elsewhere in Lévi-Strauss' writings, in an article entitled "The Mathematics of Man", where he does make reference to de Saussure, but distorts his argument:

> de Saussure had also suggested a comparison between language and certain games of strategy, such as chess. This assimilation of language to a sort of

[17] He writes also on the subject of reciprocity, where Mauss made a more significant contribution—as discussed in Chap. 12.

[18] The theory of games is, however, relevant to a very different anthropological tradition, represented by, for example, Fredrik Barth, the author of *Ethnic groups and boundaries: The social organization of culture difference* (1969). The theory of games adopts a "methodological individualist" approach to the analysis of social phenomena, while structuralism adopts a "methodological holist" approach. See Chap. 7.

> combinative process, to which we have already alluded, was to make it possible to apply directly to linguistics the theory of games. … This unexpected association … clearly brings out the fundamental factor of communication, on which all human relations are based. As the exchange of messages, in which linguistic communication consists, and the exchange of goods and services, which belongs to the realm of economics, both now admit of the same formal treatment, they begin to appear as phenomena of the same type. (Lévi-Strauss 1954: 582)

Economics, he suggests, with de Saussure's implied blessing, is analogous to "certain games of strategy". But it is clear from de Saussure's own words that he regarded the analogy between language and chess as imperfect, in one very important respect:

> At only one point is the comparison weak: the chessplayer intends to bring about a shift and thereby to exert an action on the system, whereas language premeditates nothing. (de Saussure 1974a: 89)

This intentionality on the part of the players is at the very core of game theory, so that de Saussure certainly cannot be cited in support of the view that game theory is the appropriate mathematical method for understanding language. It can certainly be argued, and indeed has been argued by many, that game theory is appropriate for understanding economic behaviour. But this is only if one adopts a very different position from that which Lévi-Strauss appears to favour, and for which structuralist analysis might be appropriate. The manner in which he argues the case for games theory is most revealing:

> When we look at the *Theory of Games* what do we find? … these players are engaged in operations which all correspond to experiences of actual life: they fight or form alliances, conspire with or against each other, cooperate or exploit each other. This, therefore, is a form of economics which … resolutely concentrates on actual beings, encountered in real life, with an immediate historical and psychological significance. … (This new economics) derives from both the great schools of thought between which economics has hitherto been divided—pure, or would-be pure, economics, which is inclined to treat *homo oeconomicus* as a properly rational individual, and

> sociological and historical economics as originated by Karl Marx, which aims, primarily, at providing the dialectical apparatus for a struggle. Both these schools are represented in von Neumann's theory. For the first time, therefore, so-called bourgeois and capitalistic economics and Marxist economics have one common language at their disposal. (Lévi-Strauss 1954: 587)

In this passage, Lévi-Strauss demonstrates his misunderstanding of *Capital* and of Marxian economics, for he seems to suggest that the "struggle" and indeed exploitation is an overt and individualistic phenomenon which may be represented as a "game"; and that this provides the basis for unifying Marxian and bourgeois economics. This is not to say that game theory has nothing to offer economics. Our understanding of bargaining processes, to take only one example, can benefit greatly from game-theory. But in *Capital* Marx was seeking to understand an economic system in which the categories conceal exploitation. The qualitative aspect of his analysis was concerned with precisely this issue: how and why does this occur? Here, other branches of mathematics might have something to contribute. Indeed, Lévi-Strauss rightly asserts that mathematics is concerned not only with the quantitative but also the qualitative; and two of the other branches of mathematics which he cites—set theory and topology—might have more to offer in this regard.

In summary, although Lévi-Strauss is a major figure in the history of structuralism, and has been an inspiration to many—even those who violently oppose his views—he has little to offer for a greater understanding either of economics—or, more specifically, of Marx—which cannot be found more clearly expressed in the works of other writers.

Godelier: A Synthesis

Having discussed the works of Althusser and Lévi-Strauss it is appropriate to turn to Godelier, who has incorporated elements from both in his writing, and who, among the ranks of those whose names have been linked with structuralism, is one of the few with some valid claim to being called an economist. He traces his own intellectual development from philosophy, through economics to anthropology (Godelier 1972: vii), a route which was determined by his final goal, an examination of the "rationality" of economics.

By the "rationality" of an economic system Godelier means "primarily the question of the 'historical necessity' for its existence". He notes that "the conditions for the rise, functioning and evolution of any system are twofold, some belonging to the sphere of men's intentional activity, while others, of more decisive importance, give expression to the unintentional properties inherent in social relations". He searches, nevertheless, for "an *ultimate* reason, an *ultimate* basis for the transformations that economic systems undergo, transformations that are governed by the relations of compatibility and incompatibility between the structures composing those systems". And, as he observes, "we know the one offered by Marx: the relations that men form among themselves in order to carry out, and in carrying out, the production of the material conditions of their existence" (Godelier 1972: ix).

This answer (which he was disposed to accept) seemed to be incompatible with the fact that "within many primitive societies it is relations of kinship between men that dominate social organization … or that religious relations seem to dominate Indian society". This led him to his study of anthropology, and his fieldwork among the Baruya of New Guinea[19] and to the conclusion that the "humane sciences" needed to be rescued "from the dead-ends of functionalist empiricism or the helplessness of structuralism in the face of history". He saw the way forward "on the basis of a Marxism that has been radically purged of all traces of vulgar materialism and dogmatism" (Godelier 1972: xiii).

After briefly summarising his objections to the various alternatives, I will examine his own proposed "way forward". I will then establish what Godelier sees as the common ground between Marxism and structuralism, and conclude by examining their differences. Godelier begins by rejecting the idealism of Hegel, and a very different alternative (associated with neo-classical economics), namely "abstract empiricism", which takes

[19] This also yielded an article on "'Salt money' and the circulation of commodities among the Baruya of New Guinea" which has been found relevant to the question: "Is there a 'historical' transformation problem?" (Morishima and Catephores 1978).

as its starting point the individual. Next in line is "functionalist empiricism" which "starts not from individuals but from the relations between them. These relations are not taken one by one, but together, and this group of relations is regarded as an 'integrated' whole to the extent these different relations are functionally complementary" (Godelier 1972: xvii). He rejects this position (which he associates with Radcliffe-Brown and Talcott Parsons) on two grounds. First, although he agrees that the "pseudo-history, the evolutionism of the nineteenth century" was rightly abandoned, he does not accept the treatment of history as "a succession of accidental events". His second objection relates to the question of the ontological status of social structure. Both structuralists and Marxists, he argues, reject the "empiricist definition of what constitutes a social structure".

> For Radcliffe-Brown and Nadel, a social structure is an aspect of *reality* itself; it is order, the ordering of the *visible* relations between men, an ordering that explains the logic of the complementariness of these visible relations. For others … (such as Leach) … the structure is an *ideal* order which the mind introduces into things by reducing the multiform flux of reality to simplified images that give one a hold upon reality and make possible social action, social practice. (Godelier 1972: xviii)

He contrasts these views with that of Marx (and Lévi-Strauss) for whom "a structure is *not* a reality that is *directly* visible, and so directly observable, but a *level of reality* that exists *beyond* the visible relations between men, and the functioning of which constitutes the underlying logic of the system". But the distinction is a complex one:

> Lévi-Strauss affirms, like Radcliffe-Brown, the 'reality' of social structures as existing outside the human mind, and so opposes Leach. But Lévi-Strauss at the same time opposes Radcliffe-Brown, since for him the reality of a social structure is not the 'ordering' of the social relations that are directly observable by the informant or the anthropologist. (Godelier 1972: xx)

This, then, is an important area of common ground between Marx and Lévi-Strauss. It is a major methodological principle which Marxism and structuralism share, against functional empiricism, "that what is visible is a *reality* concealing *another*, deeper reality". This, he claims, goes to the very heart of Marx's method as displayed in *Capital.*

> Marx shows that the reason why a commodity is a complex and obscure reality is that what makes a product of labour a commodity, namely its value, is social labour that does not *appear* as such. ... The fetishizing of commodities is not the effect of the alienation of consciousnesses but the effect *in* and *for* consciousnesses of the disguising of social relations *in* and *behind* their appearances. (Godelier 1972: xxiv)

Godelier therefore asserts that the logic of social relationships, and "at a more general level, the laws of social practice derive from the operation of these hidden structures, and this discovery should enable us to account for all the observable facts" (Godelier 1970: 341). By virtue of this insight, he regards Marx as "clearly a forerunner of the modern structuralist movement" (Godelier 1970: 343).

In elaboration of these similarities he compares the scientific practice of Marx with Lévi-Strauss' analysis of the kinship system of the Murngin tribe. Without going into the intricacies of this analysis, it may simply be noted that Lévi-Strauss introduced a wholly new interpretation, or perspective, by postulating an "implicit structure" underlying the system. As a result, it was "easy to explain all the other peculiarities of the system ... which are seen as necessary consequences of this implicit structure, as complementary facets of its internal logic" (Godelier 1970: 345).

There is also a second major principle which, says Godelier, structural analysis shares with Marx: that "the study of the internal functioning of a structure must precede and will throw light on the study of its coming into being and subsequent evolution". Godelier argues "that it is impossible to understand the architecture of *Das Kapital* without the use of (this principle)" (Godelier 1970: 347). This is in line with Althusser's interpretation, noted above, regarding Marx's method as "a sort of logical ideal genesis".[20] Godelier puts the case strongly—making the connection with linguistics:

[20] He supports Althusser's view that the basic difference between Hegel's and Marx's dialectics is that in the latter contradiction is always "overdetermined", but he does little to clarify what "overdetermined" means.

> Marx's rejection of any form of historical approach ... is total, and anticipates by more than half a century the radical rethinking in linguistics and sociology which led de Saussure and Lowie to reject the evolutionist approach of the nineteenth century. (Godelier 1970: 353)

Lévi-Strauss, making use of the structuralist method, achieved, he says, "an essential scientific gain" in his analysis of "the mechanisms by which mythical representations of reality are constructed".[21] But this is not, according to Godelier, enough.

> Marx requires of science that it not merely discover the mechanisms of mythical thought but also the mechanisms which, existing *outside of* thought, impose upon the latter the illusory conceptions which it forms of reality. (Godelier 1972: xxvi)

The key which Marx offers, and which opposes him to structuralism, is that "the underlying logic of the functioning of societies and of their history, is determined, in the last analysis, by the conditions of *production and reproduction* of their material basis, or, to use his terminology, their mode of production" (Godelier 1972: xxviii). But, as already noted above, such a view may appear difficult to reconcile with the dominance of kinship or other relations in some societies. Godelier rejects this argument, but unconvincingly:

> It is pointless to bring forward as an objection to Marxism the dominance of kinship relations in this case or politico-religious relations in that, for Marxism does not deny these facts, declines to reduce structures one to another as epiphenomena of material life, but undertakes precisely to *explain* this dominance by *seeking* the reasons for it in specific determinations of different modes of production. (Godelier 1972: xxix)

[21] Godelier indicates that Lévi-Strauss' analysis of myth has close parallels with Marx's concern with fetishism:

> Because it is constructed by analogy, the mythico-religious world represents the world in the theatrical sense of 'putting on a performance', and this corresponds to Marx's concept in *Darstellung*. Marx used this concept to indicate the spontaneous illusory representations of economic and social relations as they are perceived by the economic agents who support these social relations. (Godelier 1977: 182)

This issue deserves some discussion. I should first make it clear that Godelier certainly rejects "reductionism" or "cultural materialism", in which "the economy as a system of social relations between men … is reduced to technology and the relation between men and nature". He also rejects "simplistic functionalism which hangs all society's structures onto the one which appears to predominate—whether it be kinship, politics or religion" (Godelier 1977: 4).

Godelier argues that "in most primitive societies, kinship relations *objectively* constitute the *dominant* structure of social relations, the basic scheme for the organisation of society" (Godelier 1977: 183) and suggests that Marx's described such a pre-capitalist society in Chapter 1 of *Capital.* But he claims that "Marx, far from making the family and kinship relations in primitive or peasant societies an element of the superstructure, as certain Marxists still persist in doing, saw them clearly as relations of production, elements of the infrastructure" (1977: 172).

Thus, to the question "How can we, from a Marxist point of view, reconcile the dominant role of kinship and the ultimately determining role of the economy?" Godelier's response is that "the Marxist interpretation would be that relationships of kinship in this case are both infrastructure and superstructure. … Thus, to the extent that in this type of society kinship actually functions as a relationship of production, the determining role of the economy will be seen not to contradict the dominant role of kinship but simply express itself through it" (Godelier 1970: 356).

This is an unsatisfactory argument. In effect, Godelier says: relations of production are (of necessity) dominant. Therefore if kinship relations are dominant this must be because they "actually function as relations of production". Godelier seems to take it as axiomatic that "It is the relations of production which are the determinants in the dominance of any one element" (Godelier 1977: 36). Hence, the problem is "finding out, in a determined society, what it is that *functions as* relations of production and why this should be so" (Godelier 1977: 25). The task for social science, he says, is to discover:

> Under what circumstances and for what reasons does a certain factor assume the functions of relations of production and does it control the

> reproduction of these relations and, as a result, social relations in their entirety? (Godelier 1977: 36)

It is far from clear that Godelier achieves this challenging task here, for it certainly requires more than the mere assertion that kinship relations "function as" production relations. But he sets himself a still more ambitious task, of understanding the process of change, for he says "we must discover and examine, by ways yet to be found, the invisible network of causes linking together forms, functions, modes of articulation and the hierarchy, appearance and disappearance of particular social structures" (Godelier 1977: 2). This would release structuralism from its "helplessness in the face of history"; but it is not something which Godelier appears to have accomplished in the works cited here.

He does, however, contribute more than either Althusser or Lévi-Strauss to combining the merits of Marxist and structuralist methods, and, by way of summary, I will end by identifying his main contributions that are of relevance to my concerns in this book. First, with respect to the view that a structuralist approach is incapable of dealing with change, he rejects the hypothesis that "the appearance of internal contradictions" cannot be reconciled with "the thesis that the working of the system necessarily reproduces the conditions under which it continues to work" (Godelier 1970: 350) arguing instead that new structures appear, and this "brings about a modification of the older structures and of their role and conditions of existence" (Godelier 1970: 354).[22]

Second, he recognises the importance of "structural causality": "We have seen how the concept of structural causality in economics is at the heart of the matter" (Godelier 1977: 32). And he appreciates also the importance of fetishism, and the need for this to be better understood: "Finally, that which exists as a *void* in thought … is an analysis of forms and fundamentals in the 'fetishisation' of social relations, an analysis

[22] There is a comment in his reference to Lévi-Strauss's work on Murngin kinship which might be an instructive pointer in the direction of further work:

> He (Lévi-Strauss) then showed that such a system would be unstable and that this would determine what form and types of evolution were possible. … These capacities therefore are the objective properties of the structures. … Seen in this perspective, social evolution ceases to be a series of meaningless accidents. (Godelier 1970: 347)

which few Marxists have attempted" (Godelier 1977: 50). But he still falls short of an adequate explication of either structural causality or fetishism. For example, his analysis of why the concealment of reality behind appearance is "implicit in the structure itself" explains little:

> If capital is not a thing but a social relationship, that is, an intangible reality, it must necessarily disappear from view when presented under the tangible forms of raw materials, equipment, money etc. (Godelier 1970: 343)

But he does recognise the difficulty of getting to grips with this very complex phenomenon:

> No container-contents or internal-external metaphor seems able to express the mechanisms of intimate articulation or the reciprocal action of structures. (Godelier 1977: 4)

However, he makes rather limited use of what structuralism has to offer. And this, in summary, is my major criticism of all three writers whose work is reviewed in this chapter. In *Capital*, and indeed in most of his economic writings, Marx was trying to get to grips with complex phenomena—social phenomena. For a number of reasons which I identified at the end of Section II, he found it extremely difficult to do so. He was constrained by lack of a vocabulary, lack of appropriate analogies, lack of a methodology—largely because of the dominance in his era of natural science and mechanistic explanations. Structuralism, I have argued, has much to offer as an alternative approach. This is a view apparently shared by Althusser, Lévi-Strauss and Godelier. Yet, for a variety of reasons which I have identified in the foregoing critique of their work, all three—and especially Althusser—failed to make effective use of this approach, and as a result Structural Marxism became (with some justification) wholly discredited. I believe that structuralism has more to offer Marxian economics than has so far been extracted from it. In the next chapter I examine this possibility further.

Bibliography

Althusser, L. (1976). *Essays in Self-Criticism*. London: Verso.
Althusser, L. (1977). *For Marx*. London: Verso.
Althusser, L., & Balibar, E. (1979). *Reading Capital*. London: Verso.
Barth, F. (1969). *Ethnic Groups and Boundaries. The Social Organization of Culture Difference*. Oslo: Oslo University Press.
Benton, T. (1984). *The Rise and Fall of Structural Marxism: Althusser and His Influence*. London: Macmillan.
Godelier, M. (1970). System, Structure and Contradiction in Das Kapital. In M. Lane (Ed.), *Structuralism: A Reader*. London: Jonathan Cape.
Godelier, M. (1972). *Rationality and Irrationality in Economics*. London: New Left Books.
Godelier, M. (1977). *Perspectives in Marxist Anthropology*. Cambridge: University Press.
Lévi-Strauss, C. (1954). The Mathematics of Man. *Mathematics and the Social Sciences. International Social Science Bulletin*, Vol. VI, No. 4.
Lévi-Strauss, C. (1972). *Structural Anthropology*. Harmondsworth: Penguin University Books.
Morishima, M., & Catephores, G. (1978). *Value, Exploitation and Growth: Marx in the Light of Modern Economic Theory*. London: McGraw-Hill.
Piaget, J. (1971). *Structuralism*. London: Routledge & Kegan Paul.
Roll, E. (1973). *A History of Economic Thought*. London: Faber & Faber.
de Saussure, F. (1974a). *Course in General Linguistics*. Fontana/Collins: Glasgow.
de Saussure, F. (1974b). *Cours de Linguistique Générale* (T. de Mauro, ed.).
Schumpeter, J. A. (1954). *History of Economic Analysis*. London: Allen & Unwin.
Thompson, E. P. (1978). *The Poverty of Theory and Other Essays*. London: Merlin.

10

The Commodity as Sign

The value of a commodity is something which not only distinguishes it from or relates it to other commodities, but is a quality differentiating from its own existence as a thing, a value in use.
(Marx 1971: 128)

My purpose in this chapter is to make good the claim that structuralism has something to offer for understanding Marx's economics, and especially his qualitative theory of value. An appropriate starting point is another critique of the baneful influence of structuralism, by Perry Anderson. This will lead, once again, to a reconsideration of the work of its founder, de Saussure. In "Structure and Subject", the second of the Wellek Library Lectures, Anderson discusses "the historic local defeat of historical materialism" and considers the "hypothesis" that French Marxism "finally encountered an intellectual adversary that was capable of doing battle with it, and prevailing. Its victorious opponent was the broad theoretical front of structuralism" (Anderson 1983: 32). In that

This is a revised version of a chapter in McNeill, D (1988) *Fetishism and the Form of Value*. Unpublished thesis, University of London.

D. McNeill, *Fetishism and the Theory of Value*, Palgrave Studies in the History of Economic Thought, https://doi.org/10.1007/978-3-030-56123-9_10

article Anderson severely criticises Lévi-Strauss, and sums up his crime (and that of structuralism) in the slogan which he apparently "unloosed": "The ultimate goal of the human sciences is not to constitute man but to dissolve him" (Anderson 1983: 37). And Althusser's books "rather than engaging with Lévi-Strauss's attack on history or his interpretation of humanism, endorsed and incorporated them into a Marxism that was now itself interpreted as a theoretical anti-humanism" (Anderson 1983: 37).

Despite defending the "novelty and ingenuity of the Althusserian system" Anderson therefore regarded him as having "an intimate and fatal dependence" on structuralism—a structuralism which Lévi-Strauss had done much to promote. But Anderson also (and, as I shall argue, illegitimately) enlisted the support of de Saussure in criticising the extension of structuralism beyond its rightful bounds:

> It was Saussure himself, ironically, who warned against exactly the abusive analogies and extrapolations from his own domain that have been so unstoppable in the past decades. Language, he wrote, is 'a human institution of such a kind that all the other human institutions, with the exception of writing, can only deceive us as to its real essence if we trust in their analogy'. ... Economic relations were likewise unamenable to his categories because economic value was 'rooted in things and in their natural relations'—'the value of a plot of ground, for instance, is related to its productivity'. (Anderson 1983: 42)

But a close reading of de Saussure shows that Anderson's claim is hard to justify. I have already demonstrated that it was de Saussure himself who proposed the analogy between economics and language, based on their shared "inner duality", indicating that each could, and should, be studied synchronically as well as diachronically. This, as I have noted, is a reference to a debate current at the time he was writing. Even so, de Saussure himself indicated that the analogy was inexact, in the context with which he was concerned; and he gave as reason that in economics, in contrast to linguistics, the synchronic relations are not wholly arbitrary:

> A value—so long as it is somehow rooted in things and in their natural relations, as happens with economics (the value of a plot of ground, for instance, is related to its productivity)—can to some extent be traced in time if we remember that it depends at each moment upon a system of coexisting values. Its link with things gives it, perforce, a natural basis, and the judgments that we base on such values are therefore never completely arbitrary; their variability is limited. But we have just seen that natural data have no place in linguistics. (de Saussure 1974a: 80)[1]

It is evident that the passage from de Saussure which Anderson quotes is unrepresentative. It gives the impression that de Saussure simply wishes to reject an analogy between economics and linguistics, whereas he himself proposes such an analogy—with qualifications. It is the qualifications alone that Anderson quotes when he seeks to show that the analogy is "abusive"—as reference to the full version of the quotation immediately reveals.

But the matter does not end there. de Saussure seems to have been so eager to draw comparisons with economics that he did so on another occasion—this time in relation not to synchrony/diachrony but the signifier/signified distinction. This is never referred to by Anderson, but merits detailed discussion. The passage cited earlier in which de Saussure discusses the analogy between economics and linguistics ends with the following:

> Here, as in political economy we are confronted with the notion of *value*. (de Saussure 1974a: 79)[2]

---

[1] The last sentence refers to his earlier discussion of the arbitrariness of the sign: "the idea of 'sister' is not linked by any inner relationship to the succession of sounds s-o-r which serves as its signifier in French" (de Saussure 1974a: 67). One may agree that economic values are not wholly arbitrary, (while having reservations about the term "productivity of land") but it is surely adopting an extremely asocial view of economics to claim that economic values are "natural". Economists like Walras, of course, would agree with such a position (see Chap. 4); but it is rather surprising to find Anderson, by implication, associating himself with this view.

[2] The quotation continues: "Both sciences are concerned with *a system for equating things of different orders*—labour and wages in one and a signified and signifier in the other" (de Saussure 1974a: 79). This second part of the passage, however, is not in de Saussure's notes. (The *Cours de Linguistique Générale* was not written by de Saussure himself, but was put together by two editors, on the basis of lecture notes from his students). This, according to Mauro, is "an addition of the editors, rather

It should be made clear that de Saussure uses the word "value" in its linguistic sense, regarding this as its primary meaning—one which has an approximate counterpart in political economy. Language is "a system of pure values" whose functioning involves two elements: ideas and sounds. The idea, or concept, de Saussure calls "the signified"; and the sound, or sound-image he refers to as "the signifier". The combination of the two, the whole, he calls "the sign". The relationship between signified and signifier (signification) is complex, for each is dependent upon the other. "Without language, thought is a vague, uncharted nebula. There are no pre-existing ideas, and nothing is distinct before the appearance of language" (de Saussure 1974a: 111).

To illustrate the relationship, de Saussure likens language to a piece of paper:

> Thought is the front and the sound the back; one cannot cut the front without cutting the back at the same time; likewise in language, one can neither divide sound from thought nor thought from sound. … Language is a system of interdependent terms in which the value of each term results solely from the simultaneous presence of the others. … The observable relation between the different pieces (of paper) A, B, C, D, etc. is distinct from the relation between the front and the back of the same piece as in A/A', B/B', etc. (de Saussure 1974a: 113–115)

It is here that de Saussure spells out more fully the second parallel between linguistics and economics, deriving from the fact that both are concerned with values.

> Even outside language all values are apparently governed by the same paradoxical principle. They are always composed:

arbitrary given the comparison which it contains" (de Saussure 1974b: 451) (my translation). Mauro offers the following gloss on the first part of the passage:

> In political economy one is faced with the notion of value—but to a lesser degree than in linguistics—and with a system of values. Political economy studies equilibrium between certain social values: value of labour, value of capital. (de Saussure 1974b: 451) (my translation)

It is by no means clear that this is an improvement on the editors' version.

1. of a *dissimilar* thing that can be *exchanged* for the thing of which the value is to be determined; and
2. of *similar* things that can be compared with the thing of which the value is to be determined. (de Saussure 1974a: 115)

In elaboration of the analogy he continues:

> To determine what a five-franc piece is worth one must therefore know: (1) that it can be exchanged for a fixed quantity of a different thing, e.g. bread; and (2) that it can be compared with a similar value of the same system, e.g. a one-franc piece, or with coins of another system (a dollar etc.). In the same way a word can be exchanged for something dissimilar, an idea; besides, it can be compared with something of the same nature, another word. Its value is therefore not fixed so long as one simply states that it can be 'exchanged' for a given concept, i.e. that it has this or that signification: one must also compare it with similar values, with other words that stand in opposition to it. Its content is really fixed only by the concurrence of everything that exists outside it. Being part of a system, it is endowed not only with a signification but also with value, and that is something quite different. (de Saussure 1974a: 115)

This lengthy quotation provides rich material for more detailed discussion of the relationship between economic value (and the unity of use-value and exchange-value), and linguistic value (and the unity of signified and signifier) which will be pursued in this chapter. Reference will also be made to other writers, some of whom allude specifically to Saussure.

My aim, then, is to show how semiotics can contribute to an understanding of value and the commodity, and hence of Marxian economics. By contrast with much of the work of Althusser and his followers, my concern is therefore with the "inner logic" of the capitalist system.[3] I am not qualified to engage in debate about the distinction between semiotics and structuralism, but it does appear that the former more accurately describes my concern—and it has the added advantage of distinguishing my position from that of Structural Marxism.

[3] As indicated in the previous chapter, I believe that structuralism has less to contribute to an understanding of history, and that Althusser's difficulties arose largely from trying to apply his ideas to the doctrine of historical materialism.

It may be helpful to begin with a definition. Semiotics, according to one of its leading proponents, Umberto Eco, "is concerned with everything that can be taken as significantly substituting for something else" (Eco 1977: 7). And the sign, one of the central concepts of semiotics, is similarly defined by Eco as "*everything* that, on the grounds of a previously established social convention, can be taken as *something standing for something else*" (Eco 1977: 16). I shall argue that the commodity satisfies this definition, and that it is enlightening to regard it as a sign—with all that this implies.

Eco puts forward the view that all cultural processes may be viewed as processes of communication, which are made possible by the existence of a code—"a system of signification, insofar as it couples present entities with absent units" (Eco 1977: 8). He supports this proposition with a long list of areas of research in semiotics, of which the study of "systems of objects" is of particular interest.[4]

He begins by considering three "elementary cultural phenomena" (apart from language) which do not appear to be "communicative": the production and use of tools, kinship relations and the economic exchange of goods. He then sets out to show that these three are, in fact, concerned with "communication and signification". To this end, he discusses each of the three in turn, beginning with an example of an "Australopithecine" who uses a stone (S1) to split the skull of a baboon, and,

> having discovered its possible function, comes across a second stone (S2) some days later and recognizes it as a token, an individual occurrence of a more general model (St), which is the abstract type to which S1 also refers. Encountering S2 and being able to subsume it (along with S1) under type St, our Australopithecine regards it as the sign-vehicle of a possible function F. (Eco 1977: 23)

The "type-stone" is given a name, which is applied every time it occurs. It is then the *relations* between F, St, S1, S2 and the name that are of interest, and these may be abstracted from this specific example. In structural terms, the situation is the same as that encountered in economic exchange,

[4] In this field he cites Baudrillard, whose work is discussed in Chap. 13, as a major figure.

which can be analysed in the same way.[5] As Eco points out, Marx showed how all commodities "can become signs standing for other commodities". Thus a commodity system is very similar to a language, for "this relation of mutual significance is made possible because the commodity system is structured by means of oppositions (similar to those which linguistics has elaborated in order to describe—for example—the structure of phonological systems)" (Eco 1977: 25).[6]

In linguistics, as de Saussure says, value comes "from the reciprocal situation of the pieces of the language". Similarly, in a commodity system, there is a complex reciprocal situation obtaining between commodities by virtue of the social context within which they are set: a context in which values are like meanings.[7]

Another famous structuralist, Roland Barthes, also draws attention to this analogy, which de Saussure himself first made, and discusses the similarity between value in linguistics and value in economics, and de Saussure's example of the five-franc coin. Barthes focuses particularly on the act of signification—the binding together of "signifier and signified, an act whose product is the sign" (Barthes 1967: 48). It is this act, in the context of Marxian economics, which is of particular interest, for it is the starting point of the whole process; that which sets off the dialectic which begins with the commodity, and develops, through money and capital, as Marx describes, to the full complexity of the capitalist system.

This draws attention back to Eco's example. For the significant step in his first story (of the Australopithecine) is, surely, the establishment of a connection between S1 and S2, which simultaneously links S1 and St. This step—which might justifiably be called a primal act of

---

[5] See Chap. 6.

[6] Eco also very briefly considers a third example, the exchange of women, but, making reference to Lévi-Strauss, notes that the exchange in this case is not of "physical objects": "The woman, the moment she becomes 'wife', is no longer merely a physical body: she is a sign which connotes a system of social obligations" (Eco 1977: 26).

[7] Indeed in a sense perhaps values *are* meanings, see below. Although it is important not to go too far. As Eco puts it, "to look at the whole of culture *sub specie semiotica* is not to say that culture is only communication and signification, but that it can understood more thoroughly if it is seen from the semiotic point of view. And that objects, behaviour and relationships of production and value function as such precisely because they obey semiotic laws" (Eco 1977: 27).

classification—is directly analogous to the starting point of Marx's analysis in the first chapter of *Capital Vol I.*[8]

It should be noted that the analogy between language and economics discussed here is drawn not by economists, but by representatives of other disciplines. It has been a one-way traffic. Economists have, of course, often said that money is a sign, or at least a symbol; but their subsequent work has not carried them down the road of semiotics, to consider the full implications of such an apparently simple statement. This is perhaps not surprising in the case of neo-Classical economists, who have little interest in treating economics as a *social* science. But Marxist economists might have been expected to pursue the matter rather further.

Perhaps no-one has come nearer than Adam Schaff, from Poland—a Marxist expert on linguistics, who has also written widely on Marxist philosophy. I turn now to his contribution, but note that he too draws the analogy in the same direction. He does not start from a problem in Marxian economics and find enlightenment in the study of language, but rather considers, in his study of language, a possible parallel with Marx's work.

Schaff's work is of interest for a number of reasons. First, it provides information about some Marxists' contributions to the development of linguistics; or, rather, their lack of contribution for, as he puts it: "Marxist philosophical studies on language, and in particular on meaning and the theory of signs, are very scanty. … Hence I have to admit that the problem is controversial and to present my own view as one of the possible solutions" (Schaff 1962: 263).

Secondly, Schaff has some interesting points to make about Marx's own views on "the philosophical aspect of the communication process", referring, for example, to Marx's remarks, in *The German Ideology*, about how consciousness and speech distinguish man from animals. As one might expect, he lays great stress on the crucial role of the social in Marx's work. Thus:

---

[8] To call this a "primal act of classification" is not to claim that someone, at some time in history, really performed such an act. (In other words, to suggest that Eco is adopting something akin to Marx's "logico-historical" method). To avoid the appearance of a creation myth it might be better to analyse the learning rather than the "invention" of language; see Wittgenstein's discussion of ostensive definition, and of language games (Wittgenstein 1969).

> In criticizing Feuerbach's naturalistic tendencies Marx objected that he had assumed 'an abstract—*isolated*—human individual', and drew attention to the fact that 'the abstract individual whom he analyses belongs in reality to a particular form of society'. This is a criticism of all 'Robinson Crusoe concepts' in the social sciences. (Schaff 1962: 143)

Asserting that "consciousness, and conseqently speech as well, are products of labour, products of social life" Scaff conforms to Marx's attribution of primacy to labour.

But his argument lacks conviction: "human labour is based on co-operation, which is impossible without thinking in terms of ideas, and without communication". This is rather weak glue with which to unite labour, thought and language, for labour seems a superfluous addition—justified only by the demands of Marxist orthodoxy (see Chap. 11).

Schaff is more interesting in his discussion of linguistics, and its analogy with economics. Indeed, he draws precisely the same analogy, between meaning and value, which I have been seeking to establish. Here again the analogy is drawn *from* economics *to* linguistics, while my aim is to develop the analogy in the other direction. Schaff has the merit, by comparison with most of the other writers to whom I have referred, of being very well acquainted not only with economics but with Marxian economics. But his concern is with the meaning of meaning, not the meaning of value. Nevertheless, it is possible to use his work on meaning as a basis for further exploring the concept of value.[9]

Thus, as he says,

> One of the ways of interpreting 'meaning' is to conceive of meaning as a specific relation between the persons who communicate with one another. It is within this conception that I intend to expound the Marxist standpoint on the issue under discussion. (Schaff 1962: 263)

[9] The analogy is relevant not only to the Marxian concept of value. Schaff offers a long and interesting list of possible interpretations of meaning. Among them is that "meaning is a relation between the sign and human action" (Schaff 1962: 227), so that the meaning of a term is found "by observing what a man does with it, not by what he says about it". "Psychological categories are here replaced by categories of objective behaviour, the action of human organism, and in this way we acquire objective data which enable us to define meanings and differentiate between them, data which can be observed intersubjectively" (Schaff 1962: 262). There are parallels here with the replacement of utility theory in neo-Classical economics by "revealed preference".

He elaborates further by saying that meaning is "a definite social relation", and notes that

> material objects or events become signs only when they enter into definite intricate relations with men who use them as signs; with reality to which they are somehow referred (as names, pictures, etc.); with the system of signs, i.e., language, within which they function. It is only in such a context that an object or event becomes a sign or, in other words, has a meaning. … It is always a certain system of *social relations* which is involved. (Schaff 1962: 265)[10]

Perhaps the most effective way of demonstrating the force of the analogy between meaning and value in the context of Marxian theory is to transpose some of the key passages from Schaff relating to meaning and assess how accurately they then refer to value. The following brief list seems to confirm the validity of the enterprise (in each case the word in brackets conforms to Schaff's own wording):

> Only what we call value (meaning) turns material objects … into commodities (signs). (Schaff 1962: 227)

> Value (meaning) is a definite relation between men who exchange (communicate) with one another. (Schaff 1962: 265)

> But material objects … become commodities (signs) only when they enter into definite intricate relations with men who use them as commodities (signs). (Schaff 1962: 265)

> It is only in such a context that an object … becomes a commodity (sign) or, in other words, has a value (meaning). (Schaff 1962: 265)

---

[10] This seems a good description of meaning (and, indeed, of value). My only criticism is that he goes on to say that "meaning is, first, a relation or a system of relations between men on the psychological plane". If the term "psychological" is simply intended to contrast with material, then the word "social" would surely be better.

> Thus, if we do not believe in the mysticism of inherent values (meanings) ... we have to admit that ... it is always a certain system of *social relations* which is involved. (Schaff 1962: 265)

Such passages, together with the discussion earlier in this chapter, are surely sufficient to indicate that de Saussure's eagerness to establish parallels between economics and language was well-founded. It is unfortunate that the least interesting one (based on the synchrony/diachrony distinction) should have been that which was taken up most energetically by Marxist commentators—with or without reference to de Saussure. But this should not deter attempts to develop the others, which seem potentially more enlightening.

Perhaps a more powerful argument against doing so is that Marx himself considered, and rejected, the analogy with language. To conclude this chapter I will seek to show that Marx was wrong to do so, and hence delineate with more precision the parallels which have been already outlined above. The passage in question is to be found in the *Grundrisse*, where, after criticising an analogy between money and blood, Marx adds:

> To compare money with language is not less erroneous.[11] Language does not transform ideas, so that the peculiarity of ideas is dissolved and their social character runs alongside them as a separate entity, like prices alongside commodities. Ideas do not exist separately from language. Ideas which have first to be translated out of their mother tongue in order to circulate, in order to become exchangeable, offer a somewhat better analogy; but the

[11] From the phrasing of this passage it might seem that the comparison is one which has been proposed by someone else; but there is no reference to another work. According to Lepschy (1985: 200) "Marx and Engels did not have much to say about language", and I have found only few relevant references in Marx's writings, for example Marx (1975: 190–1; 1973: 145). One relevant quote (see Chap. 12) is: "Production by a solitary individual outside society ... is just as preposterous as the development of speech without individuals who live *together* and talk to one another". There is one other interesting reference—in Marx's critique of Bailey; but this is not exactly about language:

> 'It is impossible to *designate* or *express the value* of a commodity except by *a quantity of some other commodity.*' (As impossible as it is to '*designate*' or '*express*' a thought except by a quantity of syllables. Hence Bailey concludes that a thought is—syllables.) (Marx 1973: 146)

analogy then lies not in language, but in the foreignnness of language. (Marx 1973: 163)

This appears to be a clear rejection of my argument. I suggest, however, that it is incorrect. This is partly because Marx does not accurately spell out the analogy (it is, indeed, only a passing comment, written in parentheses). And it is partly because linguistics in his time was not greatly developed, so that he could hardly have been expected to appreciate the potential of the analogy. To support my argument I will consider each sentence in turn.

> Language does not transform ideas, so that the peculiarity of ideas is dissolved.

Correct; but words transform individual things, so that the peculiarity of the individual thing is dissolved. Thus this thing (ostensively defined, or called by its individual name "Jack") is called *a* rabbit; the peculiarity of this particular thing is dissolved. (Similarly, this rabbit is called an animal, so that the peculiarity of the *rabbit* is dissolved—although this is a further step, and a conceptually distinct phenomenon).

> Their social character runs alongside them as a separate entity, like prices alongside commodities.

Similarly, the social character of Jack (its being as "a rabbit") runs alongside it as a separate entity, like prices alongside commodities.

> Ideas do not exist separately from language.

This is not self-evident.[12] But the issue at stake parallels the question of whether values can exist without exchange-values. Exchange-value is only

[12] Thus, for example, Whorf (1956) examines implicit categories which have no corresponding name. This might be claimed as evidence of ideas without words; but such "ideas" are, nevertheless, set within a language—and *can* be expressed in that language, albeit not by a single word. A more controversial issue is the causal relationship between words and ideas. As de Saussure asks: "do ready made ideas exist before words?" (de Saussure 1974a: 65). Here, there is a close parallel with the relationship between money and exchange-value.

the manifestation of value; but it is hard to see how value in capitalism can exist—even conceptually—without exchange-value.

> Ideas which have first to be translated out of their mother tongue in order to circulate, in order to become exchangeable, offer a somewhat better analogy; but the analogy then lies not in language, but in the foreignness of language.

Marx here comes close to accepting his analogy; and it is indeed valid, for signifieds have to be "translated" into signifiers in order to circulate, in order to become exchangeable.

The force of the analogy which I am seeking to defend becomes very clear from innumerable passages by de Saussure. A few examples will suffice.

> Take a knight, for instance. By itself is it an element in the game? Certainly not, for by its material make-up—outside its square and the other conditions of the game—it means nothing to the player; it becomes a real, concrete element only when endowed with value and wedded to it. (de Saussure 1974a: 110)

So too, a use-value is not an "element in the game"—it must be produced for the market, and be exchanged; only then does it have value.

> Can it be replaced by an equivalent piece? Certainly. Not only another knight but even a figure shorn of any resemblance to a knight can be declared identical provided the same value is attributed to it. We see then that in semiological systems like language, where elements hold each other in equilibrium in accordance with fixed rules, the notion of identity blends with that of value and *vice versa*. (de Saussure 1974a: 110)

A loaf of bread produced for the market is identical with anything else of the same value. The notion of commensurability blends with the notion of value. And value is of necessity a social phenomenon:

> The community is necessary if values that owe their existence solely to usage and general acceptance are to be set up; by himself the individual is incapable of fixing a single value. (de Saussure 1974a: 113)

Perhaps it would be more effective, rather than simply proliferating examples of the similarity between language and economics, to specify with more rigour the structural equivalences, by reference to Marx's terminology and his attempts—especially in the first chapter of Volume 1 of *Capital*—to come to grips with the concept of value.

The key to the problem is that value, in economics as in linguistics, has two inseparable "dimensions"; it consists of two relations in combination. One is the relation of signification (between signified and signifier). The other is the relation between signifiers. This distinction is recognised by Marx but not always clearly spelled out. He rightly stressed that the commodity may be seen as "a complex of two things—use-value and exchange-value" (*Capital* 1: 48), that is the commodity is a sign—a combination of signified and signifier. He also stressed that exchange-value exists by virtue of the totality of exchange-values, that is that the value of a commodity (in his terminology) is expressed in terms of other commodities for which it can be exchanged. But these two relations are intimately connected, and arise simultaneously. They must be distinguished conceptually, but recognised as both integral parts of the concept of value. Marx deals with both types of relation, but sometimes fails to clarify how they in turn are connected.

The act of signification is that with which Marx was concerned in his analysis of the *form* of value. "What remains is the form of value which transforms value into exchange-value." Value has no means of manifesting itself except through exchange-value. But Marx also examined *forms* of value—the process of transition to the general form of value and the money-form. The exchange-value of a commodity finds expression in its relation to all other commodities. There are other commodities of equal value for which it can be exchanged. And with money, exchange-value can be expressed not in terms of other commodities but in terms of prices.

Similarly, there are other things, rabbits, which can be "exchanged" for this rabbit ("Jack") as long as we are concerned not with this, my rabbit, but the concept rabbit. Although this "exchangeability" is conceptually possible without language, words play a crucial role in the process. Money plays a similar role in a commodity system. And just as Marx traced the process of the development of money in the first chapter of *Capital*

Volume 1, one could discuss the emergence of the concept and the word rabbit; as Eco does, to some extent, in the passage quoted above, where the stone S2 is seen as a "token" for the general model, which is given a name.

Where the analogy with language breaks down is with regard to the quantitative as opposed to the qualitative aspect. Money is capable not only of indicating equivalence but also of measuring. In this respect words are more limited in their power. In language an "uncharted nebula" is transformed into a structured whole. But according to Marx, in a capitalist system, this whole is a bounded, measurable whole—the aggregate of social labour. The "common unity" in which commodities participate can actually be measured. This is where the analogy ceases, for there is no equivalent in language of this quantitative aspect. In capitalism, according to Marx, "the relation of the producers to the sum total of their own labour is presented to them as a social relation, existing not between themselves but between the products of their labour" (Marx 1954: 77).[13] This is a social (qualitative) relation, but also a quantitative relation. Thus money is like words—but only up to a point; for money is homogeneous, divisible—capable of acting as a measure.

To complete the discussion of the parallels between economics and language, brief mention should be made of the third important distinction to which de Saussure drew attention. The sign as the unity of the signifier and signified parallels the commodity as the unity of use-value and exchange-value, as I hope is already apparent. And economics, like linguistics, is concerned with the synchronic as well as the diachronic. But the third important distinction for which de Saussure is famous is that between language (*langue*) and speech (*parole*). The former, as Barthes puts it, is "so to speak, language minus speech: it is at the same time a social institution and a system of values. As a social institution … it is the social part of language, the individual cannot by himself either

[13] This is a passage from Marx's discussion of the fetishism of commodities. It is evident that the concept of fetishism also has parallels in language—as Schaff also pointed out (Schaff 1962: 224)—and these might prove interesting to develop.

create or modify it. … Moreover, this social product is autonomous, like a game with its own rules" (Barthes 1967: 14).

This same distinction is sometimes described as that between the message and the code. The message can only be sent by virtue of the existence of the code. Yet the code cannot be changed by a single individual; and indeed a single individual may be largely ignorant of the code, just as a speaker may communicate without being fully aware of how and why the language "works". This *langue/parole* distinction is briefly discussed by another Marxist philosopher, Mepham, who also draws a parallel with Marx's work:

> So each item is intelligible only by virtue of its relations with other actual or possible items, even though we are not explicitly conscious of these networks of relationships as we speak or hear a language. Another example of this that has proved to have important theoretical as well as practical consequences is discussed by Marx in *Capital*, namely the system of signs that constitutes the value-system in a society practising generalized commodity production. (Mepham 1973: 125)

He explains that the system of relations between exchangeable objects "is itself constituted within the system of relationships called wage-labour, which is a series of social relationships between men". And it is only "because this system is generalized, that it is possible for there to be commodity production or the system of values within which consumption and exchange take place". This final sentence is of especial significance, for it demonstrates precisely the importance of the langue/parole distinction, and its relevance to Marx's analysis of the capitalist system:

> No awareness of these structural relationships need be involved in any particular act of buying or selling even though they are the determining conditions of it. (Mepham 1973: 125)

The limited knowledge and power of those who speak a language is precisely mirrored by the limited knowledge and power of those who participate in the capitalist system.

To conclude this section of the book, it is fair to say that the analogy between economics and language extends remarkably far. And this is precisely because economics is not simply concerned with material things but with social phenomena. Words are a wholly social construct; they exist by virtue of meaning—but they also allow meaning to be expressed. Commodities are "social things"; material things set in a specific social context (and in their developed form, as money, the link with material things becomes tenuous). Commodities and money exist by virtue of value; they also allow value to be expressed.

Value, in economics, must be understood as a social phenomenon. That is why metaphors based on the material world are necessarily limiting. Marx does make use of non-material metaphors, notably religious ones—for example fetishism itself, and less importantly the Trinity Formula. But these are used more to describe than to understand; and he does not use them for elucidating the concept of value. The rabbits/animals analogy, discussed in Chap. 6, might be claimed as an exception to this generalisation; but he cut this out in the revised Second Edition of *Capital Volume I.* (See Chap. 6). My claim in this section is that non-material analogies—and most specifically the analogy with language—are capable of greatly enhancing our appreciation of the extremely complex concept of "value".

Bibliography

Anderson, P. (1983). *In the Tracks of Historical Materialism.* London: Verso.

Barthes, R. (1967). *Elements of Semiology.* London: Cape.

Eco, U. (1977). *A Theory of Semiotics.* London: Macmillan.

Lepschy, G. (1985). Linguistics. In Z. Baranski & J. Short (Eds.), *Developing Contemporary Marxism.* London: Macmillan.

Marx, K. (1954). *Capital* (Vol. I). Moscow: Progress.

Marx, K. (1971). *Theories of Surplus Value, Part III.* Moscow: Progress.

Marx, K. (1973). *Grundrisse.* Harmondsworth: Penguin.

Marx, K. (1975). *Karl Marx: Texts on Method* (T. Carver, Trans. & Ed.). Oxford: Blackwell.

Mepham, J. (1973). The Structuralist Sciences and Philosophy. In D. Robey (Ed.), *Structuralism: An Introduction*. Oxford: Clarendon.
de Saussure, F. (1974a). *Course in General Linguistics*. Fontana/Collins: Glasgow.
de Saussure, F. (1974b). *Cours de Linguistique Générale* (T. de Mauro, Ed.)
Schaff, A. (1962). *Introduction to Semantics*. Oxford: Pergamon Press.
Wittgenstein, L. (1969). *The Blue and Brown Books* Oxford. Blackwell
Whorf, B. L. (1956). *Language, Thought and Reality*. Cambridge, MA: The M.I.T. Press.

Part IV

The Social Relations of Production, Exchange and Consumption

11

Marx's Emphasis on Production

Production, distribution, exchange and consumption are … links of a single whole, different aspects of one unit. Production is the decisive phase.
(Marx 1970: 204)

My purpose in this section is to critique Marx's emphasis on production and to examine two other economic relations—exchange and consumption—so as to establish that these too may be seen as social relations, potentially broadening the scope of Marxian economics. I begin by briefly showing how Marx portrays production as dominant, if not the sole significant relation, and seek to indicate why he does so.

Marx begins his critique of capitalism with the commodity, which "appears at first sight, a very trivial thing" but is "in reality, a very queer thing, abounding in metaphysical subtleties and theological niceties" (Marx 1954: 76). This enigmatical character arises from the commodity form itself; a form attributable to the social relations of production. For, "from the moment that men in any way work for one another, their

This is a revised version of a chapter in McNeill, D (1988) *Fetishism and the Form of Value.* Unpublished thesis, University of London.

D. McNeill, *Fetishism and the Theory of Value*, Palgrave Studies in the History of Economic Thought, https://doi.org/10.1007/978-3-030-56123-9_11

labour assumes a social form" (Marx 1954: 76). Relations between persons become fetishised, and appear as relations between things—exchange-values—that lie at the heart of the capitalist system. Exchange, according to Marx, is simply the locus wherein relations of production become manifest: "The labour of the individual asserts itself as a part of the labour of society, only by means of the relations which the act of exchange establishes directly between the products, and indirectly, through them, between the producers" (Marx 1954: 78).

Here, it is true, Marx talks of the relation between producers in the act of exchange. But he is not referring to a social relationship of exchange. Rather, it is production which is the social relation, which finds its expression in the act of exchange. Although value is created in the labour process, this value is realised only in the act of exchange. Exchange therefore plays a very important mediating role; but it is not seen, in this context, as in itself a social relation of any significance.

Consumption plays an even less significant role, being associated with use-value, a relatively unproblematic concept. "So far as it (a commodity) is a value in use, there is nothing mysterious about it. ... The mystical character of commodities does not originate ... in their use-value" (Marx 1954: 76). In this aspect, a commodity is merely "a thing that by its properties satisfies human wants of some sort or another. The nature of such wants, whether, for instance, they spring from the stomach or from fancy, makes no difference" (Marx 1954: 43).

Marx does not ignore exchange and consumption, but nevertheless treats production as dominant. This emphasis on production is evident in most of his writings, but the precise relationship obtaining between production, consumption, exchange (and distribution) is spelled out most clearly, and in most detail, in the draft Introduction to the *Grundrisse,* in which, as Dobb points out in his introduction, Marx lays stress on "the primacy of production, and especially on the social relations of production" (Marx 1970: 6).

The work opens, significantly, with the words:

> To begin with, the question under discussion is *material production.* Individuals producing in a society, and hence the socially determined production of individuals, is, of course, the point of departure. (Marx 1970: 188)

And he does not fail to emphasise that production is a *social* phenomenon: "Production by a solitary individual outside society … is just as preposterous as the development of speech without individuals who live *together* and talk to one another" (Marx 1970: 189). And: "Production is always appropriation of nature by an individual within and with the help of a definite social organisation" (Marx 1970: 192).

The first two parts of the *Introduction* are entitled "Production" and "The General Relations of Production to Distribution, Exchange and Consumption" and these merit detailed study. Marx argues that consumption and production are identical in three respects; first, because production *is* consumption, and vice versa. Thus one may speak of consumptive production, in which the means of production are "used and used up", or, in the case of fuel for example, "broken down into simpler components", or of raw material "which is absorbed and does not retain its original shape and quality" (Marx 1970: 195). One may also speak of productive consumption, for, in consumption "man produces his own body", for example by feeding. (Economists, Marx notes, use this one term to refer to both phenomena, that is including what he himself calls "consumptive production".)

Second, production and consumption "each appears as a means of the other, as being induced by it … production provides the material which is the external object of consumption, consumption provides the need i.e. the internal object, the purpose of production" (Marx 1970: 198).

Third, and more obscurely, "each of them … creates the other, it creates itself as the other". Thus, consumption "produces" production "because a product becomes a real product only through consumption. For example, a dress becomes really a dress only by being worn" (Marx 1970: 196). And production "gives consumption a distinct form, a character, a finish. *For one thing*, the object is not simply an object in general, but a particular object which must be consumed in a particular way, a way determined by production. … Production therefore produces not only the object of consumption but also the mode of consumption." Production creates consumption in another way also, for "it also provides the need for the material" (Marx 1970: 197).

Marx thus establishes a threefold identity between production and consumption.[1] Certainly he does not ignore consumption; but he clearly relegates it to a secondary role, for he concludes that production is "the decisive phase, the action epitomising the entire process" (Marx 1970: 199).

He then moves on to distribution. He has earlier criticised "the crude tearing apart" of production and distribution by economists, who have presented the former as "governed by eternal natural laws which are independent of history" while associating the latter "with a certain amount of free choice" (Marx 1970: 192). Under this misguided interpretation, "production is determined by general laws of nature; distribution by random social factors" (Marx 1970: 195). This position had already been rejected by others before him, but, as Marx points out, critics either argued that distribution is just as important as production, thus falling into the same error of separating the two; or that "the different factors are not considered as a single whole" as though this "separation had forced its way from the textbook into real life, and not, on the contrary, from real life into the textbook" (Marx 1970: 195). Thus, distribution must not be portrayed as a separate phenomenon—but integrally connected with production.

Finally he turns to exchange, which he regards as "simply an intermediate phase between production and distribution … and consumption". Since the former (production and distribution treated as a single entity) "is determined by production", and the latter, "consumption is … itself an aspect of production", it may be concluded that production "obviously comprises also exchange as one of its aspects" (Marx 1970: 204).

So far the argument lacks conviction, but Marx elaborates it further:

> Firstly, it is evident that exchange of activities and skills, which takes place in production itself, is a direct and essential part of production. Secondly, the same applies to the exchange of products in so far as this is a means to manufacture the finished product intended for immediate consumption. …

[1] He rejects two other simplistic views of this identity. The first is the metaphysical argument. ("After this, nothing is simpler for a Hegelian than to assume that production and consumption are identical.") The second is the accounting identity, put forward by "prosaic economists, such as Say who claim that "if one considers a nation … then its production is its consumption".

> Thirdly, what is known as exchange between dealer and dealer ... is entirely determined by production. (Marx 1970: 204)

And he concludes that: "Exchange appears to exist independently alongside production and detached from it only in the last stage, when the product is exchanged for immediate consumption". But even here production is found to have primacy over exchange: "all aspects of exchange ... appear either to be directly comprised in production, or else determined by it" (Marx 1970: 204).

Marx summarises his position in the words quoted as the introduction to this chapter, where he commits himself to the view that "production is the decisive phase".

> That exchange and consumption cannot be the decisive elements, is obvious; and the same applies to distribution in the sense of the distribution of products. Distribution of the factors of production, on the other hand, is itself a phase of production. A distinct mode of production thus determines the specific mode of consumption, distribution, exchange and the *specific relations of these different phases to one another*. Production *in the narrow sense,* however, is in its turn also determined by the other aspects. ... There is an interaction between the various aspects. Such interaction takes place in any organic unity. (Marx 1970: 205)

Marx is thus asserting that, at one level, production, consumption, exchange and distribution are all on a par; while at a higher level, or in a wider sense, production is determinate. This view, though not always spelled out so clearly, continues to be evident throughout his later work. Although there may be debate among commentators as to the precise nature of the complex relationship between production, consumption, exchange and distribution, there can surely be no doubt that Marx assigns primacy to production.

Why does he do so? There are, I suggest, several related reasons. The first I wish to consider is Marx's concept of man: man as worker, producer—relating to nature by transforming it.[2] This is a view which he derives in large measure from Hegel, as Taylor notes[3]:

> This idea of the crucial importance of work, which is central to Marx's theory, originates with Hegel. … It is clear that for both writers man forms himself, comes to realize his own essence in the attempt to dominate and transform nature. (Taylor 1975: 119)

This is evident from many of his works, though expressed perhaps most strongly in his earlier writings; for example:

> As individuals express their life, so they are. What they are, therefore, coincides with their production, both with *what* they produce and with *how* they produce. (Marx and Engels 1974: 42)

How, more precisely, Marx regards "human nature", and whether this constitutes an adequate ground for his emphasis on labour and production, is not an issue to be resolved within the confines of a few pages; certainly I cannot do justice to the debate here. I shall, in this section, merely offer some evidence that Marx's conception of man's sociality is somewhat limited not extending to exchange or consumption.

The emphasis which Marx puts on "Man" is, nevertheless, one of the factors which sets him apart from the many who seek to exclude such issues as intractable and irrelevant. Certainly Marx is unusual, for an economist, in the attention he devotes to the subject of man and society; and what he has to say about human nature has attracted considerable attention among commentators. But his portrayal of man sometimes makes him appear as an individual interacting with Nature, rather than as a member of a social group.

In the *1844 Manuscripts*, Marx refers to man's "species-being", and reveals wherein the particularity of this species lies:

---

[2] Marx uses the term "man" to refer to humankind. In discussing his works, I adopt the same inappropriate terminology.

[3] Fromm suggests a longer list: "For Spinoza, Goethe, Hegel as well as for Marx, man is alive only inasmuch as he is productive" (Fromm 1961: 29).

> It is just in his work upon the objective world, therefore, that man really proves himself to be a *species-being*. (Marx 1977: 74)

Hence, it is by virtue of labour that Man is human; and more precisely because such labour is *conscious*[4]:

> Labour is, in the first place, a process in which both man and Nature participate, and in which man of his own accord starts, regulates, and controls the material re-actions between himself and Nature. … We are not now dealing with those primitive instinctive forms of labour that remind us of the mere animal. … We presuppose labour that stamps itself as exclusively human. … What distinguishes the worst architect from the best of bees is this, that the architect raises his structure in imagination before he erects it in reality. (Marx 1954: 173)

Thus Marx distinguishes "human" labour from the "mere animal" not by virtue of its social aspect, but because the activity is planned in advance—conscious. Elsewhere, indeed, he uses the word human as if it meant ahistorical, asocial:

> The production process in general, such as is common to all social conditions, that is without historic character, *human*, if you like. (Marx 1973: 320)

This raises the question of whether it is part of man's species-being to be social—or merely to be human. In this regard, it is surely significant that one type of alienation suffered by man is alienation from his species-being. This is distinct, in Marx's view, from his alienation from other men. Thus it is not too much to claim that rather than referring to the alienation of man from society, Marx distinguishes two forms of alienation—from his "species-being", and from other (individual) men. And the latter follows from the former:

[4] See next footnote for further discussion of the significance of "consciousness" here.

> In fact, the proposition that man's species-nature is estranged from him means that one man is estranged from the other, as each of them is from man's essential nature. (Marx 1977: 75)

Although the word "social" appears with great frequency throughout Marx's economic writings (e.g. consider the first chapter of *Capital*), it may nevertheless be argued that Marx emphasises man as human (as one who works on nature) more than man as social; certainly in some of his works he seems to lay more emphasis on the former.

Since most economists, especially in the neo-Classical tradition, lay heavy emphasis on the individual, it is not surprising that criticisms of Marx as taking insufficient account of the social are not commonly found in their writings. Support for this view is, however, to be found in other disciplines; and I shall briefly consider the works of an anthropologist and an historian in support of my claim.

I begin with the anthropologist, Dumont, who argues, with strong textual support, that Marx adopts "a predominantly individualistic view of man—I mean a view according to which humanity is embodied in each particular human being" (Dumont 1977: 128). Dumont's particular interest is in hierarchy, and in *From Mandeville to Marx* he tentatively proposes:

> Two almost identical formulations of Marx's hierarchical judgment: (1) the individual is primary as against society; (2) the relation between man and nature (work, labor) is primary as against relations between men. (Dumont 1977: 153)

Thus he posits a link between precisely the two objects of my criticism in this chapter. Whether or not one accepts this link, the case that Dumont makes for Marx's stress on the individual as against the whole is a strong one. His critique of Marx is set against a historical analysis of the development of economic thought. Indeed his main thesis is summarised in the sub-title of his book: *The Genesis and Triumph of Economic Ideology*. According to Dumont, Marx "succeeds in removing what blocked the way to revolution, … but he remains within the limits of economic thought" (Dumont 1977: 153)

> Marx has insisted, against the economist, on the social nature of man; yet he does not take society as the real subject of the production process but follows the economists in concentrating on the individual subject. (Dumont 1977: 157)

Perhaps Dumont relies unduly on the early works of Marx. Certainly his argument rests very largely on *The German Ideology* and the *1844 Manuscripts*. Passages from Marx's other works (some of which Dumont quotes) are less easy to reconcile with his major claim. But a somewhat similar charge is also levelled against Marx by the historian Edward Thompson, who argues that "*Capital* was not an exercise of a different order to that of mature bourgeois Political Economy, but a total confrontation within that order" (Thompson 1978: 65). Such an approach, he says, cannot provide the necessary answers:

> A unitary knowledge of society (which is always in motion, hence a historical knowledge) cannot be won from a 'science' which, as a presupposition of its discipline, isolates certain kinds of activity only for study, and provides no categories for others. And the structure of *Capital* remains marked by the categories of its antagonist, notably *economy* itself. (Thompson 1978: 65)

Capital makes use of history to provide examples and illustrations, but it is not itself a historical work. Thompson does not underestimate the importance of historical materialism, but argues that its development very largely came after *Capital* and after Marx. Thompson, too, addresses the issue of Man in the abstract, but does not wholly accept the standard version known by "any first-year student".

> As a matter of fact, it is a question, and a very difficult one, how far Marx and Engels ever did fully reject the concept, 'man', which reappears in the concept of alienation, in the notion of a 'truly human morality', and in what some scholars detect as an historical teleology of human immanence. (Thompson 1978: 149)

Thompson is unwilling to ignore "all those dense, complex and elaborated systems by which familial and social life is structured and social consciousness finds realisation and expression (systems which the very rigour of the discipline in Ricardo or in the Marx of *Capital* is designed to exclude)" (Thompson 1978: 170). He might well take exception to the emphasis of Dumont the anthropologist on "the whole", a perspective which tends to lay correspondingly less stress on the individual person. Yet they both criticise Marx for being too much of an economist:

> To the end of his life, when confronting, in his anthropological researches, problems manifestly demanding analysis in terms not derivative from Political Economy, Marx—while acknowledging the problems—was always trying to shove them back into an economic frame of reference. (Thompson 1978: 172)

Thompson sharply criticises Marx for his claim that moral influences are "economical before everything else" a judgment which is "derived from a particular and limited definition of the 'economic'". Indeed, he goes further, arguing that this "was transmitted to the subsequent Marxist tradition in the form of a repression (which) made it more easy for the major tradition to … capitulate to an economism which, in fact, simply took over a bourgeois utilitarian notion of 'need'" (Thompson 1978: 172).

Against the argument of Dumont, and to some extent Thompson also, it is relevant to consider an alternative interpretation put forward by Meikle, who stresses the "essentialism" of Marx. In his view:

> (i) … History is the process of coming-to-be of human society. Its essence is human labour, and its different 'principles' are the social forms in which that labour is historically supplied. … (ii) Marx also has a view of man as a natural kind; a species of the mammalian order, whose essence is differentiated from others of that and other orders by the essential property of being conscious and social. (Meikle 1985: 57)[5]

Meikle claims that these two views are fused in one, that "the essence of this mammalian species is realised only in the degree to which the

[5] The interpretation of the term "conscious" is important. The earlier quotation (see previous footnote) implies that it means no more than capable of planning; but it could be taken far more broadly to refer to social consciousness.

essence of society has been realised" (Meikle 1985: 59) and criticises those who seek to divorce them. Dumont (and perhaps also Thompson) would presumably fall into this group—not merely divorcing the two processes, but ignoring the latter. My own view is that the two must be distinguished, and that Marx makes an error by "fusing" them. The latter view of man is (contra Dumont) evident in Marx's writings; but it *is* given less emphasis, not only in the early works but even in *Capital.* Marx's theory is concerned with what Meikle calls "human" labour, and "the social forms in which that labour is historically supplied". His starting point is man as worker, not man as a social being.

In this context it is important to note the distinction between labour in the sense of alienated labour (as in the *1844 Manuscripts*) and labour in its more general sense, as in *Capital.* This is well analysed by Arthur (1986) who points out than many commentators, including Lukács, Marcuse and Oizerman, have failed to observe this crucial difference. He himself chooses the term "productive activity" to refer to the most general phenomenon—which, under capitalism, is alienated. According to Arthur, the "ontological underpinning" of *Capital* is to be found in the *1844 Manuscripts*, for:

> In 1844 a turning point occurs in Marx's philosophical development. For the first time he attributes fundamental ontological significance to *productive activity*. Through material production humanity comes to be what it is. (Arthur 1986: 5)

I believe this is a correct interpretation of Marx. Arthur quotes Marx's reference to "the emergence of nature for man", describing this as "a genuine advance beyond that state in which man is sunk in the natural, unable to perceive his own specificity as an acting subject and to grasp nature as an object of purposeful activity" (Arthur 1986: 130). This, for Marx, is how Man is distinct from the "natural"—not, primarily, as a social being, but as a human being. The key to this humanity is labour. "Labour", in Marx's later writings is "one of his fundamental ahistorical categories" (Arthur 1986: 13). This is evident from the following quotation:

> The general features of the labour process … are all independent of every historical and specifically social conditioning. … They are in fact immutable natural conditions of human labour. This is strikingly confirmed by the fact that they hold good for people who work independently. … Thus they are in fact absolute determinants of *human* labour as such, as soon as it has evolved beyond the purely animal. (Marx 1976: 1022)

Under capitalism, human labour is alienated; it becomes social labour. But, according to Arthur, it is labour in the sense of "productive activity"—ahistorical, "human" labour—that has fundamental ontological significance. This is, I believe, a correct interpretation of Marx.

I will conclude this chapter by considering some other reasons why Marx emphasised labour. One was that Marx believed it was the proletariat that had the power to change the system. This might be called a political reason, for by emphasising the significance of labour, Marx identified the potential for change, for revolutionary action.[6]

There were also what might be called "economic" reasons. Ricardo, and other economists before him, had also emphasised labour. Certainly it is one of the technical inputs into production. It is also the case that all inputs into production can be expressed in terms of labour. But neither of these arguments justifies giving it pride of place; the emphasis on labour cannot be based on technical, material grounds alone. Marx was fully aware of this. Certainly the emphasis which Ricardo and other economists put on labour appealed to him, but not merely as a matter of methodological convenience. He had better grounds for regarding it as basic.

Marx's "economic" reason for focussing on labour is methodological in a more important sense: the emphasis on production cuts straight to the heart of the capitalist system, wherein exploitation occurs by the extraction of surplus value by the capitalist class from the workers. The concept of surplus value, which is essential to his critique of the system, rests on the role of labour. The exploitation occurs in production, not in exchange. The sphere of circulation is the "noisy sphere, where everything takes

[6] Alternatively, adopting an essentialist interpretation, this might be more closely linked with the previous point—the nature of man; thus, the proletariat is important not simply because it is a politically effective force, but because of its role in the necessary unfolding of events.

place on the surface … within whose boundaries the sale and purchase of labour power goes on, … a very Eden of the innate rights of man". This is the sphere which "furnishes the 'Free-trader Vulgaris' with his views and ideas" (Marx 1954: 172). For the purposes of laying bare the exploitation in capitalist society, the crucial sphere is that of production, and the crucial social relation is that between the capitalist and the worker.

Thus there were several, closely interlinked reasons why Marx placed such an emphasis on labour and production. And it was as a result that he was able to integrate the different strands of his argument. (It is therefore something of a distortion to present these as separate "philosophical" "political", and "economic" reasons, as I have done here.) It is evident, however, that Marx's originality did not lie in his emphasis on labour. Indeed, he could hardly avoid such an emphasis, given the era he lived in and the ideas prevalent at the time. Lenin identified three influences on Marx: German philosophy, British political economy and French Socialism.[7] In each case, one could argue, labour was the key. The authors whose works exerted influence on Marx—whether philosophers, economists or socialists—all focussed on it. It is true that Marx brought these together; and here, certainly, there was great originality. But how was it possible for him to do so? And where, in relation to economics specifically, did his originality lie? The answer, I suggest, is in Marx's emphasis on the social. This was original. This gave the power to his critique of economic categories. This was where he had to break new ground, and go beyond Ricardo, to investigate "what labour it was that produced value". (See Chap. 5.) His obsession with labour, however, blinded him to other types of social relations—of exchange and consumption—as discussed in the following two chapters.

Bibliography

Arthur, C. (1986). *Dialectics of Labour: Marx and His Relation to Hegel*. Oxford: Blackwell.

Cohen, G. (1978). *Karl Marx's Theory of History*. A Defence: Oxford Clarendon.

---

[7] Lenin's "The Three Sources" (quoted in Cohen 1978: 1).

Dumont, L. (1977). *From Mandeville to Marx: The Genesis and Triumph of Economic Ideology*. Chicago: University Press.
Fromm, E. (1961). *Marx's Concept of Man*. New York: Ungor.
Marx, K. (1954). *Capital* (Vol. I). Moscow: Progress.
Marx, K. (1970). *A Draft Introduction to Grundrisse*. Moscow: Progress.
Marx, K. (1973). *Grundrisse*. Moscow: Progress.
Marx, K. (1976). *Capital* (Vol. I). Harmondsworth: Penguin.
Marx, K. (1977). *Economic and Philosophic Manuscripts of 1844*. Moscow: Progress.
Marx, K., & Engels, F. (1974). *The German Ideology* (C. J. Arthur, Ed.). London: Lawrence and Wishart.
Meikle, S. (1985). *Essentialism in the Thought of Karl Marx*. London: Duckworth.
Taylor, C. (1975). *Hegel*. Cambridge: Cambridge University Press.
Thompson, E. P. (1978). *The Poverty of Theory and Other Essays*. London: Merlin.

12

Exchange and Reciprocity

For neither would there have been association if there were not exchange, nor exchange if there were not equality, nor equality if there were not commensurability.
(Aristotle, as quoted by Marx in Marx 1970b: 68)

The expression "an Indian giver" means "one who gives a present and later asks for its return, as American Indians did, if they got nothing in exchange for their presents" (Brewer 1981: 589). Newcomers to North America, from the continent of Europe, found this a very bizarre phenomenon, but it is not, by any means, restricted to American Indians. It is an example of a very widespread practice involving what is known in anthropology as "reciprocity", a complex concept which can best be explained by reference to Marcel Mauss, who, in his pioneering work *The Gift*, did more than any other to establish its significance and to show how it could enlighten our understanding of both "traditional" and "modern" society.

This is a revised version of a chapter in McNeill, D (1988) *Fetishism and the Form of Value*. Unpublished thesis, University of London. A modified version of that chapter was also published in *Public Affairs Quarterly*, 1969. Vol 4, no. 1, pages 55–68.

D. McNeill, *Fetishism and the Theory of Value*, Palgrave Studies in the History of Economic Thought, https://doi.org/10.1007/978-3-030-56123-9_12

Mauss begins with a long quotation from the *Edda*, of which the third paragraph is particularly striking: "A man ought to be a friend to his friend and repay gift with gift. People should meet smiles with smiles and lies with treachery." He then goes on:

> The foregoing lines from the Edda outline our subject-matter. In Scandinavian and many other civilizations contracts are fulfilled and exchanges of goods are made by means of gifts. In theory such gifts are voluntary but in fact they are given and repaid under obligation. (Mauss 1970: 1)

Much of the book then consists of ethnographic material from selected areas—Polynesia, Melanesia and North-West America—by which "Mauss sought to show that exchange in primitive societies consists not so much in economic transactions as in reciprocal gifts, that these reciprocal gifts have a far more important function in these societies than in our own, and that this primitive form of exchange is not merely nor essentially of an economic nature but is what he aptly calls 'a total social fact'" (Lévi-Strauss 1949: 54).

To appreciate the context within which such a phenomenon occurs, consider the situation in a "traditional" society.[1] Each person occupies a certain position, and by virtue of this relates to all other persons. (Those outside the society are excluded from consideration, and may indeed be excluded from the category of human beings.) Each person belongs to society as a whole by virtue of such ties, and belongs more particularly to a specific group within society by virtue of his or her kin and affine relations with others. Typically, the most important determinants of such groups are marriage rules; thus a person belonging to one group should not marry a member of certain specified groups, but may (or perhaps should) marry a person from another.

The exchange of things frequently reflects, and may also be said to express and even reinforce, such relations between persons and relations between groups of persons. Thus the type and (to a lesser extent) amount

[1] The picture that follows is idealised and static. My aim is to demonstrate a major difference in *emphasis*; the cost is severe over-simplification.

of things which should be given by one person to another under certain circumstances are specified. In the case of marriage, such rules are particularly common and particularly clear. A marriage between two persons is also, and more importantly, a link between two groups; a link which may also be seen as an *exchange* of persons (typically portrayed by commentators as an exchange of women) between two groups. Marriage may thus be seen as an important relation between persons—though not as isolated individuals—a relation which reflects, expresses and reinforces the relationship between the two groups (and indeed expresses and reinforces membership of the society itself). And the exchange of things which accompanies it may be seen in the same light.

Marriage is by no means the only circumstance in which things are exchanged. It does, however, usefully exemplify the point that I wish to emphasise, which may be briefly summarised as follows. There are societies in which exchange of things is very different from its apparent counterpart in modern Western society. The relation between such things exchanged reflects a relation between persons; the relation between persons is primary, the relation between things secondary. This relation between persons is one which obtains between them not as persons but as members of groups; it may more accurately be seen as a relation between groups. Exchange of goods and services in such societies is thus not best understood in modern "economic" terms, but rather as establishing or maintaining a social bond.

But Mauss does not restrict his study entirely to contemporary, non-Western societies. He includes also a chapter on "Survivals in Early Literature" which is of particular interest.

> Likewise Greek, Roman and Semitic civilizations distinguished clearly between obligatory prestations and pure gifts. But are these distinctions not of relatively recent appearance in the codes of the great civilizations? (Mauss 1970: 46)[2]

[2] Mauss refers to customs of gift-exchange "in which persons and things become indistinguishable". This is a theme of considerable interest which I cannot pursue further here: that the distinction between things and persons, which is fundamental to our own society—"the very condition of part of our system of property, alienation and exchange"—is "foreign to the customs we have been studying" (Mauss 1970: 46).

He then discusses ancient Rome, the Hindu classical period, Germanic societies and (very briefly) Chinese law. With regard to Ancient Greece he notes:

> We have not given enough attention to Greek law or the law which preceded the great Ionic and Doric codifications, so we cannot say whether or not the various peoples of Greece knew these rules of the gift. (Mauss 1970: 121)

He does, however, refer briefly to Aristotle's *Nichomachean Ethics*—to section 1123, on the "magnanimous citizen, his public and private expenses, his duties and responsibilities" (Mauss 1970: 121). Whether or not this fragment is taken as evidence of Mauss' support for my case, I wish to argue that Greek society at the time of Aristotle was more "traditional" in this respect than many modern commentators allow; and that a more famous passage in Aristotle, quoted by Marx and much discussed by others, can be better understood in the light of the concept of reciprocity. It is to this that I now turn. I shall discuss it at some length because it adds weight to both my claims. First, it shows that exchange merits consideration not merely as an expression of a social relation of production. Second, it shows that Marx failed to recognise this point.

In the first volume of *Capital*, Marx praises "the great thinker who was the first to analyse so many forms of thought, society, or Nature, and amongst them also the form of value, I mean Aristotle" (Marx 1954: 65). But he suggests that Aristotle's analysis is nevertheless inadequate, attributing this to "the peculiar conditions of the society in which he lived", that is that Greek society was based upon slavery. He quotes Aristotle directly:

> 'Exchange,' he (Aristotle) says, 'cannot take place without equality, and equality without commensurability'. Here, however, he comes to a stop, and gives up the further analysis of the form of value. (Marx 1954: 65)

Marx claims that Aristotle was unable to understand value because "Greek society was founded upon slavery, and had, therefore, for its natural basis, the inequality of men and their labour-powers. The secret of the expression of value, namely, that all kinds of labour are equal and equivalent, because and so far as they are human labour in general, cannot be deciphered, until the notion of human equality had already acquired the fixity of a popular prejudice" (Marx 1954: 65).

This quotation shows Marx to be a sympathetic interpreter of Aristotle, in the sense that he takes into account, indeed makes much of, the fact that Greek society in Aristotle's day was significantly different from our own. But he makes a notable omission in his quotation from Aristotle—an omission which he did not make earlier in *A Contribution to the Critique of Political Economy*. Here he quoted Aristotle more fully, including the introductory sentence:

> for neither would there have been association if there were not exchange. (Marx 1970b: 68)[3]

This first sentence is, I wish to argue, a reference to reciprocity. Why, then, did Marx omit it when he cited this quotation on the second occasion? I am not claiming that he recognised its significance and deliberately cut it out. Quite the contrary; I suggest that he thought it unimportant. Whereas, if my hypothesis is correct, it is of considerable significance for our understanding of what Aristotle meant. Thus, Marx's sensitivity to Greek society did not, I suggest, extend to a full understanding of the place of reciprocity in that society. (Although his point about slavery was, in a sense, entirely pertinent.) To support this hypothesis I need to set the quotation from Aristotle in its context by examining in more detail the passage from the *Nichomachean Ethics*:

> Men seek to return evil for evil—and if they cannot do so, think their position mere slavery—or good for good—and if they cannot do so there is no exchange, but it is exchange that they hold together. This is why they give a prominent place to the temples of the Graces—to promote the requital of services; for this is characteristic of grace—we should serve in return one

[3] See head of this chapter for the full quotation.

> who has shown grace to us, and should another time take the initiative in showing it. (Aristotle 1980: 1133a, b)[4]

This text, I suggest, supports the view that Aristotle is describing a society in which, to use Evans-Pritchard's words in his introduction to Mauss 1970, "exchange of goods was not a mechanical but a moral transaction, bringing about and maintaining human, personal, relationships between individuals and groups" (Introduction to Mauss 1970: ix). Such an impression is strengthened by the fact that Aristotle is concerned also with retaliation ("returning evil for evil") which has close affinity with Mauss's quote from the *Edda* cited above.

The section from which this extract is drawn—on reciprocal justice—is complex and has been the subject of considerable debate. It is therefore necessary to argue the case more fully; and in so doing, I hope, cast more light on a society which, though in some ways similar to our own, was also in important respects, very different.

To set Aristotle's argument in context: it occurs in Book 5 of *The Nichomachean Ethics* where his concern is with justice—that subset of virtue concerned with relations to one's neighbour (1130a). After a brief section on "universal justice" he turns to "particular justice", that is, the just as the fair and the equal. Under this heading he first discusses distributive and rectificatory justice, before turning to "justice in exchange, reciprocity in accordance with proportion".

He understands justice in terms of balance—it is "a kind of mean" (1133b). And his analysis of the fair and equal, with strong Pythagorean influence, is presented largely in mathematical terms. Thus he distinguishes the geometrical (proportionate) from the arithmetic: certain types of transaction are just if the things concerned stand in an appropriate *ratio*; others are just if the things concerned are *equal*. But it must be stressed that the relationship in each case is *first* a relation between persons, and then, and as a result, a relation between things. He is perfectly at home with relations between persons: "among men who are free and either proportionately or arithmetically equal" (1134a). The problem for

[4] Unless otherwise specified, references are to the Ross translation (Aristotle 1980). Rather than giving page references to this edition, however, I will follow common practice and henceforth refer only to the original version.

Aristotle arises with relations between things; to Aristotle, things are not commensurable.

Distributive justice, the first type which Aristotle discusses, applies in a situation where benefits are to be shared among a number of people. Here, he argues, it is the relative status of the people concerned which should determine their shares. For example, a sum of money, perhaps booty from war, is to be distributed—between two people:

> The just, therefore, involves at least four terms; for the persons for whom it is in fact just are two, and the things in which it is manifested, the objects distributed, are two. And the same equality will exist between the persons and the things concerned; for as the latter—the things concerned—are related, so are the former. (1131a)

The distribution is just if it is done according to the merit of the persons concerned, although, as Aristotle notes, there is some dispute as to the sort of merit: "democrats identify it with the status of freeman, supporters of oligarchy with wealth (or with noble birth) and supporters of aristocracy with excellence" (1131a).

He also expresses his argument mathematically:

> and the ratio between one pair is the same as that between the other pair; for there is a similar distinction between the persons and between the things. As the term A, then, is to B, so will C be to D, and therefore *alternando*, as A is to C, B will be to D. … The conjunction, then, of the term A with C and of B with D is what is just in distribution … the just is proportional. (Mathematicians call this kind of proportion geometrical). … This, then, is one species of the just. (1131b)

The next type of justice to be considered is rectificatory. Here the issue is not the distribution of common possessions but the righting of an injury; for example where one person has defrauded another. Here "the law looks only to the distinctive character of the injury, and treats the parties as equal, if one is in the wrong and the other wronged" (1132a). Justice is achieved in such circumstances by making good the damage: "the judge restores equality" (1132a); the just "consists in having an equal amount before and after the transaction" (1132b). Again Aristotle expresses the idea in mathematical terms, but using geometry (division of a straight line) rather than algebra.[5] This relates to the importance of "the whole" in Aristotle's thinking, which causes him to express some of the mathematics in what appears to modern eyes as an unnecessarily complex or even distorted manner. Thus his exposition of arithmetic equality (1132b) seems to make very heavy weather of what is in our time a very simple idea. And in discussing geometrical proportion he concludes that "Therefore also the whole is in the same ratio to the whole" (1131b) which adds nothing to our modern understanding.

He also describes the case of rectificatory justice by reference to "loss" and "gain", which terms, he notes, "have come from voluntary exchange … e.g. in buying and selling and in all other matters in which the law has left people free to make their own terms". This indicates how novel the concepts of "gain" and "loss" appear to Aristotle; matters in which individuals are free to make their own terms—rather than referring to law—are, by implication, the exception. Aristotle is describing a society in which the law plays an immensely important role; an exchange of goods of the type described here is a rather new and unusual phenomenon which raises novel problems for one who is concerned to determine what is just.

But according to Aristotle, justice in exchange "fits neither distributive nor rectificatory justice". But he determines that what is appropriate is "reciprocity in accordance with a proportion and not on the basis of precisely equal return. For it is by proportionate requital that the city holds together" (1132b). How is this to be achieved? Aristotle's analysis here is rather similar to that which he applied in the case of distributive justice. Exchange, like the sharing of booty, should be on a geometrical (proportionate) basis—reflecting the merit of the parties concerned. But the situation of exchange is nevertheless not the same as the sharing of booty.[6]

[5]The interpretation of fairness as appropriate *division* is central to Aristotle's thinking; thus: "It is for this reason also that it is called just (*dikaion*) because it is division into two equal parts (*dikha*) … and the judge (*dikastes*) is one who bisects (*dikhastes*)" (1132a).

[6]Aristotle's text here, and indeed in many places, is open to other interpretations. I suggest that both his argument in this section, and the fact that he treats reciprocal justice as a separate category, support the view that reciprocal justice is distinct from both the other kinds—indeed a sort of mixture of the two. Unlike the case of booty, the goods are not initially held in common. There are, as discussed below, other important differences also between exchange and the other transactions

In the case of distributive justice there was "*conjunction*" of the term A with C and of B with D—the ratio between the things reflected the (unequal) ratio between the persons. But in the case of exchange Aristotle determines that there should be "*cross-conjunction*":

> Now proportionate return is secured by cross-conjunction. … If, then first there is proportionate equality of goods, and then exchange[7] takes place, the result we mention will be effected. If not, the bargain is not equal and will not hold. (1133a)

That I have rightly interpreted the expression "cross-conjunction" is confirmed by the later passage:

> There will, then, be reciprocity when the terms have been equated so that as farmer is to shoemaker, the amount of the shoemaker's work is to that of the farmer for which it exchanges. (1133a)[8]

Thus the just is achieved where A is to B, as D is to C; hence, where farmer A is to shoes D, as shoemaker B is to food C. This has confused many commentators, who cannot understand why there should be "cross-conjunction"—the link between farmer and shoe rather than farmer and food. The reason appears to be that the important connection for Aristotle is *need*. Those who "associate for exchange" are "in general people who are different and unequal". Otherwise they would have no cause to exchange. Each *needs* what the other has. Thus the persons who are party to an exchange are different and unequal, but in the act of exchange they are equated—a situation which appears to Aristotle as somewhat paradoxical, both because persons are not equal and because things are not commensurable.

---

discussed, and it is perhaps a matter of speculation which of these is of most significance for Aristotle.

[7] The word "exchange" here ("*to antipeponthos*") is translated by Ross as "reciprocal action"; but according to Scaltsas (1985) Aristotle is using the term to describe "just the process of exchanging". I am greatly indebted to Scaltsas for his advice in interpreting Aristotle, without wishing to commit him to the views expressed here.

[8] Aristotle first uses the example of a housebuilder rather than a farmer to make the same point, but the argument is unaffected.

> This is why all things that are exchanged must be somehow comparable. It is for this end that money has been introduced, and it becomes in a sense an intermediate; for it measures all things. … All goods must therefore be measured by some one thing, as we said before. Now this unit is in truth, need,[9] which holds all things together. … But money has become by convention a sort of representative of need. (1133a)

Aristotle's solution to the paradox, then, relies on the concepts of need and money. With regard to the first, it should be stressed that, contrary to what many have written, Aristotle regards this, and not production, as the important link between person and thing. Consider the situation in the abstract. A farmer possesses food and a shoemaker shoes. Initially we have two unequal persons (the farmer, A, and the shoemaker, B) and two incommensurable things (the food, C, and the shoes, D).[10] Each person is related to each thing in two different ways: either by virtue of having produced it, or by virtue of needing it. It is the latter link which Aristotle seizes upon. This many translators and commentators have found difficult to accept, preferring to impute to him some sort of early labour theory of value, implying that the significant link is between the farmer (or more precisely his labour) and the food that he produces. Some (such as Ross) concede that Aristotle does not expressly state it in these terms. Another (Rowe) describes the passages in question as "very strange" and attributes them to "mere carelessness" on Aristotle's part (Rowe 1971: 103). An extreme case is Chase, who seems to find the text so contrary to common sense that he actually inverts the relevant ratios (Chase 1911: 114). And an early nineteenth-century writer not only alters the text but *ad libs* extravagantly as well, to give further (spurious) weight to his inaccurate translation (Gillies 1813: 375).

Despite these various translations and commentaries it is clear that Aristotle is not suggesting that the amount (or even the quality) of labour

[9] "Need" is a translation of the Greek "*khreia*", whereas Ross, like Rackham and other earlier translators, has "demand" here. It seems widely accepted that "need" is more accurate (ref Meikle, and Miller.), although the moral connotations of the word "*khreia*" are not fully captured by this word either. As Finley notes: "The semantic cluster around *chreia* … includes 'use', advantage', 'service'" (Finley 1970: 8).

[10] The distinction between "unequal" and "incommensurable" is important, as becomes more evident below.

embodied in each thing is of significance. No emphasis on production and labour can be sustained by even the most cursory reading of the text. This is not to say, however, that he is an early marginal utility theorist—a view favoured by Soudek (1952) and others. Certainly he emphasises need; but to claim that Aristotle was a precursor of the Austrian school is no less anachronistic than to portray him as an early Political Economist (though perhaps not quite so distortive of the texts themselves).[11]

But even if need is identified as the significant link, this does not solve Aristotle's dilemma. He brings money also into the discussion, and seeks an answer there. He seems to recognise its significance and yet cannot adequately explain how it resolves the issue. Money, he says, becomes "in a sense an intermediate; for it measures all things". This is in keeping with his analysis of distributive and rectificatory justice, each of which also required some "intermediate".[12] He does not elaborate, however, on how money plays a role analogous to that of the arithmetic or geometric in these two cases. Nor does he explain the relationship between need and money. Indeed, each in turn seems to be given the credit for relating the incommensurable:

> This is why all things that are exchanged must be somehow comparable. It is for this end that money has been introduced. (1133a)

> All goods must therefore be measured by some one thing, as we said before. Now this unit is in truth need … which holds all things together. (1133a)

And he appears finally to admit the inadequacies of his own analysis:

---

[11] In addition to the many translations, with accompanying notes, there are numerous articles concerned with this particular section of the *Nichomachean Ethics*, some of which I have referred to. It should perhaps be noted that there is no evidence that the Greek text, on which so much of this debate centres, was corrupt.

[12] Distributive justice: "*qua* intermediate it must be between certain things (which are respectively greater and less" (1131a); and "the proportional is intermediate" (1131b). Rectificatory justice: "The equal is intermediate between the greater and the lesser line according to arithmetical proportion" (1132a). In each case there are two amounts allotted on a basis which is fair; in the first instance they are fair because "intermediate" on a geometrical basis; in the second case, fair because "intermediate" on an arithmetical basis.

> Now in truth it is impossible that things differing so much should become commensurate, but with reference to need they become so sufficiently. (1133b)

Thus, he recognised that money achieved—somehow—a measurement or mediation, but he could not fully appreciate how or why. And we should hardly blame him for that. He was seeking to analyse a rather new and anomalous phenomenon. As Marx noted "Even among the Greeks and Romans … money reaches its full development … only in the period of their disintegration" (Marx 1970a: 208). Aristotle was seeking to understand a society in which money was only beginning to exert its influence, and market trading was only incipient.

This is a point well accepted by several more modern commentators (e.g. Finley, Polanyi, Meikle) although they would not all agree on precisely how far Greek society had developed. Meikle seems to suggest more than my interpretation allows, claiming that "products had, in very considerable part, acquired this social form (of 'commodities') in Aristotle's Athens" (Meikle 1979: 67). But he bases his analysis on the *Politics*, where, he argues "we find Aristotle looking at exchange in quite a different way. … Aristotle is analysing the evolution of social relations of exchange through their successive historical forms" (Meikle 1979: 61). If Meikle claims too much, Polanyi goes in other the direction in asserting that "the supply-demand-price mechanism escaped Aristotle" (Quoted by Finley 1970: 13). Whether or not Meikle's reading of the *Politics* is correct, however, need not affect my main argument; that in the *Ethics* Aristotle is trying to comprehend what is in our society seen as a purely "economic" transaction in terms of justice. This view draws further support from the fact (stressed by Finley and conceded also by Meikle) that in the *Ethics* the word trade is not used.

Aristotle's concern was with justice, and he considered exchange as a type of transaction which should be analysable in terms of the just. It is not surprising that he found it difficult. In his society, relations between persons were clearly established, and it was these that determined behaviour and governed all types of transactions—including those which involved things. Giving, magnificence and so on were clear examples (ref discussion of Mauss above); the rules regarding these were determined by the status of the person concerned. Exchange of goods, such as we have been discussing, appeared to Aristotle as somewhat anomalous.

Not only was exchange incipient, so too was the economy itself (each in our modern sense of the term). With Finley, I would "insist that the ancients did not (rather could not) have the concept" (Finley 1970: 22). In Aristotle's day, the economy was "imbedded" in a social whole, to quote Polanyi; and it became disembedded only gradually, in step with the emerging distinction between status and contractus. "Status is set by birth—a man's position in the family—and determines the rights and duties of a person. … But *status* was gradually replaced by *contractus*, i.e. by rights and duties derived from bilateral agreements" (Polanyi 1968: 83).

> Transactions in early times are public acts performed in regard to the status of persons. … Great as the economic significance of such transactions was, it ranked second to their importance in establishing the position of the persons in the social context. (Polanyi 1968: 91)[13]

But here was a new type of transaction—exchange between two persons each of whom needed the other's good. Aristotle understood that it did not fit easily into the existing categories; but he could not know quite how radically different it was. And this point has escaped many commentators on Aristotle, who appear to be far more at home discussing traditional, "non-economic" transactions—such as giving to the temple of the graces. These they can classify as "religious" or "moral" acts (perhaps equally anachronistic terms). But they find it hard to understand that Aristotle was trying to analyse exchange in much the same way.[14]

---

[13] Polanyi's description of Aristotle's method, which relates closely to this point, is very enlightening:

> In mapping out a field of study he (Aristotle) would relate all questions of institutional origin and function to the totality of society. Community, self-sufficiency and justice were the focal concepts. The group as a going concern forms a community (*koinonia*) the members of which are linked by the bond of good will (*philia*). … *Philia* expresses itself in a behaviour of reciprocity (anti-peponthos). … The rate at which the shared services (or, eventually, the goods) are exchanged follows from the requirement of *philia*, i.e. that the good will among the members persist. For without it community would cease. (Polanyi 1968: 97)

[14] A possible exception, apart from Polanyi, is Miller who, in arguing for a new "consequentialist" interpretation of Aristotle's theory of justice, asserts:

Aristotle sought to understand this new phenomenon in relation to, and even in terms of, others with which he was more familiar. The result was not wholly satisfactory. But he had the merit of recognising the problem, and seeing something of the solution (in money). This is more than can be said for most commentators, who have sought rather to interpret Aristotle in modern terms. What he describes is indeed, in incipient form, a modern phenomenon. But his explanation of it is not; how could it be? The "same" transaction is looked at from two wholly different perspectives: from that of a society in which it is the exception, and from one in which it is the rule.

Due weight, surely, should be given to Aristotle's own explanation of the phenomenon. It may be misguided; more likely, I suggest, it is simply very difficult to comprehend, since modern words do not accurately map onto ancient concepts.[15] This problem of translation from one era to another was commented on by Marx in a letter to Engels:

> Philologists of the stature of Grimm translated the simplest Latin sentences wrongly, because they were influenced by Moser etc. … For example, the well-known passage in Tacitus: … They change (by lots i.e. lottery) the fields and common land … remains, which Grimm etc. translate as: 'They cultivate new fields every year, and there is always (uncultivated) land left over!' (Marx and Engels 1983 to Engels March 25th, 1868)

And Marx rightly saw this as a symptom of a deeper problem—of understanding societies different from our own (whether separated in time or in space). His comment on Grimm follows a discussion of the

---

> We must take seriously Aristotle's introducing the notion of reciprocal justice in terms of its political function. Reciprocal justice, he says, is justice concerning exchanges which hold the city together. How does it do so? By promoting exchanges in which people rely on each other to satisfy one another's needs. (Miller 1981: 336)

I do not quite agree with his term "political", but his interpretation seems very similar to my own—although he appears to be unaware of the crucial concept of reciprocity as I have described it above.

[15] Thus the word "*metadosis*" was taken to be exchange or barter, while patently meaning its opposite, namely, giving one's share" (Finley 1970: 112). This not only provides a good example of the problem, it also reinforces the picture of exchange as concerned with participation in society as a whole, as a member of a group.

different reactions to the French Revolution—first the Romantic view, then the tendency "to look past the Middle Ages to the pre-history of every nation" finding "the most modern things in the most ancient". He discussed this same issue at greater length in the draft Introduction to *Grundrisse* in relation to the emerging concepts of labour and money.

In keeping with Marx's criticism of those who projected the present onto the past, I suggest that we need a well-informed as well as a sympathetic translation of Aristotle's text. By "sympathetic" I imply a willingness to try and understand Aristotle in his own social context; to accept that there may be no simple one-to-one mapping of concepts, and hence words, from Ancient Greece to modern Europe—rather than distorting those passages which are difficult to understand, or dismissing them as "weaknesses" attributable to "mere carelessness".

Marx's own interpretation of this passage from the *Ethics* is sympathetic in the sense just defined. He seeks to understand it in Aristotle's own terms. His conclusion is that Aristotle is, in the final analysis, wrong (though excusably so):

> Aristotle is aware of the fact that the different things measured by money are entirely incommensurable magnitudes. What he seeks is the oneness of commodities as exchange-values, and since he lives in Ancient Greece it was impossible for him to find it. He extricates himself from this predicament by making essentially incommensurable things commensurable—by means of money. (Marx 1970b: 68)

That Aristotle failed to solve the problem seems incontrovertible. Indeed he himself found the analysis unconvincing, saying that it is impossible "that things so widely different should become commensurable", and concluding lamely that "they may become so for practical purposes".

As well as being sympathetic, Marx's interpretation was also well-informed in that he took account of conditions in Greek society at this time: the inequality of men, most evident in the existence of slavery. And he used this to explain why Aristotle was unable to understand the concept of value in exchange. I nevertheless do not wholly agree with Marx. What I am suggesting is that exchange in Aristotle's time actually was *different*—not that he simply did not understand it. Thus Marx only partially appreciated the significance of the different social context with which he was dealing.

It is indeed very difficult—perhaps impossible—for a modern commentator fully to understand the text. It is not only a question of lack of words, and hence lack of concepts. Aristotle's world is in some sense inaccessible to the modern mind, which is steeped in notions which can never be fully eliminated. As Finley notes: "The first principle of a market economy is, of course, indifference to the *persons* of the buyer and seller: that is what troubles most commentators on Aristotle" (Finley 1970: 10). But can this problem ever be fully resolved? Can we fully understand what relations between persons meant in Aristotle's time? Even sympathetic commentators admit to serious difficulty in this regard. Thus, Meikle: "Cross-conjunction remains a mystery since nobody knows what the ratio of producers means" (Meikle 1979: 60). And Finley: "I must confess that, like Joachim, I do not understand what the ratios between the producers can mean, but I do not rule out the possibility that 'as a builder is to a shoemaker' is somehow to be taken literally" (Finley 1970: 13).

In our modern society relations between persons are very different; and exchange of goods is a "purely economic" phenomenon. In Aristotle's society, by contrast, this type of exchange was only beginning to emerge; a development in which money played a key role. To this extent Aristotle was right to emphasise money, but he either would not or could not explain exchange in this way. To claim that he *would* not is to favour the view that Greek society at his time was relatively well developed in this regard but that Aristotle was somehow blinkered. To claim that he *could* not is to argue that even though this type of exchange was emergent, it was very little developed, so that the time was not yet ripe for the major shift of categories required; just as one might argue that the breakthrough which Adam Smith achieved, in recognising labour in general, could not have been achieved until society itself had changed sufficiently (Ref Marx's discussion in the draft Introduction to *Grundrisse*).

What seems incontrovertible is that Aristotle was seeking to describe a society in transition, in which relations between persons were in the process of being replaced by relations between things. Whether or not he recognised the emergent tendency, he sought to explain the new phenomenon (or perhaps more accurately to judge it) in terms of the old, well-established rules. The resulting argument is unsatisfactory but instructive, perhaps best summed up in the rather puzzling passage which Marx chose to truncate:

> Money, then, acting as a measure, makes goods commensurate and equates them; for neither would there have been association if there were not exchange, nor exchange if there were not equality, nor equality if there were not commensurability. (Marx 1970b: 68)

Of the three links in the logical chain, the first and third are fairly straightforward: "Association would be impossible without exchange" is a statement about reciprocity—asserting that the specific type of relation between persons which is under discussion can occur only by virtue of the exchange of goods.[16] "No equality without commensurability" is a statement about relations between things; that things cannot be equated unless they are also commensurable (a problem to which Aristotle's solution is money). The middle link in the chain—"no exchange without equality"—is, however, more open to different interpretation. It links the relations between persons with the relations between things; but where, precisely, is the crucial connection? Does "equality" here refer to equality between persons or equality between things, or both?

To summarise, and conclude: there has been a very gradual shift—if one can trace Greek society through to our own—from a society in which the emphasis was on persons and relations between persons, to one in which the emphasis is on things and relations between things. Persons were members of groups, to which they perhaps belonged by virtue of birth, and because of which they enjoyed a certain status. They reinforced and gave expression to this status partly by transactions involving things (and either gods or other persons). Exchange such as we have been discussing was a rather incongruous type of transaction which did not fit into this pattern. Relations between persons were well understood and established; relations between things less so.

[16] The relation itself, however, is still paradoxical for Aristotle. Association should, since the parties are unequal, be based on proportionate requital (unequal in arithmetic terms).

But with the development of trade and the market came the emergence of independent producers. Then production for sale increasingly became the norm; and persons acquired social standing by virtue of what they produced. Persons related to one another through exchange—as independent commodity producers.

This type of society—simple commodity production—is one which Marx makes some reference to; but the society with which he was mainly concerned, capitalism in nineteenth-century Europe, was different again. There were indeed some independent producers, but the majority of workers sold their labour to capitalists.[17] Thus there were two great groups: the proletariat and the capitalist. The status of each was very simply determined. Capitalists were owners of capital; workers were "owners" only of their own labour-power, which they sold on the market. There is here an important relation between persons—namely the relation of exploitation. But this relation took the form of a relation between things. It was masked and concealed. The situation appeared, in this respect, reversed; relations between things were (apparently) clear, while relations between persons were concealed.

In his comments on Aristotle, Marx rightly emphasised the social, and more specifically the different social context which Greek society provided. And he rightly noted that persons were, in that society, unequal. But, I suggest, he was wrong to stress the importance of labour, for the inequality of men did not derive from this. Marx, although far less constrained than other economists by the categories of his time, was still unable fully to appreciate the society which Aristotle was seeking to describe. He was able to step outside the confines of his own society to a very great extent. But he laid undue emphasis on labour and production as the keys to understanding society. For nineteenth-century capitalism such an emphasis was justified; far less so, however, for Ancient Greek society. Further, I wish to argue, such an emphasis may be increasingly inappropriate in modern western society. In the next chapter I shall argue this point with regard to a third type of relation: consumption—or more accurately, need.

[17] His society was, in this sense, "mixed". The same was true of Aristotle's, and indeed of the idealised "traditional" society I described at the outset—ref. footnote (1) in this chapter.

Bibliography

Aristotle. (1980). *The Nichomachean Ethics* (D. Ross, Trans.). Oxford: University Press.

Brewer, E. (1981). *Brewer's Dictionary of Phrase and Fable*. London: Cassell.

Chase, D. (1911). *The Nichomachean Ethics of Aristotle*. London: J.M. Dent & Co.

Finley, M. I. (1970). Aristotle and Economic Analysis. *Past and Present*, Vol. 47.

Gillies, J. (1813). *Aristotle's Ethics and Politics* (3rd ed.). London: T. Cadell and W. Davies.

Lévi-Strauss, C. (1949). *The Elementary Structures of Kinship*.

Marx, K. (1954). *Capital* (Vol. I). Moscow: Progress.

Marx, K. (1970a). *A Draft Introduction to Grundrisse*. Moscow: Progress.

Marx, K. (1970b). *A Contribution to the Critique of Political Economy*. Moscow: Progress.

Marx, K., & Engels, F. (1983). *Letters on "Capital"*. London: New Park.

Mauss, M. (1970). *The Gift: Forms and Functions of Exchange in Archaic Societies*. London: Routledge & Kegan Paul.

Meikle, S,. (1979). Aristotle and the Political Economy of the Polis. *Journal of Hellenic Studies. Vol 99.*

Miller, R. W. (1981). Marx and Aristotle: A Kind of Consequentialism. *Canadian Journal of Philosophy, VII*(Suppl), 323–352.

Polanyi, K. (1968). Aristotle Discovers the Economy. In G. Dalton (Ed.), *Primitive, Archaic and Modern Economies*. Boston: Beacon Press.

Rowe, C. (1971). The Endemion and Nichomachean Ethics. A Study in the Development of Aristotle's Thought. *Proceedings of the Cambridge Philological Society. Supplement No. 3.*

Scaltsas, D. (1985). *Reciprocal Justice in Aristotle's Nichomachean Ethics*. Mimeo notes for paper delivered to the Philosophy Department, University of Edinburgh.

Soudek, J. (1952). Aristotle's Theory of Exchange: An Inquiry into the Origins of Economic Analysis. *Proceedings of the American Philosophical Society, 96*(1), 45–75.

13

Consumption, Need and Use-Value

the using up of commodity C, its consumption … is of purely physical interest, expressing no more than the relation of the individual A in his natural quality to an object of his individual need.
(Marx 1973: 274)

The emphasis on the social in Marx's analysis of the capitalist economic system does not extend to consumption—or at most indirectly, via production. Marxian theory is here almost as impoverished as neo-Classical utility theory. I will begin this section with a brief critique of the latter, which, I suggest, can be applied with almost equal force to Marx. The authors of *The World of Goods: Towards and Anthropology of Consumption* make the case for treating consumption as a social phenomenon:

> First, the very idea of consumption itself has to be set back into the social process, not merely looked upon as a result or objective of work. Consumption has to be recognized as an integral part of the same social

---

This is a revised version of a chapter in McNeill, D (1988) *Fetishism and the Form of Value*. Unpublished thesis, University of London.

D. McNeill, *Fetishism and the Theory of Value*, Palgrave Studies in the History of Economic Thought, https://doi.org/10.1007/978-3-030-56123-9_13

> system that accounts for the drive to work, itself part of the social need to relate to other people, and to have mediating materials for relating to them. (Douglas and Isherwood 1980: 4)

As they rightly assert, "economists carefully shun the question of why people want goods", using the empty term "tastes" to refer to the unexplained (but assumed unchanging) behaviour of consumers. They note that some neo-Classical economists have themselves been harsh critics of economic theory in this respect, quoting, for example, Lancaster:

> The theory of consumer behaviour in deterministic situations as set out by, say, Debreu or Uzawa is a thing of great aesthetic beauty, a jewel set in a glass case. … it now stands as an example of how to extract the minimum of results from the minimum of assumptions. (Lancaster 1966: 132)

They attempt to build up a theory of consumption based on the view that "goods in their assemblage present a set of meanings, more or less coherent, more or less intentional" (Douglas and Isherwood 1980: 5) arguing that "consumption is the very arena in which culture is fought over and licked into shape" (Douglas and Isherwood 1980: 57). "Man is a social being. We can never explain demand by looking only at the physical properties of goods. Man needs goods for communicating with others and for making sense of what is going on around him" (Douglas and Isherwood 1980: 95).

Their work is less compelling when it moves from critique to the positing of an alternative, and they contribute little not already offered by such writers as Veblen (1925), Weber (1970) or even Packard (1960). Nevertheless, their attack on conventional theory is valid. And more importantly, in the context of this book, their criticisms of the neo-Classical concept of utility could to a large extent be applied also to the Marxian concept of use-value, to which I now turn. Many writers in the Marxist tradition portray use-value in terms which take little or no account of the social context. Thus, for example, Hilferding:

> A use value is an individual relationship between a thing and a human being. (Hilferding, in Sweezy 1984: 131)

And Sweezy:

> Use value is an expression of a certain relation between the consumer and the object consumed. (Sweezy 1968: 26)

In both cases the author goes on to contrast the individual relationship of use-value with the *social* relationship—value or exchange-value. Thus both writers counterpose use-value against exchange-value precisely on the grounds that the former is not to be seen as involving a social relation. Their conception of use-value is therefore hard to distinguish from that of "bourgeois economists". Perhaps the early utility theorists laid undue stress on the thing itself rather than the relationship between the thing and the individual. (Consider, e.g., Jevons' definition of utility as "a circumstance of things arising out of their relation to man's requirements" (Jevons 1871: 43).) But it was not long before other economists in the same tradition made good this deficiency. Thus Smart, who quotes the foregoing definition of Jevons, comments that "It is a commonplace that value is not inherent in things; it is not so well recognised that neither is utility. There is nothing 'useful' except in relation to a being who finds it so" (Smart 1893).

Many similar quotations could be cited from economists of both Marxist and non-Marxist schools. In summary, despite the crucial contrasts between them in other respects, when it comes to consumption there is remarkably little difference in their analysis or lack of it. Both describe a relation obtaining between a thing and a person. (From the point of the thing this is use-value; from the point of view of the person it is need.) It is recognised that the use-value does not inhere in the thing, independently of the person. But what economists of both schools generally fail to analyse is the social context within which this relation obtains. The person is seen as an autonomous human being, endowed with tastes or needs and relating on an individualistic basis with things with which he or she comes into contact.

In Marxian economics this is consistent with the relegation of use-value to a minor role. Indeed, it may even be excluded altogether. Thus, to quote Hilferding, and Sweezy, again: "The natural aspect of the commodity, its use-value, lies outside the domain of political economy"

(Hilferding 1984: 130). "Marx excluded use-value (or as it would now be called, 'utility') from the field of investigation of political economy on the ground that it does not directly embody a social relation" (Sweezy, quoted in Rosdolsky 1980: 73).

Thus it would appear that Marx treats use-value in terms which are asocial, psychologistic; an approach which is very much associated with bourgeois economists, and is rightly criticised by Marx in the context of exchange-value.

It is notable that even Rubin, who lays such stress on the social (in relation to production) certainly does not extend this to the realm of consumption and need.[1] In *Essays on Marx's Theory of Value* he discusses the question of demand, but is at pains to link it very directly with the forces of production. Thus, the three causes for variation in demand which he identifies are:

> 1) changes in the *value* of a given commodity, for example its cheapening as a result of the development of productive forces in a given productive branch; 2) changes in the *purchasing power* or the income of different social groups ... which in turn changes in relation to the change in productive forces; 3) finally, changes in the intensity or urgency of *needs* for a given commodity. (Rubin 1982: 193)

He recognises that "at first glance it seems that in the last case we make production dependent on consumption" but refutes this argument by tracing back to what "causes changes in the urgency of needs for a given commodity". It is here that his argument is at its weakest. He begins with a straightforward example of a technical, material kind, where iron ploughs replace wooden ones. Next he takes two more challenging cases, which I will discuss in reverse order. Demand for goods can be influenced by the weather:

> Sharp and long-term changes in climatic conditions could strengthen or weaken the need for winter clothes. ... But even such cases do not

[1] I make this claim in spite of the fact that Rubin's is one of only two works which Rosdolsky cites as exceptions to the rule that the role of use-value "has been very neglected in previous Marxist literature" (Rosdolsky 1980: 73).

> contradict the view of primacy of production over consumption. … the *objects* with which man satisfies his needs and the *manner* of satisfying these needs are determined by the *development of production*, and they, in turn, modify the character of the given *needs* and may even create *new* needs. (Rubin 1982: 194)

The strength of his argument is visibly declining. In this example he claims only that needs are "modified" by non-social factors (although it is not immediately clear how the development of production would modify the *type* of winter clothes needed). But he then turns to a still more challenging example, where "successful anti-alcoholic propaganda decreases the demand for alcoholic beverages". Here he has "purposely chosen an example where the reduction of production is brought about by social causes of an ideological and not an economic character".

> It is obvious that the successes of anti-alcoholic propaganda were brought about by the economic, social, cultural and moral level of different social groups, a level which in turn changes as a result of a complex series of social conditions which surround it. These social conditions can be explained, in the last analysis, by the development of the productive forces of society. (Rubin 1982: 194)

Here he is surely on still weaker ground. The need for warmth at least may be regarded as physiological. But what of the need for alcohol? Even if the *character* of such needs is "determined by the preceding development of society and, in the last analysis, of its productive forces", this still leaves the needs themselves to be accounted for. They certainly cannot all be traced back to animal, physiological needs. It is notable that this last example appears to represent the limit of Rubin's imagination as regards the possible influence of the social in the sphere of consumption. And this is in spite of the fact that he stands out amongst Marxian commentators in his recognition of the crucial importance of the social in Marx's work.

Some commentators on Marx have denied that he relegated use-value to a minor role. A major proponent of this alternative view is Rosdolsky, who claims that this is an issue which "has been very neglected in previous Marxist literature" (Rosdolsky 1980: 73). "Many of Marx's pupils", he argues, fell into the same error for which Marx criticised Ricardo, of abstracting from use-value. And he singles out Sweezy (quoted above) for presenting a "clumsy distortion of Marx's real view" (Rosdolsky 1980: 74). Given some of the passages from Marx's writings, such as those I have quoted, this seems difficult to justify. But Rosdolsky's argument deserves to be considered in some detail. First he argues that in simple commodity production it is correct that use-value is of no significance for the economist.

> How exactly the commodities to be exchanged were produced ... and how they will be consumed after exchange is incidental to the economic study of simple commodity circulation. ... The social change of matter takes place in the change of form of the commodities themselves. And in this situation the change of form is the only social relation between the commodity owners. ... As far as the content outside the act of exchange is concerned, this 'content can only be ... 1) the natural particularity of the commodity being exchanged 2) the particular natural need of the exchangers or both together, the different *use-values* of the commodities being exchanged'. (Rosdolsky 1980: 81)

In the case of capitalism, by contrast, use-values acquire "economic significance" in various ways, as Rosdolsky demonstrates. He notes how the material nature of the product affects the duration of the working period and the circulation period, and then cites Marx's comments in *Grundrisse* on fixed capital: "this aspect of its use-value (its durability, or its greater or lesser perishability) here becomes a form-determining moment i.e. a determinant for capital as regards its form, not as regards its substance" (Rosdolsky 1980: 85). In Volume III of *Capital* Rosdolsky finds more examples of "the significance of use-value as an economic category"; he discusses ground-rent, the effects of seasonal variations on agricultural produce, and the productivity of labour varying with "the exhaustion of forest lands, coal and iron mines etc." These arguments to indicate the economic significance of use-values may be valid, but they all relate to use-values in production. What is surely more relevant, and certainly for the purposes of this chapter, is use-values in consumption.

Rosdolsky does, however, have a further line of argument, which he supports with extracts from *Marginal Notes on Wagner*. Here, Marx seems to confront the criticism directly, claiming that "use-value plays a far more important part in my economics than in economics hitherto", but adds that "it is only ever taken into account when this arises from the analysis of given economic forms". Rosdolsky provides examples of such references to use-value by Marx: his discussion of the concrete form of labour; and the money-form, in which "the value of a commodity is represented in the use-value of the other, i.e. in the natural from of the other commodity" and surplus-value, which "derived from a 'specific' and exclusive use-value of labour power, etc. etc." (Rosdolsky 1980: 76).

The case of labour-power is, Rosdolsky claims, "of decisive importance"—concerned, as it is, with the relation between capital and labour. Here, "it is precisely the use-value of the commodity purchased by the capitalist (i.e. labour-power) which constitutes the presupposition of the capitalist production process and the capital relation itself" (Rosdolsky 1980: 84). Here, use-value, in Marx's words "appears as a particular economic relation". It "falls within the economic process because the use-value here is itself determined by exchange-value". This is therefore put forward as the most compelling of the several arguments which Rosdolsky presents.[2]

In summary, Rosdolsky describes Marx's position as follows:

> Whether use-value should be granted economic significance or not can only be decided in accordance with its relation to the social relations of

[2] It is not clear how much importance should be attached to the words "appears as" in the former quote, which are absent in the second. This may be of no significance, but the question arises more clearly from the contrast between two other passages which Rosdolsky cites from *Grundrisse* (without, apparently, noticing the distinction):

> This material (of wealth) … falls within its (political economy's) purview only when it is modified by the formal relations, or appears as modifying them. (Marx quoted in Rosdolsky 1980: 80)

> Use-value falls within the realm of political economy as soon as it becomes modified by the modern relations of production, or as it in turn intervenes to modify them. (Marx quoted in Rosdolsky 1980: 80, footnote)

> production. It is certainly an economic category to the extent that it influences these relations or is influenced by them. (Rosdolsky 1980: 80)

This is not a compelling argument. If a sufficient condition for being granted the status of "economic significance" is that something be "influenced by" social relations of production, then the term is too broad to merit further debate. Even if the direction of causality is reversed (i.e. it is suggested that use-value influences the social relations of production). Rosdolsky's claim is still of little interest, for he appears to interpret use-value very widely to refer simply to material conditions and constraints.

The argument on the basis of labour-power is more compelling. Certainly the use-value of labour-power is of crucial importance; one could indeed argue that it is the special nature of labour in this respect that lies at the basis of the capitalist system. But precisely because this is special it cannot be used as the basis for the more general claim that use-value plays a central role in Marx's economics.

Whatever may be the merits of Rosdolsky's case, it is clear that use-value is a problematic concept, which cannot be regarded as relating solely to material and natural phenomena. Consider again the quote from Hilferding, which begins: "The object of economics is the social aspect of the commodity, of the good, insofar as it is a symbol of social interconnection" (Hilferding 1984: 130). My claim is that a use-value, too, can be "a symbol of social interconnection". There are, it is true, a few Marxist commentators who lay stress on the social in discussing consumption. (Typically, and perhaps not unexpectedly, they are those who approach the issue from the aspect of need rather than use-value.) The most obvious to cite is Heller, author of *The Theory of Need in Marx*. In this work, she starts with a critique of the Keynesian style of economics which treats needs as "a sort of instinctive endowment" armed with which the individual buyer and seller puts in to the market "'unwanted' work (disutility) and take(s) out 'wanted' commodities (utility)" (Heller 1974: 7). Against such a view, she says, the works of Marx constitute "an overwhelmingly powerful proof that the commodity-based structure of capitalism would have to be superseded by some new social structure if the needs of men and women as *human beings* are to be met" (Heller 1974: 9).

In Marx, according to Heller (in contrast to many other commentators), "the concept of need plays one of the main roles, if not actually *the* main role" (Heller 1974: 25). In support of this unusual assertion she claims that Marx himself lists the discovery of the significance of use-value as one of his three original economic discoveries.[3] Heller defines the concept of "natural needs" to refer to "the simple maintenance of human life … a limit (different for different societies) beyond which human life is no longer reproducible as such". But, as she notes, "the mode of satisfaction makes the need itself social" (Heller 1974: 32).

> 'Necessary needs' are not distinct from 'natural needs' in the *Grundrisse*, "but in *Capital* they include a cultural element. 'Necessary' needs *develop*, historically, they are not dictated by mere survival; the cultural element in such needs, the moral element and custom, are decisive." (Heller 1974: 33)

Thus she does allow that needs have an important cultural element. Indeed she later distinguishes Marx's "naturalistic conception" of the concept of utility (in which it always appears with a positive value judgement—"synonymous with usefulness"—from the "non-naturalistic conception" (Heller 1974: 59). And she claims that this is Marx's own position, even though she quotes *Capital*, where "use value is defined as the 'natural form' of the commodity, which expresses the relation between the individual and nature", and *Theories of Surplus Value*: "Use value expresses the natural relation between things and men, the existence of things for men. Exchange value is … the social existence of the thing" (Heller 1974: 35).

The crucial point, according to Heller, is that for Marx "it is production which creates new needs" (Heller 1974: 40). "Man's need and the

[3] Her claim cannot easily be refuted since she gives no reference to substantiate it. The standard reference in this connection is Marx's letter to Engels of August 24, 1867, "The best thing about my book". But here he lists only two things: the two-fold character of labour and the treatment of surplus value independent of its special forms. A later letter to Engels (January 8, 1868) refers to "three brand new elements of the book". Here he adds that "wages are presented as an irrational manifestation of a concealed relationship", and phrases the point about labour power more generally: "If the commodity has a double character—the use-value and the exchange-value—then labour contained in the commodity must also be of double character". It is true that Marx here makes reference to use-value; but it is hardly enough to justify Heller's claim—if this quotation is indeed its basis.

object of the need are correlated. … The objects 'bring about' the needs, and the needs bring about the objects." Here she seems to endow the objects themselves with strange, fetishistic powers: "The objects of need 'guide' and 'steer' man, who is born in human society, in the formation of his needs" (Heller 1974: 41).

Despite these pitfalls and possible inconsistencies, she argues convincingly that there is, in Marx, something called "social need", of which she distinguishes four varieties:

> The most important meaning (and the most frequently used) is that of 'socially produced' need … the needs of individual human beings. (Heller 1974: 69)

To these she adds the need of man for communism, the average needs for material goods in a society or in a class, and needs satisfiable only by the creation of corresponding social institutions (e.g. education, health care)" (Heller 1974: 70). Finally she turns to the concept of "radical need", which, she asserts, "appears for the first time in a detailed form in the Introduction to … *A Critique of Hegel's 'Philosophy of Law*" (Heller 1974: 88). This is need of a very different sort, and to use the same term to refer to both is somewhat confusing. According to Heller:

> Capitalist society … produces not only alienation but the consciousness of alienation, in other words, radical needs. (Heller 1974: 94)

> The need of the slave to be a free man. … The bourgeoisie's need to take political power. (Heller 1974: 97)

It would seem that radical needs are best understood in the context of an essentialist reading of Marx. The drive of history, and more particularly the supersession of one mode of production by another, would seem to be attributable to such "radical needs". This may be an accurate interpretation of Marx's view; but it is a use of the term "need" which tells us little about consumption. On this issue Heller's contribution is of very limited value:

> It is assumed that the needs of individuals that are directly oriented towards consumption [i.e. under capitalism] are, both qualitatively and quantitatively, roughly equal. It is therefore extraordinarily easy to account for them: with the aid of random samples, both quality and quantity can be determined. … But human beings in communist society, in Marx's view, are characterised above all else by the fact that their needs, considered *individually*, … will, be qualitatively and quantitatively extremely varied. (Heller 1974: 121)

She seems, to judge from this passage, to see no problem in understanding what determines needs—and certainly gives little indication of these being subject to any social influence. Under capitalism, needs are "extraordinarily easy to account for"; and under communism they are, it would seem, determined solely by the individual.

The concept of social need in Marx is discussed also by Elster, who makes reference to Heller's four types, and suggests one addition:[4]

> To these I add … the needs whose objects essentially involve a reference to other people. They are social in content rather than in origin. … Consider first the need for positional goods, that is the need for relative excellence, to have more or to be better than other people. Next, consider the need to be like other people, or to differ from other people, that is conformism and anti-conformism. And finally one may cite the need to impress other people, for example by conspicuous consumption. (Elster 1985: 69)

These are pertinent additions to the list. Elster's interest in them, however, reflects his own individualistic perspective on such phenomena (discussed in Chap. 7); thus, he goes on to note that "an important feature of (this last type of) needs is that they may be individually or collectively self-defeating" (Elster 1985: 70).

Cohen, in an admirably clear exposition of the social/material distinction, appears to defend Marx's view that "the consumption of use-value is of 'purely physical interest', 'expressing no more than the relation of the individual in his natural quality to an object of his individual need'"

[4] It is perhaps significant that he also subtracts two of Heller's types: the need of man for communism and the average needs for material goods in a society or in a class.

(Cohen 1978: 103). He discusses the example of 'socially engendered needs' such as a man's need for a deodorant, and although conceding that such a need "is (partly) social in origin" concludes:

> We may prescind from the social genesis and represent the result as a relation between man and nature. Society alters human nature, and it may become part of a man's nature to want a deodorant. (Cohen 1978: 103)

It is surely too much to suggest that it becomes "part of man's nature to want a deodorant". This transports demand and need into the unassailable realm of the "natural".

It would not be sufficient, however, simply to recognise that needs are in some sense social. Marx himself, if not all his commentators, was at least aware of the fact that needs are not just physiological—that "socially necessary" labour time does not refer merely to what is required to keep a person able-bodied. But how are these needs determined, if not by the individual?

Marcuse was one who sought a more radical approach to such questions, arguing that in modern society "the prevalence of repressive needs is an accomplished fact" (Marcuse 1968: 5).[5] In *One-Dimensional Man*, his attack on the "system of domination" of technological society, he distinguishes between so-called true and false needs. False needs are "those which are superimposed upon the individual by particular social interests in his repression" (Marcuse 1968: 5). In advanced industrial society, he asserts, "the social controls exact the overwhelming need for the production and consumption of waste; the need for stupefying work where it is no longer a real necessity" (Marcuse 1968: 7). Despite the validity of much of the argument, his analysis of need does not cut very deep. For a far more incisive approach it is necessary to turn to the work of Baudrillard.

In *Beyond Use Value* Baudrillard contrasts Marx's treatment of exchange-value (as "abstract and general") with use-value ("concrete and particular") and suggests that "use value—indeed utility itself—is a fetishized social relation" (Baudrillard 1981: 131).

[5] Marcuse was apparently too radical for Rosdolsky who claims that he "goes to the other extreme" (from Sweezy) (Rosdolsky 1980: 75, footnote).

> the same logic (and the same fetishism) plays on the two sides of the commodity specified by Marx: use value and exchange value. … Marxist analysis has contributed to the mythology … that allows the relation of the individual to objects conceived as use values to pass for a concrete and objective—in sum, 'natural'—relation between man's needs and the function proper to the object. (Baudrillard 1981: 134)

He criticises, to good effect, the concept of need itself, and the view that it is "constitutive of the very structure of the individual". It is this which "produces the commodity system in its general form" and which causes the social being to be one who "autonomizes himself and rationalizes his desire, his relation to others and to objects, in terms of needs, utility, satisfaction and use value" (Baudrillard 1981: 136). Baudrillard, like Marx, stresses the importance of the social. But by contrast with Marx he is not content to restrict social relations to the domain of production:

> Robinson Crusoe is the outcome of a total mutation that has been in progress since the dawn of bourgeois society. … Man was transformed simultaneously into a productive force and a 'man with needs'. The manufacturers and the ideologues of Nature divided him between themselves. In his labour he became a use value for a system of production. Simultaneously, goods and products became use values for him, taking on a meaning as functions of his needs, which were henceforth legalized as 'nature'. He entered the regime of use value, which was also that of 'Nature'. … The myth of Robinson Crusoe is the bourgeois avatar of the myth of Terrestrial Paradise. … political economy is sustained on the great myth of human fulfillment according to the natural law of needs. (Baudrillard 1981: 141)

He criticises Marx for allowing "this moral law of use value to have escaped the critique of political economy"; and argues that "there is nothing clear and natural in the fact of 'transforming nature according to one's needs'". As he puts it in an apt concluding sentence:

> The whole system and its 'mystery' were already there with Robinson Crusoe on his island, and in the trumped-up immediacy of his relation to things. (Baudrillard 1981: 142)

From this analysis Baudrillard derives what he calls his "critique of the political economy of the sign". He draws attention to "a structure of control and of power much more subtle and more totalitarian than that of exploitation" and stresses that the important question is "the symbolic destruction of all social relations not so much by the ownership of the means of production but by *the control of the code*" (Baudrillard 1975: 122).

> Far from the individual expressing his needs in the economic system, it is the economic system that induces the individual function and the parallel functionality of objects and needs. ... Needs, far from being articulated around the desire or the demand of the subject, find their coherence elsewhere: in a generalized system that is to desire what the system of exchange value is to concrete labour, the source of value. (Baudrillard 1981: 133, 135)

This concept of the "code" and the "hegemony of the code" is central to Baudrillard's thesis. He identifies a "new ideological structure ... much more illegible than that which played on productive energy" where the "form-commodity" is replaced by the "form-sign". He stresses that he is not referring to the conscious psychology of prestige and differentiation, but to a hidden, unrecognised code which structures our behaviour without our being aware of it, the manipulation of which is "more radical; than that which plays on labour power" (Baudrillard 1975: 122).

Consumption is very much a social phenomenon; and needs are far from natural and unproblematic, explicable by an individualistic, Robinson Crusoe model of behaviour. At a somewhat superficial level such an argument might be widely accepted; it is now almost a commonplace that people use goods to establish or consolidate their status.[6] But Baudrillard (and perhaps Douglas and Isherwood also) is saying far more

[6] An apparently similar point appears also in Aristotle's Nichomachean Ethics (1980):

> The man who goes to excess and is vulgar exceeds, ... by spending beyond what is right. For on small objects of expenditure he spends much and displays a tasteless showiness. ... And all such things he will do not for honour's sake but to show off his wealth. (1122b)

The matter is not so simple, however, for Aristotle contrasts such a man with "the magnificent man"—the man who makes honourable expenditures "e.g. those connected with the gods—votive offerings, buildings and sacrifices" (1122b). Such expenditure may, paradoxically, be better understood not as consumption but as exchange. See Chap. 12.

than this. Economics is not about relations between men as mere things, and it is impoverished insofar as it treats them as such. Marx recognised the importance of treating economics as a system of social relations, but he emphasised only production. The commodity is presented as "a very queer thing, abounding in metaphysical subtleties and theological niceties" but these subtleties are in no way attributed to its status as an object of utility. "The mystical character of commodities does not originate … in their use-value" (Marx 1954: 76). He fails to see consumption itself as an important social relation, and, furthermore, one which allows the exercise of power and control.

Lest I appear to overstate the case, I should again stress that Marx did not regard the needs of man as simply those of an advanced mammalian species—for food, drink, clothing and habitation.[7] Indeed, he notes as one of the effects of man's alienation, as described in the *1844 Manuscripts*, that "man (the worker) only feels himself freely active in [such] animal functions—eating, drinking, procreating, or at most in his dwelling and in dressing-up etc."

> Certainly eating, drinking, procreating, etc., are also genuinely human functions. But taken abstractly, separated from the sphere of all other human activity and turned into sole and ultimate ends, they are animal functions. (Marx 1977: 71)

From this passage (which, strictly speaking, refers to "functions" rather than "needs") it would seem that the context of "all other human activity" is necessary to raise eating and drinking above the animal level. In another passage, Marx makes a rather similar distinction, between human needs within and without society:

> The meaning of an object for me goes only so far as *my* sense goes … for this reason the *senses* of the social man *differ* from those of the non-social man. … The *sense* caught up in crude practical need has only a *restricted* sense. For the starving man, it is not the human form of food that exists,

[7] Although there may be some who do. Marx refers to Liebig to offer a particularly graphic example: the "brutal South Americans" who force their workers to eat beans as well as bread, though they themselves would prefer bread alone, since this enables them to work harder (Marx 1954: 537).

> but only its abstract existence as food. It could just as well be there in its crudest form, and it would be impossible to say wherein this feeding activity differs from that of *animals*. (Marx 1977: 102)

Thus there is a recognition that man's needs are not simply the same as those of animals. Wherein does this difference lie? Marx seems to locate it in productive activity. He rejects the picture of man as a passive being, and takes Wagner to task on this point:

> On no account do men begin by 'standing in that theoretical relation to the *things of the external world*'. They begin, like every animal, by *eating, drinking* etc., hence not by 'standing' in a relation, but by *relating themselves actively*, taking hold of certain things in the external world through action, and thus satisfying their need. (Therefore they begin with production.) (Marx 1975: 190)

Marginal Notes on Wagner provides what is perhaps Marx's most imaginative ideas on need. Here he goes so far as to describe a phenomenon which resembles the fetishism of commodities—but in the context of consumption:

> Through the repetition of this process, the property of those things, their property 'to satisfy needs', is impressed upon their brains. … Perhaps they call them 'goods', or something else which expresses the fact that they need these things practically, that these things are useful for them, and they believe that this useful character is possessed by the thing, although it would scarcely appear to a sheep as one of its 'useful' properties that it is edible by man. (Marx 1975: 190)

But Marx's view, even in this late work, is that insofar as "need" entails any social relation, this relation is production. There is a role for society, or "social organization"—but this simply means "the level of the social process of production" (Marx 1975: 204). It is clear that he was well aware of cultural variations in the pattern of need:

> But if Rodbertus wants to state only the triviality that use-value, which actually confronts the individual as an object of use, confronts him as an

> individual use-value for him, then this is a trivial tautology or false, since for an individual, the need for a professorial title, or the title of privy councillor, or for a decoration, not to speak of such things as rice, maize, or corn, or not to mention meat (which does not confront the Hindu as the means of nourishment), is only possible in some quite definite 'social organization'. (Marx 1975: 205)

What is not clear is how the mode of production, or "the level of the social process of production", relates to the pattern of consumption; the fact, to cite his own example, that meat is not food to the Hindu.

The dominant impression which Marx clearly leaves, despite some of the qualifications which must be acknowledged on the basis of the quotations cited here, is not merely that production is dominant over consumption, but that consumption itself is relatively unproblematic. Indeed, Marx is often far less subtle than the extracts above suggest. He adopts, at times, a blinkered, even fetishistic, view of needs and consumption:

> When consumption emerges from its original crudeness and immediacy—and its remaining in that state would be due to the fact that production was still primitively crude—then it is itself as a desire brought about by the object. The need felt for the object is induced by the perception of the object. An *objet d'art* creates a public that has artistic taste and is able to enjoy beauty—and the same can be said of any other product. (Marx 1970: 197)

Typically, however, Marx recognises the importance of the social, but traces all back to production as original and determinant. This is most clearly expressed in a much-quoted passage from the draft Introduction to *Grundrisse* which immediately precedes the one just cited:

> The object is not simply an object in general, but a particular object which must be consumed in a particular way, a way determined by production. Hunger is hunger; but the hunger that is satisfied by cooked meat eaten with knife and fork differs from hunger that devours raw meat with the help of hands, nails and teeth. Production thus produces not only the object of consumption but also the mode of consumption, not only

> objectively but also subjectively. Production therefore creates the consumer. (Marx 1970: 197)

Against this view, I have argued, in this chapter, that there is a strong case for treating consumption also as a social relation; that need is not simply a "natural" phenomenon but, to a very large extent, a social phenomenon.

There are good reasons why Marx sought to establish the primacy of production over need, but this sometimes led him into quite crude argumentation, as here:

> But life involves before everything else eating and drinking, a habitation, clothing and many other things. The first historical act is thus the production of the means to satisfy these needs, the production of material life itself. … The satisfaction of the first need … leads to new needs; and this production of new needs is the first historical act. (Marx and Engels 1974: 48)

Even accepting the view of Bhaskar, who also cites these passages (Bhaskar 1979: 137), that the "first historical act" must here be understood in an analytical not a chronological sense, the case for the primacy of production appears rather weak.

Bibliography

Aristotle. (1980). *The Nichomachean Ethics* (D. Ross, Trans.). Oxford: University Press.

Baudrillard, J. (1975). *The Mirror of Production*. St. Louis: Telos.

Baudrillard, J. (1981). *For a Critique of the Political Economy of the Sign*. St. Louis: Telos.

Bhaskar, R. (1979). *The Possibility of Naturalism*. Brighton: Harvest.

Cohen, G. (1978). *Karl Marx's Theory of History: A Defence*. Oxford: Clarendon.

Douglas, M., & Isherwood, B. (1980). *The World of Goods: Towards an Anthropology of Consumption*. Harmondsworth: Penguin.

Elster, J. (1985). *Making Sense of Marx*. Cambridge: University Press.

Heller, A. (1974). *The Theory of Need in Marx*. London: Allison & Busby.

Hilferding, R. (1984). *Bohm-Bawerk's Criticism of Marx*. Lifton NJ: Kelley.

Jevons, W. (1871). *The Theory of Political Economy*. London: MacMillan.
Lancaster, K. (1966). A New Approach to Consumer Theory. *Journal of Political Economy, 74*, 132–157.
Marcuse, H. (1968). *One-Dimensional Man Jevons Theory of Political Economy*.
Marx, K. (1954). *Capital* (Vol. I). Moscow: Progress.
Marx, K. (1970). *A Draft Introduction to Grundrisse*. Moscow: Progress.
Marx, K. (1973). *Grundrisse*. Harmondsworth: Penguin.
Marx, K., & Engels, F. (1974). *The German Ideology*. (C. J. Arthur Ed.) London: Lawrence and Wishart.
Marx, K. (1975). *Karl Marx: Texts on Method* (T. Carver, Trans. & Ed.). Oxford: Blackwell.
Marx, K. (1977). *Economic and Philosophic Manuscripts of 1844*. Moscow: Progress.
Packard, V. (1960). *The Hidden Persuaders*. Harmondsworth. Penguin.
Rosdolsky, R. (1980). *The Making of Marx's 'Capital'*. London: Pluto.
Rubin, I. I. (1982). *Essays on Marx's Theory of Value*. Montreal: Black Rose Books.
Smart, W. (1893). Preface. In F. von Wieser (Ed.), *Natural Value*. London: Macmillan.
Sweezy, P. (1968). *The Theory of Capitalist Development: Principles of Marxian Political Economy*. New York: Modern Reader Paperbacks.
Veblen, T. (1925). *Theory of the Leisure Class*. New York: MacMillan
Weber, M. (1970). Essays in Sociology. (Gerth and C. Wright Mills Ed.). London. Routledge & Kegan Paul.

Part V

Marx in the Twenty-First Century

14

Marx and the Environment

One part of society thus exacts tribute from another for the permission to inhabit the earth, as landed property in general assigns the landlord the privilege of exploiting the terrestrial body, the bowels of the earth, the air, and thereby the maintenance and development of life.

(Marx 1959: 774)

Introduction

The aim of this book has been to study Marx's theory of value, and especially his concept of fetishism, and assess the relevance of these ideas today. In this concluding section, I bring this work up to date by reviewing more recent literature. I will begin, however, by briefly summarising my findings. I have argued that the qualitative aspect of the theory of value is a crucial part of Marx's contribution to economics which has not been given due attention. It finds expression in his analysis of the value-form and fetishism. These provide the starting point of his 'logico-historical' analysis of the capitalist system and his critique of economic categories. Marxian economists have not, I suggest, made sufficient efforts to study and develop this aspect of his work. There has been a

D. McNeill, *Fetishism and the Theory of Value*, Palgrave Studies in the History of Economic Thought, https://doi.org/10.1007/978-3-030-56123-9_14

tendency to regard the qualitative theory of value as falling outside the domain of economics proper: brilliant, perhaps—but to be classified as the work of "Marx the sociologist" or "Marx the philosopher". I have argued, however, that they occupy a central place in his analysis of capitalism and 'bourgeois economics'.

In Part I (Chaps. 2, 3, and 4), I traced how Marx uses the term fetishism in his writings, from almost his first published work as a journalist to the first volume of *Capital*; and how its significance developed, from a mere rhetorical device to an analytical tool of central importance to his critique of political economy: the concept of commodity fetishism. In Part II (Chaps. 5, 6, and 7) I examined how he extends the concept, from the commodity to money, capital and interest-bearing capital; and how—in theorising exchange-value in *Capital Volume I*—he walks a narrow path between the 'bourgeois economics' of Samuel Bailey and the mystification of Hegel. Throughout these chapters I was concerned with the question: what is the ontological status of value; what is it that renders something valuable—transmuting it from an object to a commodity? And here the concept of the fetish is a useful analogy; for a fetish is, in a sense, 'real'; it has real effects, not because of its material but its social qualities: the shared beliefs and practices of society. This is Marx's strength, by comparison with bourgeois economics: he recognises, and seeks to come to grips with, the social aspect of capitalism—and the implications for relations of power.

In Parts III and IV, I discussed what I regard as some shortcomings in his work. In Chaps. 8, 9, and 10, I noted that all the various analogies that Marx uses for explaining exchange-value are physical, material and argued that comparison with language would have been more enlightening. The aptness of this analogy rests precisely on the fact that language is the epitome of the social. This is largely why approaches which have developed from the study of language—structuralism and semiotics—have proved enlightening in some of the social sciences. But they have not proved so successful in economics. Structural Marxism could, I suggested, have successfully built on such an approach, but failed to do so. In Part IV, Chaps. 11, 12, and 13, I showed that Marx's conception of the social is associated primarily, if not exclusively, with labour and production, and that this causes him to ignore the fact that exchange and consumption also are social phenomena.

My purpose in this final section is to assess the relevance of fetishism and the theory of value for contemporary capitalism by reviewing some of the Marx-inspired literature of recent decades. I limit myself to two areas of work—the environment and financialisation. These topics account for the greater part of the literature;[1] not perhaps surprising in view of the financial crisis of 2008 and the escalating crisis of climate change and other environmental challenges.

I will first very briefly summarise the significance of the term 'fetishism' as an analytical tool.[2] In *Capital Volume I*, Marx begins with exchange-value and the commodity, which constitute the very foundations of the capitalist system. Exchange-value is the form that value takes, a form which conceals its origins in labour. As Marx expresses it, in exchange-value: "a social relation between persons assumes the fantastic form of a relation between things" (Marx 1954: 77). This is the phenomenon that he refers to as the fetishism of commodities.[3] This is a very apt metaphor, for the power of the fetish (among the people of West Africa whence the term arose) did not derive from its natural, material properties but rather from the beliefs and practices of that society. So too in capitalism: what appears to be natural—the market price of a commodity—is very far from being so. It is in fact social; 'social' in the sense that it is dependent on the shared beliefs and practices of society. The fetishism of commodities allows the exploitation of labour to be concealed: the fact that surplus value accrues to the capitalist as profit appears natural, unchallenged.

In reviewing the recent literature my interest has been in two questions: To what extent do these works, on the environment and financialisation, draw on Marx's theory of value and his concept of fetishism? And, conversely, is our understanding of Marx's theory of value and his

[1] This is supported by a Google search, which shows that writing on the environment is especially well represented.

[2] As discussed earlier in this book, there is an important difference in ontological status between the various manifestations of fetishism. What appears to be the case with commodity fetishism is, in a sense, 'real'.

[3] I use this term interchangeably with 'commodity fetishism', although Schulz (2012) asserts, based on Marx's original German text, that Marx used only the term 'fetishism of commodities'.

concept of fetishism enhanced by these works? With regard to both the two topics—environment and financialisation—Marx's analysis of the sources of revenue is of particular relevance. This is summed up in the famous Trinity Formula to which I shall make frequent reference:

> Capital—profit (profit of enterprise plus interest), land—ground-rent, labour—wages, this is the trinity formula which comprises all the secrets of the social production process. (Marx 1959: 814)

Here, Marx includes in his analysis not only capital and labour but also land (in the broad sense to include mines, forests etc.). While capitalists receive profits, landowners receive rent and workers receive wages. This appears to be 'natural'. But this is far from the case; the secrets are hidden by the mystifying way in which the relations are presented.[4]

Marx and Nature

In recent years, a great deal has been written about nature and the environment that draws on Marx's work. Most of this is to be found not in economics, but rather in geography, or interdisciplinary studies such as political ecology and critical agrarian studies. What these works generally share is a recognition that capital's relation to nature has both widened and deepened dramatically. It has 'widened' in geographical terms:

> Under capitalism the appropriation of nature and its transformation into means of production occur for the first time at a world scale. (Smith 2008: 71)

> capital has expanded its range and depth with the passing of time. (Harvey 2014: 56)

> Recurrent waves of socio-ecological exhaustion … motivate recurrent waves of geographical expansion. (Moore, 66)

[4] Marx uses a variety of formulations to caricature such mystifying categories, suggesting that they are as meaningless as 'yellow logarithms', or have as little relation to each other as 'lawyer's fees, red beets and music'.

And it has 'deepened' in terms of extending property rights over a larger range of goods and services:

> Production 'all the way down' into the level of molecular biology and DNA sequencing. (Harvey 2014: 248)

This extension of the phenomenon with regard to the environment, may also combine with financialisation, as in the case of carbon emissions trading which, according to some, could overtake oil as "the world's biggest commodity market, and it could become the world's biggest market over all" (Kanter 2007).

In this Marxist-inspired literature there is a broad consensus in rejecting market-based environmental policies such as emissions trading. But there are also major disagreements, largely between what are sometimes referred to as Reds and Greens—either applauding or criticising Marx's writings on nature. It is notable, however, that while these writers often quote Marx, the majority make little or no reference to his labour theory of value. "Value is central to the political economy of capitalism, but Marxian value theory has generally been abandoned when it comes to including nature in the analysis" (Walker 2017: 53). "The Marxist tradition makes occasional reference to 'a law of value'—but this 'law' can scarcely be detected in most radical analyses of capitalism, its historical movements, and its relation to the web of life. Greens, even Marxist Greens, tend to avoid the question of value in some ways, but embrace it in others" (Moore 2015: 51).

To cite Christophers:

> Recent years have seen forceful calls for political ecologists and other scholars concerned with the political economy of the environment to engage more actively with value theory in general and Marxian value theory in particular (Robertson 2012; Büscher 2012; Robertson and Wainwright 2013). Claiming that a generation of such scholars has generally avoided 'constructive engagement with value theory', Robertson and Wainwright (2013: 894) argue that it is high time this neglect is put right. (Christophers 2018: 330)

Several scholars have attempted the task of summarising Marx's views of nature. Useful overviews of this literature are to be found in Castree

(2000) and Dolenec (2018) on which I mainly draw in the following brief review of Marxian writing relating to the environment.

According to Castree (2000: 5) it is "difficult to distil a coherent Marxian position on the question of nature", despite—or perhaps because of—the fact that "Marxists have spent more than a century mining his texts in order to piece together otherwise disparate, and often gnomic, comments and asides on capitalism and nature" (Castree 2000: 5). As Smith puts it: "The discussion of *Capital* was not intended to analyze nature, specifically, under capitalism. … Pursuing his primary task, however, did not require him to present or even develop a completed conception of nature" (Smith 1984: 52).

Apart from Engels himself, Alfred Schmidt (1971),[5] Sebastiano Timparano (1975) and Norman Geras (1983) were early contributors to the debate. In summarising their works I will refer mainly to some few who appear to dominate the field. Writing on the topic increased rapidly with a growing international interest in the environment that is generally dated back to the first Earth Summit in Stockholm in 1972, and the hugely influential *Limits to Growth* (Meadows et al. 1972). An important landmark was the journal *Capitalism, Nature, Socialism* initiated in 1988 by James O'Connor.

Much of the literature may be described as 'eco-Marxist', defined by Castree (2000: 18) as "a growing corpus of work, largely fashioned in the last decade, which seeks to read Marx as an actual or potential critic of capitalism's environmental consequences". He names Elmar Altvater, Reiner Grundmann and James O'Connor as examples of scholars in this tradition. The growth of eco-Marxism parallels, and counters, the evolving capitalist response to the problem, summarised by Bakker as follows: "First, a new, intense phase of privatization and 'accumulation by dispossession' began. Its most recent, well-publicized iteration is a series of 'land grabs' and 'water grabs' by globalized corporations." Second, 'ecological fixes', moving polluting industries to developing countries. Third, "fram(ing) environmental externalities as opportunities for profit by, for

[5] "It is not necessary … to scour Marx's entire collective works in order to isolate his different treatments of nature. This painstaking and ambitious project has already been accomplished by Alfred Schmidt in his difficult but definitive study of *The Concept of Nature in Marx*" (Smith 2010[1984]: 32–3).

example, turning waste into a resource". Fourth, attempting to "commodify new types of socio-natures, from the global climate to genes" (Bakker 2015: 449).

Although sharing an antipathy towards capitalism, the so-called Red-Green alliance was not always a comfortable one. Some writers criticised Marx for either ignoring nature or adopting a 'Promethean' attitude, committed to industrial progress irrespective of natural limits. While some argued that his work was fully compatible with ecological thinking, others sought to reinterpret and adapt his writings to develop a new synthesis.

Anthony Giddens (1981) is generally identified as the one who characterised Marx's thinking as Promethean. Foster (1999) identifies a number of other writers who held the same view: Ted Benton, Kate Soper, Robyn Eckersley, Murray Bookchin and David Goldblatt. Against these he poses Elmar Altvater, Paul Burkett, Michael Perelman, Michael Lebowitz, David Harvey and himself (Dolenec 2018). Dolenec distinguishes between "a first stage of ecosocialist writing in the 1970s, which was critical of and distant towards Marxism" from a second stage, from the 1990s onwards, which "fleshed out a more comprehensive Marxist analysis of nature and sought a synthesis of red and green ideas" (Williams 2017). Examples of these are Benson's edited volume *The Greening of Marxism* (1996), Burkett's *Marx and Nature: a Red and Green Perspective* (1999) and Foster's *Marx's Ecology* (2000). "These volumes testified to the growing recognition that Marx's political economy represented a valuable framework for dealing with the present ecological crisis. Since then, two decades of scholarship have accumulated, arguing that Marx and Engels embedded ecological thinking deep within their critique of capitalism" (Williams 2017).

The claim that Marx's attitude to nature was Promethean can find support in some quotations from his work, but be readily countered by others. A detailed analysis by Smith (2010 [1984]) argues convincingly against the charge. It is not Marx that is the villain. "Contrary to many who accuse Marx of ignoring the value of nature, his theory suggests it is capitalism" (Huber 2016).

A more complex question, and one which dominates much of the debate, concerns the relationship that *people* have to nature. Here, scholars use a number of inter-related terms: first/second nature, internal/external nature, the production/construction of nature, the metabolic rift. These terms all, to varying extents, involve binaries, and the debates about them are supplemented by a sometimes vituperative meta-debate about Cartesian dualism that I will not include in my account. To limit the scope of my review, I also exclude related debates about space—a topic of interest especially to Marxist geographers.[6]

The terms 'first' and 'second' nature derive from Schmidt (1971), 'reintroduced and reworked' from Hegel (Castree 2000). This distinguishes nature at its most elemental from nature as transformed by society.

The term 'production of nature' derives from (Smith 1984). Expressed in simple terms it refers to the fact that pristine nature no longer exists, if indeed it ever did. Nature has been hugely transformed by human beings and—more specifically and dramatically in recent centuries—by capitalism: hence the suggestion that the term 'anthropocene' might better be replaced by 'capitalocene'.

A related issue is the 'construction of nature' as an idea, a social category. Confusingly, the term is used by some to refer to construction in the material sense. But as Smith emphasises "While the 'production of nature' thesis certainly stresses the veins of social agency that run through nature, it is not in any way assimilable to, or to be confused with, the constructionist paradigm that has become fashionable since the 1980s" (Smith 1984: 246). Castree identifies "a persistent polarity between naturalistic and social constructionist views" (Castree 2000). Although Malm (2018) asserts that no one seriously and consistently occupies either of the two polarised positions regarding this issue—that nature is entirely produced, literally, by humans, or that it exists only as an idea—he includes quotations from Latour and Haraway that seem close to the latter extreme.[7]

[6] According to Smith, Marx does not make much reference to space, except in relation to use-value. He quotes Marx, concerning the transportation of people or commodities, wherein "a material change is effected in the object of labour—a spatial change, a change of place … and along with this goes a change in its use-value. … Its exchange-value increases in the same measure this change in value requires labour" (Smith 1984: 112). Other authors who have written on space from a Marxist perspective include Lefebvre (1991), Castells (1977) and Harvey (2008).

[7] For example, Haraway (quoted in Malm 2018: 25) nature is "a powerful discursive construction", it is "a trope. It is figure, construction, artefact, movement, displacement, Nature cannot pre-exist its construction." (Haraway 1992: 298)

The term 'metabolic rift' was coined by Marx. He wrote of a 'rift' between town and country, and—in a passage which clearly demonstrates his appreciation of the capitalist threat to sustainable agriculture—he notes that "it disturbs the metabolic interaction between man and the earth, …. it hinders the operation of the eternal natural condition for the lasting fertility of the soil"[8] (Marx 1975: 637–38). The term was taken up by Schmidt, and recently extended by other scholars, most notably Foster (e.g. Foster 1999). According to Malm (2018: 179) "the metabolic rift school has come under sustained fire from Jason Moore. … He seeks to demonstrate that Foster and colleagues repeat the original sin of Cartesian dualism."

In the substantial body of material that I have attempted to summarise, only few scholars relate their work to Marx's theory of value. Those that do discuss it, and recognise its central place in his work, usually seek to adapt it—either by complementing it with a parallel theory, or expanding it to include things other than labour. I will now briefly describe these alternatives.

Theories of Value

Many of those whose work I have reviewed use words such as 'production', and 'work' (though seldom 'labour'), which confuses the debate, since this would seem to imply a link with Marx's theory of value. Or they adopt new terms such as 'abstract social nature'. But they often display an equivocal relationship to the labour theory of value, if they engage with it at all.

O'Connor is the best example of one who sought to supplement Marx's theory of value with another. He posits a 'second contradiction of capitalism' (1998: 127) relating not to the production of surplus value but to global environmental destruction. In O'Connor (1998) he proposed that

[8] Late in his life, Marx took great interest in the work of the German agricultural chemist, Justus von Liebig, whom he quotes in *Capital Volume 1*, ch 15, footnote 246: "To have developed from the point of view of natural science, the negative, i.e., destructive side of modern agriculture, is one of Liebig's immortal merits". Recent work by Saito (2017) has made available previously unknown writing by Marx on this topic.

the "capital-nature relation" was no less fundamental than the capital-labour relation in analysing how capitalism reproduces and, ultimately, undermines itself. In his journal *Capitalism: Nature: Socialism* in which he sought to expand value to include the contribution from nature (Collins 2016; Mariyani-Squire 2000), O'Connor's purpose was to combine the works of Marx and Polanyi (including the latter's concept of 'fictitious commodities').[9] This involved "A massive review of the labour theory of value" (Castree 2000: 112).

The other alternative, to propose an extended theory of value, is based on the premise that the labour theory of value fails to take account of the contribution made by nature. Moore is one of the most well-known in this tradition, seeking "a productive synthesis of Marxist and Green thinking" (2015: 51)

> Value relations incorporate a double movement to exploitation and appropriation. Within the commodity system, the exploitation of labor-power reigns supreme. But this supremacy is only possible, given its tendency towards self-exhaustion, to the degree that the appropriation of uncommodified natures counteracts this tendency. This has been difficult to discern because value *relations* are necessarily much broader than the immediate production of commodities. … The centrality of wage-work in certain Marxist perspectives is not wrong but partial, given the unsustainability of the circuit of capital as closed system. (Moore 68–69).

He argues that "capitalism can be comprehended through the shifting configuration of the exploitation of labor-power and the appropriation of Cheap Nature" (Moore, 2015: 64). His proposal is indeed radical. "Marxists have taken value to be an *economic* phenomenon with systemic implications. This, I think, inverts the reality. Value-relations are a *systemic* phenomenon with a pivotal economic moment" (Moore 2015: 193).

The law of value, Moore argues, "far from reducible to abstract social labor, finds its necessary conditions of self-expansion through the creation and subsequent appropriation of Cheap Natures" (66). These, he lists as labour, food, energy and raw materials—the 'four cheaps'.[10] (This

[9] For discussion of Polanyi's influence see also Prudham (2013).

[10] With regard to unpaid labour, Moore draws in part on earlier work by Mies (1986).

was subsequently, in a book with Raj Patel, extended to seven cheaps (Moore and Patel 2017).) Moore's work has been sharply criticised, for example by Nayeri (2017), but others share his views.

> A blind spot in the labour theory of value is its treatment of the unpaid work of animals, fuel, household workers, workers in the informal sector, or forced labour. … The work of resources, for example, is categorized as rent accruing to the owners of land. (Kallis and Swyngedouw 2018: 51)

Kallis, who promotes the idea of degrowth, suggests to extend the term exploitation "beyond class-based appropriation to include other forms of undue transfers based on race, gender or ethnicity, including the unpaid appropriation of resources and the services of ecosystems" (Kallis 2018).

Sometimes based on the work of Georgescu-Roegen, attempts have also been made to develop an energy-based theory of value, which have been "hotly debated" (Burkett 2003; Daly and Umana 1981).[11]

The key issue in the debates reviewed in the foregoing pages is whether Marx's theory can, and should, be 'extended', 'reinterpreted', 'updated' to better incorporate the role of nature. One way to address this issue is in the form of a question: 'is nature productive?' Two contrasting positions regarding this issue are well expressed in "Do Bees Produce Value? A Conversation Between an Ecological Economist and a Marxist Geographer". The problem is, as Kallis rightly states, in seeking to clarify the debate: "much of the misapprehension between ecological and Marxist economists has to do with the fact that terms such as 'Value' … do not have the same meaning for us ecological economists" (Kallis and Swyngedouw 2018: 11).

The motivation for many eco-Marxists in promoting a revised theory of value is to seek a way of countering the damage that capitalism is imposing on the environment.[12] Marx's solution is a "higher economic

---

[11] There has even been proposed an animal labour theory of value, as noted by Foster and Burkett (2018).

[12] It is clear that Marx was aware of the threat that capitalism posed for the environment. His analysis helps to explain its endless striving for profit and hence increased production. But one aspect that he fails to examine is the drive to ever-increasing consumption, which is the necessary corollary to production (ref Chap. 13). Some Marxist economists have addressed the issue, and most notably Fine (e.g. Fine and Leopold 2002; Fine 2017) who has developed a theory of consumption, inspired by Marx's work, that demonstrates the power that producers exert over consumers. But

form of society" in which private property is abolished, as indicated in the following passage, which concludes with a very apt expression of the modern concept of sustainability:

> private ownership of the globe by single individuals will appear quite as absurd as private ownership of one man by another. Even a whole society, a nation, or even all simultaneously existing societies taken together, are not the owners of the globe. They are only its possessors, its usufructuaries, and, like boni patres familias, they must hand it down to succeeding generations in an improved condition. (Marx 1959: 776)

Accumulation by Dispossession

David Harvey has been an important scholar in bringing the works of Marx to a wider audience—not only within his own discipline, geography—most notably through his clear and rigorous account of Marx's work in *Limits to Capital* (1982). To a greater extent than many of those referred to above, Harvey does relate his analysis to Marx's theory of value. In recent years, he has been particularly influential owing to his writing on 'accumulation by dispossession' (Harvey 2004: 64).

This expression, coined by Giovanni Arrighi replaced the former term 'continuous primitive accumulation'. Primitive (or original) accumulation is "the historical process of divorcing the producer from the means of production [and subsistence]" Karl Marx (1977: 875). The argument for preferring the new term was that the word 'primitive' is misleading; the phenomenon is still very much a reality in the poor countries of the world: "The so-called 'land grabs' throughout Africa, Latin America and much of Asia … are just the most obvious symptom of a politics of accumulation by dispossession run riot in ways that even Polanyi could not have imagined" (Harvey 2014: 36). Indeed, as Harvey argues, the concept is also applicable to what is happening today in rich countries—even if it is less apparent, and manifested less brutally.

---

this cannot be the whole picture; a fuller understanding of this (very social) phenomenon is required if the environmental challenge is to be effectively confronted.

According to Brenner (2006: 102) "Harvey has done an impressive job of reviving Marx's primitive accumulation, adapting it for the present day, and demonstrating its value in understanding" not only contemporary capitalism but also "contemporary neoliberal imperialism". The term has certainly been taken up very widely.[13]

Part of the attraction of the concept 'accumulation by dispossession' is that it relates so directly to politically urgent issues, such as land grabs in poor countries: "some of its most vicious and inhumane manifestations are in the most vulnerable and degraded regions within uneven geographical development" (Harvey 2003: 173). But it appeals also, no doubt, because of the rhetorical power of the words themselves. This may, however, come at a cost—at least according to one of its critics, Das who describes it as 'a chaotic concept' and argues that Harvey "inflates the causal significance of the concept far too much" (Das 2017).[14] Das acknowledges the validity of Harvey's point—that Marx mistakenly relegates "accumulation based upon predation, fraud, and violence … to an 'original stage' that is considered no longer relevant" (Harvey 2003: 144). But he notes that Harvey, at his own admission, "inflate(s) the idea somewhat" (Harvey 2003: 165) and "worr(ies) about the indiscriminate way in which it might be (and already has been!) used" (Harvey 2003: 158–59).

A number of authors have applied the concept in an analysis of land grabbing (e.g. Hall 2013), or its more specific variant 'green grabbing',[15] "where 'green' credentials are called upon to justify appropriations of land for food or fuel" (Fairhead et al. 2012: 238). This is an increasingly urgent topic to study and critically analyse: the ever-expanding global reach of private property, and the varying—often extra-economic—means by which this is exercised; and not least the role of the state in this process.

[13] According to Google scholar, usage of the term has increased about fifty times since 2006, two years after Harvey's original article.

[14] In support of his claim that this is a concept out of control, Das lists eight different applications, ranging from (1) the commodification and privatization of land and the forceful expulsion of peasant populations; to … (8) usury, the national debt, and … the use of the credit system.

[15] Or even 'green/blue grabbing' (Benjaminsen and Bryceson 2012).

Nature as Accumulation Strategy

Many recent articles relate to ways in which nature is being 'commodified' and 'financialised' by, for example, carbon markets. Robert Costanza, one of the most influential advocates of placing a money value on the environment, argues that the Earth is "a very efficient, least-cost provider of human life-support services", the entire value of which is between 16 and 54 trillion dollars (Costanza et al. 1997: 255). (This, as Robertson notes, was more than the then-current global GNP.) As Swyngedouw (2010: 220) notes, "The commodification of CO_2—primarily via the Kyoto Protocol and various offsetting schemes—in turn, has triggered a rapidly growing derivatives market of futures and options".[16] In his article 'Nature as Accumulation Strategy' Smith (2007) identifies a number of such 'ecological commodities', as he calls them. On the same theme, Bram Büscher and Robert Fletcher (2015) propose the term 'Accumulation by Conservation' whereby: "public, private and non-governmental sectors seek ways to turn the non-material use of nature into capital that can simultaneously 'save' the environment and establish long-term modes of capital accumulation" (2015: 273). They list numerous examples: carbon markets (Paterson 2010; Lohmann 2011), ecotourism (Fletcher and Neves 2012), species and wetlands banking (Robertson 2004, 2012; Sullivan 2013), Reducing Emissions from Deforestation and Forest Degradation (REDD+) (Angelsen 2009). In addition, "Derivatives of all of the above (and more) extend markets still further (Cooper 2010)" (Büscher and Fletcher 2015: 274).

As Robertson (2004: 365) describes it, "Imposing market relations on uncapitalized environmental phenomena requires techniques by which a dollar value can be placed on 'environmental services', and such techniques have proliferated over the past decade on the strength of the imagined consensus on the need to price nature" (Robertson 2004). One of the most important such techniques is, of course, cost-benefit analysis,

[16] He adds "The extraordinary complexity of state and regulatory procedures forcing the commodification of CO_2 exemplifies par excellence what Marx once defined as commodity fetishism" (Swyngedouw 2010: 220). This, I suggest, is a rather inaccurate interpretation of the concept.

which has been used to place a money value not only on nature but also human life and future generations (McNeill 2018).

The phenomenon of payment for environmental services may be seen as reflecting the latest move down a slippery conceptual slope—or perhaps more accurately a broken ladder—that leads irresistibly from 'nature' to 'the environment' (a more scientific term); from 'the environment' to 'environmental services' (a still more technical term); and finally to 'payment for environmental services'—the incorporation of nature into the world of economics (and of finance, as discussed in the following chapter).

Payment for environmental services, and more broadly the commodification of nature, is critiqued in an article by Kosoy and Corbera (2010) which is of particular interest for my review since it explores the issue "through the lens of commodity fetishism, understood here as the masking of the social relationships underlying the process of production" (Kosoy and Corbera 2010). They identify "three inherent invisibilities in the commodification of ecosystem services": simplifying the complexity of natural ecosystems, prioritising a single exchange-value that denies the multiplicity of values which can be attributed to these services, and masking the social relations (power asymmetries) embedded in the process of 'producing' and 'selling' ecosystem services (Kosoy and Corbera 2010: 1229). Although the article claims that it "draws inspiration from the concept of commodity fetishism" I would argue that only the third of these "invisibilities" is directly comparable with the term as Marx employed it.

As long ago as 1990, David Harvey urged geographers to "deploy the Marxian concept of fetishism with its full force" (Harvey 1990: 423), but few have taken up his challenge. Noel Castree has invoked the term in several articles, though he is seemingly sceptical of "all Marx's huff and puff about 'metaphysical subtleties and theological niceties'" (2001: 1521) and the way that "many Marxists since Marx have arguably confined it" in an "epistemic straight jacket" (1519). But understanding the phenomenon of commodity fetishism can, he argues, help to "to make visible the geographical lives of commodities" (1519).[17] Castree uses the

[17] As Harvey expressed it: The grapes that sit upon supermarket shelves are mute; we cannot see the fingerprints of exploitation upon them or tell immediately what part of the world they are from.

example of bioprospecting to ask the question "Where, more generally, do public or common resources and knowledges begin and where do they end": "the kind of difficult question a contemporary Marxist critique of the commodity fetish allows us to ask" (1524).

Like Harvey in his original article from 1990, Castree and others to whom he refers are concerned to "highlight the displacements—geographical, temporal and phenomenal—that are … part and parcel of capitalist commodification" (2003: 282) and hence reveal the exploitation of the system. Castree states, however, that for a number of reasons "most contemporary social, cultural, and economic geographers prefer metaphors other than fetishism in the pursuit of commodity analysis; using terms such as 'commodity displacement', 'the social geography of things', 'commodity chains' and 'actor-networks'. He refers to the work of Hartwick (1998), whose analysis focuses not only on the concealed exploitation of labour but also of nature, adding a comment which, I suggest, somewhat misrepresents the concept of commodity fetishism: "Hartwick's point, like Marx's, is that the spatiotemporal separation of commodity producers and commodity consumers in capitalism means that the latter cannot 'see' what is 'contained' in the physical form of the commodities they purchase" (2003: 282).[18]

Marx on Rent

While the writings referred to above do draw inspiration from Marx, they in many cases make little or no reference to what was surely central to Marx's analysis of nature under capitalism, namely his theory of rent, as Christophers has noted. "Consider, meanwhile, the fate of the one substantial strand of conceptual political economy that does emphasis land:

"Christophers, like Castree (2001) has been inspired by Harvey and suggests "to apply the critique of commodity fetishism to the circulation of money" in a way that "should look broadly like the attempts that have been made to follow nonmonetary commodities and hence to trace their socio-spatial backgrounds" (2011: 1075).

[18] Adopting a similar approach, Hudson and Hudson (2003: 413) suggest that the alternative-trade movement "represents an initial attempt to counter the pervasiveness of commodity fetishism, working to make visible and relevant the social relations that underlie production and exchange".

rent theory. Given a fillip by Harvey's exposition in *Limits* (1982: 330–72) … such theory enjoyed a brief period in the spotlight in the 1980s before essentially disappearing off the radar, circumscribed gesturing at 'rent gaps' (Smith 1987) aside" (Christophers 2016: 136). This is surprising since however one may interpret Marx's writing on nature it is clear that the concept of rent occupies a central position. Harvey (2010: 183) asserted that 'rent has to be brought forward into the forefront of the analysis'. Perhaps this is now beginning to happen. According to (Andreucci et al. 2017): "the rent question is returning with a vengeance".

In the totality of his works, Marx's writing on rent is relatively brief. It is set out in most detail in *Capital Vol III* and, to a lesser extent, *Theories of Surplus Value Vol III*. As many commentators have noted, the exposition is rather repetitive and sometimes hard to follow: "appallingly muddled" to quote Harvey (1982: 68). Engels, who composed both of the above works after Marx's death, writes in the Preface to *Capital Vol II*: "In the case of the third volume there was nothing to go by outside a first extremely incomplete draft". He does, however, add: "The part on ground-rent was much more fully treated (than Part V), although by no means properly arranged".

In what follows I will present a brief review of Marx on rent, starting with the famous Trinity Formula: 'Capital—profit (profit of enterprise plus interest), land—ground-rent, labour—wages, this is the trinity formula which comprises all the secrets of the social production process' (Marx 1959: 814). This formula constitutes a highly condensed summary of Marx's key argument. It brings together two triads: the three classes (capital, labour and landowners) and their respective 'returns' under capitalism. Presented in this way, the relations capital-profit and labour-wages are fetishised—appearing as if they were natural. The exploitative nature of the relation between capital and labour is thus concealed. This is the main focus of Marx's analysis: how capitalists exploit workers, cheating them out of the surplus value that they create. But what of the relations between capitalists and landowners, and between landowners and workers? Are these also antagonistic? How do they appear in the mystical world of capitalism and bourgeois political economy?

In his writing, Marx concentrates primarily on the capital-labour relationship, and the two fetishised relations: capital-profit and labour-wages.

But Marx's theory of rent includes also the relationship between capitalists and landowners. This is accorded relatively limited attention; and the relation between landowners and workers even less. But to analyse capitalism and the environment it is in fact these relations that are of most relevance.

In brief, Marx's analysis is that the landowner appropriates a part of the surplus value from the capitalist. By contrast, in Marx's theory, the landowner and the worker have no direct relationship. This is because he is analysing the situation in fully blown capitalism, where people are already removed from the land. The relationship between landowner and worker is treated as a historical one, in which the former appropriated land from the latter. But in pre-capitalism, of course, the relationship is direct and important: the landowner exerts power over the worker—for example as slave or serf. As Coronil (1997) forcefully pointed out, this phenomenon is very much ongoing in many countries, which is why the debate about accumulation by dispossession is important. (As noted above, if 'land' is much more broadly defined—to include, e.g., genes—the phenomenon is still relevant in very advanced countries.)

Marx's theory of rent shows how it developed historically with the expansion of capitalism. As labour was removed from the land, under the influence of capital, a new triangular relationship was established: between capital, land and labour. (As he notes, the categories 'rent' and 'labour' unlike 'capital' existed also before capitalism.)[19] Marx shows how the property-owner, thanks to ownership of the land, is able to divert some of the surplus value generated in production to his own pocket. But what of the process whereby the landowner exerts exclusive property rights over the land? Although he does rail against the institution of private property and devotes space to describing its historical development, Marx does not theorise much about it. Perhaps for this reason, an important distinction has sometimes been blurred—between "two organically related but analytically distinct 'moments': the creation of property rights, … (and) the struggle over the appropriation and distribution of

[19] "the land on the one hand and labour on the other, two elements of the real labour process, which in this material form are common to all modes of production, which are the material elements of every process of production and have nothing to do with its social form" (Marx 1959: 591).

surplus value generated by the rent relation itself" (Andreucci et al. 2017: 28). Scholars have used different words to refer to these: 'expropriation', 'exploitation' and so on. To avoid confusion I shall use the term 'appropriation', distinguishing between two distinct phenomena: Appropriation 1, the extraction of rent, and Appropriation 2, the institution of private property. (I believe that some of the confusion regarding the concept of accumulation by dispossession is that this term actually conflates the two.)

Appropriation 1

> This capitalist farmer pays the landowner, the owner of the land exploited by him, a sum of money … for the right to invest his capital in this specific sphere of production. This sum of money is called ground-rent, no matter whether it is paid for agricultural land, building lots, mines, fishing grounds, or forests, etc. (Marx 1959: 618)

Appropriation 1 enables the landowner to appropriate a part of the surplus value that accrues in the production process: "Wherever natural forces can be monopolised and guarantee a surplus-profit to the industrial capitalist using them, be it waterfalls, rich mines, waters teeming with fish, or a favourably located building site, there the person who by virtue of title to a portion of the globe has become the proprietor of these natural objects will wrest this surplus-profit from functioning capital in the form of rent" (Marx 1959: 773).

Marx appears to be even more critical of the landowner than the capitalist; he describes the former as "a class that neither works itself, nor directly exploits labour, nor can find morally edifying rationalisations, as in the case of interest-bearing capital, e.g., risk and sacrifice of lending capital to others" (Marx 1959: 829).

While ground rent is that which is paid simply for the use of the land, the situation is complicated by the fact that capitalists may—typically will—invest in the land. "Capital may be fixed in the land, incorporated in it either in a transitory manner, as through improvements of a chemical nature, fertilisation, etc., or more permanently, as in drainage canals, irrigation works, leveling, farm buildings, etc." (Marx 1959: 618). Marx refers to these payments for improvements as differential rent 1 and 2. Such differential rent "does not constitute the actual ground-rent, which is paid for the use of the land as such—be it in a natural or cultivated state" (Marx 1959: 619).[20] Marx makes a further distinction by identifying 'absolute rent' as that which is attributable to some resource being the subject of monopoly, for example champagne.[21]

As Marx notes, there is a certain symmetry between this phenomenon and the exploitation of labour: "Just as the operating capitalist pumps surplus-labour, and thereby surplus value and surplus-product in the form of profit, out of the labourer, so the landlord in turn pumps a portion of this surplus-value, or surplus-product, out of the capitalist in the form of rent in accordance with the laws already elaborated" (Marx 1959: 820).

According to Joan Robinson, Ricardo made the same point: "in taking pains to show that the landlords were parasites on society … he was to some extent the champion of the capitalists. They were part of the productive forces against the parasites. He was pro-capitalist as against the landlords more than he was pro-worker against the capitalists" (Robinson 1973: 267, quoted in Christophers 2019).

Some of the Marxist literature concerns rather technical issues relating to varying forms of differential rent, and sometimes also absolute rent. These debates, as indeed many of the others discussed in this chapter, are complicated by the uneasy fit between conceptual categories and empirical reality. Even if the former are clear-cut, which is not always the case, it is often difficult to apply them in an unequivocal way to the world as it is; especially when the categories were developed 150 years ago. An extreme example of this is the category 'land' itself. How is this to be understood? In his discussion of rent, Marx usually talks about agriculture, but notes that the same argument also applies to other natural 'resources'. For example, he writes:

[20] Marx writes that "Ground-rent might seem to be a mere form of distribution, because landed property as such does not perform any, or at least any normal, function in the process of production itself" (Marx 1959: 883). The phrase 'or at least any normal' seems equivocal.

[21] Harvey (1982) elaborates on the issue of absolute rent, in relation to real estate.

> It should be noted for the sake of completeness that we also include water, etc., in the term land, in so far as it belongs to someone as an accessory to the land. (Marx 1959: 615)

> This sum of money is called ground-rent, no matter whether it is paid for agricultural land, building lots, mines, fishing grounds, or forests, etc. (Marx 1959: 618)

> (Or, instead of agriculture, we can use mining because the laws are the same for both). (Marx 1959: 615)[22]

Appropriation 2

By 'Appropriation 2', I refer to the establishment of exclusive private property over land, broadly defined as "the monopoly by certain persons over definite portions of the globe, as exclusive spheres of their private will to the exclusion of all others" (Marx 1959: 615). This is also referred to by Marx as 'legal fiction'.[23] As he notes, "Free private ownership of land (is) a very recent product" (Marx 1959: 616). In England a crucial example was the "communal lands turned successively into private property through the Enclosure Bills", thanks to "the opportunity which makes the thief; the more or less plausible legalistic subterfuges of the big landlords to justify their appropriation" (Marx 1959: 770). This led to the removal of workers from the land, and their reappearance as capitalist wage-labour:

> the monstrous power wielded by landed property, when united hand in hand with industrial capital, enables it to be used against labourers engaged in their wage struggle as a means of practically expelling them from the earth as a dwelling-place. One part of society thus exacts tribute from another for the permission to inhabit the earth, as landed property in general assigns the landlord the privilege of exploiting the terrestrial body, the bowels of the earth, the air, and thereby the maintenance and development of life." (Marx 1959: 774)

[22] And yet he also writes: "For instance, in the extractive industries, *which must be clearly distinguished from agriculture*, raw material as an element of constant capital is wholly absent, and even auxiliary material rarely plays an important role" (Marx 1959: 759) (my emphasis).

[23] The "legal fiction by grace of which certain individuals have an exclusive right to certain parts of our planet" (Marx 1959: 634).

It is important to emphasise the complementary roles of capitalist and landowner in creating the mystified category of rent, based on the institution of private property. As Marx puts it, the fact that "the title of a number of persons to the possession of the globe enable(s) them to appropriate to themselves as tribute a portion of the surplus-labour of society … is concealed by the fact that the capitalised rent, … appears as the price of land, which may therefore be sold like any other article of commerce. … But the title itself is simply transferred, and not created by the sale. … *What created it in the first place were the production relations*" (Marx 1959: 776) (my emphasis).

In its historical development, the capitalist mode of production "totally separates land as an instrument of production from landed property and landowner; … it dissolves the connection between landownership and the land so thoroughly that the landowner may spend his whole life in Constantinople, while his estates lie in Scotland. Landed property thus receives its purely economic form by discarding all its former political and social embellishments and associations" (Marx 1959: 618).

Rent is distinguished, says Marx, "by the palpable and complete passiveness of the owner", (Marx 1959: 565). But while the landowner may be passive in relation to the capitalist (Appropriation 1), this is far from the case in relation to their role in removing people from the land (Appropriation 2), as Marx makes clear in his descriptions of the enclosures.

Fairhead et al. (2012: 238) define this type of appropriation as "the transfer of ownership, use rights and control over resources that were once publicly or privately owned—or not even the subject of ownership" thus emphasising the complexity of the concept of property. Such appropriation often occurs by so-called extra-economic means (Glassman: 2006).

As described in Chap. 2, it was precisely the phenomenon of private property that motivated Marx, as a young journalist, to attack the members of the Rhineland Assembly regarding their views on the theft of wood. It was then that he adopted the powerful metaphor of the fetish—which later became a tool in his analytical arsenal. His theorising on the topic is contained mainly in his analysis of primitive accumulation, predating nineteenth-century British capitalism. But the phenomenon remains a very relevant object of study in the contemporary world, where private property continues to be extended—both over land in the narrow sense, and in the increasingly expanded sense that includes such things as genes or the airwaves. The former is an arena for continuing, often violent, conflict; but the latter, that may be equally important, is less contested. And that which underlies both—the institution and associated concept of private property itself—appears to be immune to challenge: accepted as something 'natural'.

Brief Conclusion

According to Huber (2016): "Value is back on the agenda". This may be so. But, as I have shown, much of the recent literature that refers to Marx is concerned with his attitude to nature, and this relates only peripherally to Marx's theory of value which some, indeed, treat as erroneous or irrelevant. Many of the works that do refer to it, either try to develop a complementary theory or to expand it. In both cases, the premise is that the labour theory of value fails to take account of the contribution made by nature. But Marx's theory of value is not an investigation of how humans behave; nor is it normative—concerning how people ought to behave. It is an attempt to understand how capitalism works: what value means, in practice, in a capitalist system—and *according to the categories of bourgeois economics*. Superficially, this means that the market is king; but Marx's analysis is, of course, more fundamental.

The main way in which Marx's theory of value connects with nature is through the concept of rent. This topic too is, apparently, also back on the agenda now: "the rent question is returning with a vengeance" (Andreucci et al. 2017, quoted above). As I have argued, Marx's theory of rent, although somewhat incoherent, does indeed have continuing relevance. I have focused especially on how it relates to the qualitative theory of value, his analysis of the mysterious—and mystifying (fetishistic)—inner workings of capitalism. In this respect it concerns mainly the relationship between capitalists and landowners. This is of only limited relevance to the questions that appear to be most burning for many contemporary scholars: what I have called 'Appropriation 2'—new ways of 'commodifying' nature.

According to Christophers (2018: 331) "the political economists of nature have increasingly recognized the salience of financial institutions, practices and devices". But, with notable exceptions, "this literature has skirted, or merely fluttered its eye lashes at, value and value theory, at least in a Marxian guise. Meanwhile, those staging the human-environment tradition's 'fresh encounter' (Robertson and Wainwright 2013: 894) with value theory have thus far had very little of substance to say about finance" (Christophers 2018: 331). It is in this direction that I now turn.

Bibliography

Andreucci, D. M. G.-L., Wedekind, J., & Swyngedouw, E. (2017). 'Value Grabbing': A Political Ecology of Rent. *Capitalism Nature Socialism, 28*(3), 28–47.

Angelsen, A. (Ed.). (2009). *Realizing REDD+: National Strategy and Policy Options*. Bogor: CIFOR. Cited in Büscher, Bram and Robert Fletcher (2015).

Bakker, K. (2015). Neoliberalization of Nature. In Perreault, T., Bridge, G., & McCarthy, J. (Eds.), *The Routledge Handbook of Political Ecology*. Routledge.

Benjaminsen, T. A., & Bryceson, I. (2012). Conservation, Green/Blue Grabbing and Accumulation by Dispossession in Tanzania. *Journal of Peasant Studies, 39*, 2.

Benson, T. (Ed.). (1996). *The Greening of Marxism*. New York: Guilford Press.

Brenner, R. (2006). What Is and What Is Not Imperialism. *Historical Materialism, 14*(4), 79–105.

Burkett, P. (1999). *Marx and Nature: a Red and Green Perspective*. New York: St. Martin's Press.

Burkett, P. (2003). The Value Problem in Ecological Economics. *Organization and Environment, 16*(2), 137–166.

Büscher, B. (2012). Nature on the Move: The Value and Circulation of Liquid Nature and the Emergence of Fictitious Conservation. *New Proposals: Journal of Marxism and Interdisciplinary Inquiry, 6*(1-2), 20–36.

Büscher, B., & Fletcher, R. (2015). Accumulation by Conservation. *New Political Economy, 20*(2), 273–298.

Castells, M. (1977). *The Urban Question*. Cambridge, MA: MIT Press.

Castree, N. (2000). Marxism and the Production of Nature. *Capital and Class*.

Castree, N. (2001). Commentary. *Environment and Planning, 33*, 1519–1525.

Castree, N. (2003). Commodifying What nature? *Progress in Human Geography, 27*(3), 273–297.

Christophers, B. (2016). Land as Capital and Commodity. *Transactions of the Institute of British Geographers, 41*(2), 134–148.

Christophers, B. (2018). Risking Value Theory in the Political Economy of Finance and Nature. *Progress in Human Geography, 42*(3), 330–349.

Christophers, B. (2019). The Problem of Rent. *Critical Historical Studies, 6*(2), 303–323.

Collins, J. L. (2016). Expanding the Labor Theory of Value. *Dialectical Anthropology, 40*, 103–123.

Cooper, M. (2010). Turbulent Worlds: Financial Markets and Environmental Crisis. *Theory, Culture & Society, 27*(2–3), 167–190. Cited in Büscher, Bram and Robert Fletcher (2015).

Coronil, F. (1997). *The Magical State: Nature, money and modernity in Venezuela.* University of Chicago Press.

Costanza, R., d'Arge, R., de Groot, S. F., Grasso, M., Hannon, B., Limburg, K., et al. (1997). The Value of the World's Ecosystem Services and Natural Capital. *Nature, 387*, 253–260.

Daly, H. E., & Umana, A. F. (Eds.). (1981). *Energy Economics and the Environment: Conflicting Views of an Essential Interrelationship*. Boulder, CO: Westview.

Das, R. (2017). David Harvey's Theory of Accumulation by Dispossession: A Marxist Critique. *World Review of Political Economy, 8*(4), 590–616.

Dolenec, D. (2018). Ecology and Enviromentalism. In A. Pandakis, I. Szeman, & J. Diamanti (Eds.), *The Bloomsbury Companion to Marx*. Bloomsbury Academic.

Fairhead, J., Leach, M., & Scoones, I. (2012). Green Grabbing: A New Appropriation of Nature? *Journal of Peasant Studies, 39*(2), 237–261.

Fine, B. (2017). Consumption Matters. *Ephemera, 13*(2), 217–248.

Fine, B., & Leopold, E. (2002). *The World of Consumption: The Cultural and Material Revisited.* London: Routledge.

Fletcher, R., & Neves, K. (2012). Contradictions in Tourism: The Promise and Pitfalls of Ecotourism as a Manifold Capitalist Fix. *Environment and Society: Advances in Research, 3*(1), 60–77. Cited in Büscher, Bram and Robert Fletcher (2015).

Foster, J. B. (1999). Marx's Theory of Metabolic Rift: Classical Foundations for Environmental Sociology. *American Journal of Sociology, 105*(2), 366–405.

Foster, J. B. (2000). *Marx's Ecology: Materialism and Nature*. New York: Monthly Review Press.

Foster, J. B., & Burkett, P. (2018). Value Isn't Everything. *International Socialism*, No. 160.

Geras, N. (1983). *Marx and Human Nature: Refutation of a Legend*. London. Verso.

Giddens, A. (1981). *Contemporary Critique of Historical Materialism*. Berkeley: University of California Press.

Glassman, J. (2006). Primitive Accumulation, Accumulation by Dispossession, Accumulation by 'Extra-Economic' Means. *Progress in Human Geography, 30*(5), 608–625.

Hall, D. (2013). Primitive Accumulation, Accumulation by Dispossession and the Global Land Grab. *Third World Quarterly, 34*(9), 1582–1604.

Haraway, D. (1992). The Promises of Monsters: A Regenerative Politics for Inappropriate/d Others. In L. Grossberg, C. Nelson, & P. A. Treichler (Eds.), *Cultural Studies* (pp. 296–298). New York: Routledge.

Hartwick, E. (1998). Geographies of Consumption. *Society and Space, 16*, 423–437.

Harvey, D. (1982). *The Limits to Capital*. Oxford: Basil Blackwell.

Harvey, D. (1990). Between space and time: reflections on the geographical imagination. *Annals of the Association of American Geographers, 80* (418–434), 423.

Harvey, D. (2003). *The New Imperialism*. Oxford: Oxford University Press.

Harvey, D. (2004). The 'New' Imperialism: Accumulation by Dispossession. *Socialist Register*.

Harvey, D. (2008). The Right to the City. *New Left Review*.

Harvey, D. (2010). *The Enigma of Capital: And the Crises of Capitalism*. Oxford: Oxford University Press.

Harvey, D. (2011). *The Enigma of Capital and the Crisis of Capitalism*. Croydon: Profile Boks.

Harvey, D. (2014). *Seventeen Contradictions and the End of Capitalism*. New York: Oxford University Press.

Huber, M. (2016). Resource Geographies I: Valuing Nature (Or NOT). *Progress in Human Geography, 42*(5), 148–159.

Hudson, I., & Hudson, M. (2003). Removing the Veil? Commodity Fetishism, Fair Trade, and the Environment. *Organization & Environment, 16*(4), 413–430. https://doi.org/10.1177/1086026603258926

Kallis, G. (2018). *Degrowth*. Newcastle upon Tyne: Agenda Publishing.
Kallis, G., & Swyngedouw, E. (2018). Do Bees Produce Value A Conversation Between an Ecological Economist and a Marxist Geographer. *Capitalism Nature Socialism, 29*(3), 36–50.
Kanter, J. (2007, July 6). In London's Financial World, Carbon Trading Is the New Big Thing. *The New York Times*. Retrieved January 10, 2015, from http://www.nytimes.com/2007/07/06/business/worldbusiness/06carbon.html.
Kosoy, N., & Corbera, E. (2010). Payments for Ecosystem Services as Commodity Fetishism. *Ecological Economics, 69*(6), 1228–1236.
Lefebvre, H. (1991). *The Production of Space* (D. Nicholson-Smith, Trans.). Oxford: Blackwell.
Lohmann, L. (2011). The Endless Algebra of Climate Markets. *Capitalism Nature Socialism, 22*(4), 93–116. Cited in Büscher, Bram and Robert Fletcher (2015).
Malm, A. (2018). *The Progress of this Storm: Nature and Society in a Warming World*. London: Verso.
Mariyani-Squire, E. (2000). Natural Causes, Uncertain Consequences?: Some Critical Comments on James O'Connor's Ecological Marxism. *Journal of Australian Political Economy, 45*, 100–122.
Marx, K. (1954). *Capital* (Vol. I). Moscow: Progress.
Marx, K. (1959). *Capital* (Vol. III). Moscow: Progress.
Marx, K. (1975). *Karl Marx: Texts on Method* (T. Carver, Trans. & Ed.). Oxford: Blackwell.
Marx, K. (1977). *Economic and Philosophic Manuscripts of 1844*, Moscow: Progress.
McNeill, D. (2018). 'Natural', 'Human', 'Social': It's All Capital Now. In H. Jordheim & E. Sandmo (Eds.), *Conceptualizing the World: An Exploration across Disciplines*. New York: Berghahn books.
Meadows, D. H., Meadows, D. L., Randers, J., & Behrens III W. W. (1972). *The Limits to Growth: A Report for the Club of Rome's Project on the Predicament of Mankind*. Universe Books, New York.
Mies, M. (1986). *Patriarchy and Accumulation on A World Scale: Women in the International Division of Labour* (251pp). London: Zed Books.
Moore, J. (2015). *Capitalism in the Web of Life: Ecology and the Accumulation of Capital*. London: Verso.

Moore, J., & Patel, R. (2017). *A History of the World in Seven Cheap Things*. Oakland: University of California Press.

Nayeri, K. (2017, July). 'Capitalism in the Web of Life' – A Critique. *Climate & Capitalism*.

O'Connor, J. (1998). *Natural Causes: Essays in Ecological Marxism*. New York: The Guildford Press.

Paterson, M. (2010). Legitimation and Accumulation in Climate Change Governance. *New Political Economy, 15*(3), 345–368. Cited in Büscher, Bram and Robert Fletcher (2015).

Prudham, S. (2013). Men and Things: Karl Polanyi, Primitive Accumulation, and Their Relevance to a Radical Green Political Economy. *Environment and Planning A: Economy and Space, 45*(7), 1569–1587.

Robertson, M. (2004). The Neoliberalization of Ecosystem Services: Wetland Mitigation Banking and Problems in Environmental Governance. *Geoforum, 35*(3), 361–373. Cited in Büscher, Bram and Robert Fletcher (2015).

Robertson, M. (2012). Measurement and Alienation: Making a World of Ecosystem Services. *Transactions of the Institute of British Geographers, 37*(3), 386–401.

Robertson, M., & Wainwright, J. (2013). The Value of Nature to the State. *Annals of the Association of American Geographers, 103*(4), 890–805. https://doi.org/10.1080/00045608.2013.765772

Robinson, J. (1973). An Open Letter from a Keynesian to a Marxist. In *Collected Economic Papers* (Vol. 4). Oxford: Basil Blackwell.

Saito, K. (2017). *Karl Marx's Ecosocialism: Capital, Nature, and the Unfinished Critique of Political Economy*. New York: New York University Press.

Schmidt, A. (1971). *The Concept of Nature in Marx*. London. Verso.

Schulz, G. (2012). Marx's Distinction between the Fetish Character of the Commodity and Fetishism. *Studies in Social and Political Thought, 20*, 25–45.

Smith, N. (1984). *Uneven Development: Nature, Capital and the Production of Space* (3rd ed., 2010). London: Verso.

Smith, N. (1987). Gentrification and the Rent Gap. *Annals of the Association of American Geographers, 77*(3), 462–465.

Smith, N. (2007). Nature as Accumulation Strategy. *Socialist Register*.

Smith, N. (2008). *Uneven Development: Nature, Capital, and the Production of Space*. Athens, GA: University of Georgia Press.

Sullivan, S. (2013). Banking Nature? The Spectacular Financialisation of Environmental Conservation. *Antipode, 45*(1), 198–217. Cited in Büscher, Bram and Robert Fletcher (2015).

Swyngedouw, E. (2010). Apocalypse Forever? Post-political Populism and the Spectre of Climate Change. *Theory, Culture & Society, 27*(2–3), 213–232. https://doi.org/10.1177/0263276409358728

Timparano, S. (1975). *On Materialism*. London: New Left Books.

Walker, R. (2017). Value and Nature: Rethinking Capitalist Exploitation and Expansion. *Capitalism Nature Socialism, 28*(1), 53–61. https://doi.org/10.1080/10455752.2016.1263674

Williams. (2017). *The Bloomsbury Companion to Marx* (A. Pendakis, I. Szeman, & J. Diamanti, Eds.). London: Bloomsbury.

15

Marx and Financialisation

"with the stroke of an enchanter's wand, it (the public debt) endows barren money with the power of breeding and thus turns it into capital, without the necessity of its exposing itself to the troubles and risks inseparable from its employment in industry or even in usury. … the national debt has given rise to joint-stock companies, to dealings in negotiable effects of all kinds, and to agiotage, in a word to stock-exchange gambling and the modern bankocracy."
(Marx 1954: 706)

Introduction

The second topic on which much of recent Marx-inspired literature has been written is financialisation. Again, I will be concerned especially with the extent to which these works benefit from an appreciation of Marx's theory of value and his concept of fetishism. This section builds partly on the analysis in Chap. 5 which deals with the fetishism of money, capital and interest-bearing capital.

The financial sector has grown dramatically in recent decades, in both absolute and relative terms (see below). The financial crisis of 2008 led many commentators—and not only radicals—to cast a critical eye on its

D. McNeill, *Fetishism and the Theory of Value*, Palgrave Studies in the History of Economic Thought, https://doi.org/10.1007/978-3-030-56123-9_15

activities and claim that it is parasitical on the 'real' economy. They also noted its privileged position with regard to salaries, and how government has been "prodigiously favourable to the sector over the period of neoliberalism and its Global Financial Crisis, during which returns fell to -5% before almost immediately being restored to 20%" (Christophers and Fine 2020).

A great deal has been written about financialisation, especially following the 2008 crisis. According to the *Routledge International Handbook of Financialization* (Mader et al. 2020) since 2010, the number of annually published journal articles on financialisation has more than quadrupled, to almost 400 (Web of Science 2019). The growth of financialisation scholarship coincided with a diffusion across academic disciplines. Articles in the tradition of (heterodox) economics are, in total, outnumbered by those in geography and other disciplines—such as anthropology, accounting studies, development studies, political science and sociology.

It has been claimed that as many as 17, or perhaps even 27, different definitions of the term 'financialisation' may be found (Christophers 2018). A recent survey of the literature in an economics journal concluded that "the term 'financialization' is often applied differentially across analyses despite an often-implicit pretense that the same phenomenon is analysed" (Davis 2017: 1333). Many refer to Epstein's definition: "The increasing role of financial motives, markets, actors and institutions in the operation of the domestic and international economies" (2005: 3). Or Krippner: "a pattern of accumulation in which profits accrue primarily through financial channels rather than through trade and commodity production" (2005: 174). In his aptly titled book *Fictitious Capital: How Finance is Appropriating our Future*, Durand asserts that financialisation is "above all distinguished by the accumulation of drawing rights over values that are yet to be produced" (Durand 2014: 4).

Within the Marxian literature "a straightforward definition of financialization has yet to emerge" (van der Zwan 2014). According to Ronald Dore (2008: 1097) quoted in (van der Zwan 2014): "Financialization' is a bit like 'globalization'—a convenient word for a bundle of more or less discrete structural changes in the economies of the industrialized world'".

Some other definitions—by those whose works I will be referencing most—are as follows:

Christophers: “If financialization now means anything consistent at all … it is perhaps only the hazy conviction that ‘finance’, itself variously understood (of course), today enjoys a historically unique significance” (2015: 186).

Lapavitsas: “a systematic transformation of the capitalist economy pivoting on the financial system and involving new sources of profit” (2009b: 141).

Fine, perhaps the most prolific Marxist scholar on the subject, has criticised the ‘fuzz and buzz’ that surrounds the term. He has defined it as “the process by which the various forms of capital in exchange (including financial and other assets and markets) have not only expanded in extent and diversity but become increasingly articulated with one another” (2010: 98). Or, more explicitly linked to Marx’s own terminology: “the increasing scope and prevalence of IBC (interest-bearing capital) in the accumulation of capital” (2013: 55).

In summary, there is no single agreed definition of financialisation—even within Marxist literature. However defined, it is apparent that financialisation has involved an increase in what might be called both breadth and depth (similar to the expansion discussed in the previous chapter with regard to the environment). “IBC has expanded enormously both intensively (within existing activities) and extensively (to new areas of applications) over the past three decades” (Christophers and Fine 2020).

Financialisation has spread into, indeed created, new markets; largely by creating new and increasingly complex financial instruments, aided by new technology. Because of the central role they played in the financial crisis, derivatives based on housing mortgages are perhaps the best known; but there are many others. Futures markets for agricultural products have a long history, but in recent decades these have been increasingly exceeded in size by more complex derivative forms. Payment for environmental services is another example, as discussed in the previous chapter. More recently, even more unlikely variants have appeared. In the health sector we find so-called pandemic or ebola bonds developed by the World Bank. And, based on faith in the so-called efficient markets hypothesis, the phenomenon is even linked to a new practice of ‘political prediction markets’ (Aitken 2020).

Quantification of the extent of the spread of financialisation depends, of course, on how it is defined. In his book, Durand refers to three measures: “the weight of the financial sector, the importance of this sector’s profits relative to overall profits, and the dynamic of financial profits in non-financial firms" (Durand 2014: 75). He offers the following summary statistics.

Over the period 1970–2014, the gross value added by financial and insurance activities as percentage of GDP (calculated as an average figure across eleven rich countries) increased by half, from about 4% to about 6%.[1] The proportion of overall profits accounted for by financial and insurance rose by approximately the same amount. There are wide variations between the eleven countries, especially regarding the third indicator, non-financial corporations' financial income as a proportion of gross operating profit. In France, the extreme case, this rose from 8% in the 1970s to 88% in 2008. By contrast, in the United States, income from dividends is overshadowed by income from interest (which includes revenues from liquid assets invested in highly developed monetary funds). Here, the total was about 13% in 1970, and rose to over 30%, before falling back to under 10% in 2014.

In her much-cited article Krippner (2005) provides data on the contribution of different sectors of the US economy in the period 1950–2001, based on three different measures: employment, GDP and corporate profits. The decline of manufacturing is very clear. The rise of FIRE (fire, insurance and real estate) is not notable in terms of employment, but massive (though erratic) in terms of corporate profits.

There has been some debate as to whether financialisation is a new phenomenon. Quoting Vercelli (2013) Christophers and Fine (2020) distinguish three different positions: financialisation as a 'unique' historical episode; as a recurring phenomenon, occurring in waves (Arrighi 1994; Perez 2002); or as a long-run tendency. While contemporary Marxist scholars appear to be unanimous in regarding it as dysfunctional, Durand (2014) notes, referring to earlier works by Braudel (1984), Hilferding (1990) and Gershrenkon (1962), that it has not, in the past, necessarily been associated with economic decline.

[1] In 2018, the US financial services sector accounted for 7.4% of total economic output. This compared with 6.9% in the United Kingdom, ranking it the *seventh largest in the OECD* in relative terms. In Luxembourg the figure was 26%. https://commonslibrary.parliament.uk/research-briefings/sn06193/, https://www.selectusa.gov/financial-services-industry-united-states.

Variations in the definition of financialisation tend to be linked with variations in the primary focus of interest of the commentator. Christophers and Fine (2020) identify three primary schools: "the structural shift in patterns of accumulation school (i.e. Krippner, van Treeck, etc.; the school focused on the shift in corporate imperatives toward a more singular focus on shareholder value; Froud et al. 2000); and the school focused on finance's colonization of 'noneconomic' lifeworlds (Martin 2002)". (Christophers and Fine 2020) All three issues are certainly important, but I would emphasise the distinctive significance of the third of these schools: how financialisation creates a new way of conceptualising and interacting with the world, with the concept of risk playing a central role. Financialisation extends its influence over both the world of business and everyday life through a set of practices and associated modes of thought; and these are mutually reinforcing.

In the following review of recent debates about financialisation I begin by setting out Marx's analysis of interest-bearing capital, followed by a discussion of 'the financialisation of everyday life'. Partly building on these, I then address two key questions that have been the subject of scholarly debate; first asking whether financialisation is productive, and then exploring what kind of appropriation is involved in this phenomenon. I have chosen not to include debates about crisis itself. Although this is of course of crucial importance, the issue does not, I believe, relate closely to Marx's 'qualitative' theory of value—the subject of this book.

Marx's Analysis of Interest-Bearing Capital

Without necessarily committing myself to Fine's definition of financialisation as synonymous with interest-bearing capital, I find it useful to start my analysis by examining how Marx understands this. The relevant texts are contained mainly in *Capital Volume III* and *Theories of Surplus Value Part III*. Marx writes that "*Interest* is therefore nothing but a part of the profit (which, in its turn, is itself nothing but surplus-value, unpaid labour), which the industrial capitalist pays to the owner of the borrowed capital with which he 'works', either exclusively or partially" (Marx 1971: 470). To reach this conclusion he begins, as usual, with a historical account. He relates interesting-bearing capital to "its antiquated form, usurer's capital (which) belongs together with its twin brother, merchant's capital, to the antediluvian forms of capital, which long precede the capitalist mode of production and are to be found in the most diverse economic formations of society" (Marx 1959: 593).

"As soon as manufacture gains strength" merchant's capital becomes "the servant of industrial capital, and carries out one of the functions emanating from the conditions of production of industrial capital"—in the sphere of circulation (Marx 1971: 470).

Something similar happens with interest, with interest-bearing capital becoming subordinated to industrial capital (Marx 1971: 468). Initially, this was done by force "first of all in Holland, where capitalist production in the form of manufacture and large-scale trade first blossomed" (Marx 1971: 527). "Violence (the State) is used against interest-bearing capital by means of compulsory reduction of interest rates, so that it is no longer able to dictate terms to industrial capital. But this is a method characteristic of the least developed stages of capitalist production. The real way in which industrial capital subjugates interest-bearing capital is the creation of a procedure specific to itself—the *credit system* … a form of industrial capital which begins with manufacture and develops further with large-scale industry" (Marx 1971: 468). "The credit associations established in the 12th and 14th centuries in Venice and Genoa arose from the need for marine commerce and the wholesale trade associated with it to emancipate themselves from the domination of outmoded usury and the monopolization of the money business" (Marx 1959: 601).

Marx's description of the early days resonates with accounts of contemporary capitalism:

> With the development of interest-bearing capital and the credit system, all capital seems to double itself, and sometimes treble itself, by the various modes in which the same capital, or perhaps even the same claim on a debt, appears in different forms in different hands. (Marx 1959: 470)

The kernel of Marx's analysis of interesting-bearing capital is contained, I suggest, in the following:

> Interest is, therefore, the expression of the fact that value in general—materialised labour in its general social form … confronts living labour-power as an independent power, and is a means of appropriating unpaid labour; and that it is such a power because it confronts the labourer as the property of another. But on the other hand, this antithesis to wage-labour is obliterated in the form of interest, because interest-bearing capital as such has not wage-labour, but productive capital for its opposite. The lending capitalist as such faces the capitalist performing his actual function in the process of reproduction, not the wage-worker, who, precisely under capitalist production, is expropriated of the means of production. Interest-bearing capital is capital as property as distinct from capital as a function. But so long as capital does not perform its function, it does not exploit labourers and does not come into opposition to labour. (Marx 1959: 379)

Two points deserve emphasis here. Firstly, the lender of interesting-bearing capital, the money-capitalist, though apparently divorced from the production process, appropriates a part of the surplus value created. Secondly, the lender appears to appropriate this not from the wage-worker that created it but from the productive capitalist. (This 'mystification' is discussed in Chap. 5, on the fetishism of interesting-bearing capital.) Marx makes a third important point shortly before this passage:

> Interest is then net profit, as Ramsay calls it, which the ownership of capital yields as such, either simply to the lender, who remains outside the reproduction process, or to the owner who employs his capital productively. But in the latter's case, too, capital yields this net profit to him not in his capacity of productive capitalist, but of money-capitalist, of lender of his own capital as interest bearing capital to himself as to a functioning capitalist. (Marx 1959: 379)

Here, Marx seeks to distinguish between actors and roles; thus a productive capitalist can 'act in the capacity of' a money-capitalist. This can often be a source of confusion in interpreting Marx: theoretical categories do not easily fit with the 'messy' empirical reality.

As the capitalist system develops further, there arises what Marx calls "fictitious capital". This is a legally-based claim on a future stream of revenues generated by an asset, which can be bought and sold independently of the asset itself.

"Fictitious capital was Marx's term for financial assets like a company's debt and equity securities (bonds and stocks/shares, respectively). These were deemed fictitious forms of capital precisely in the sense that they did not embody 'real' value" (Christophers 2018: 334).

These financial assets were "Marx claimed, merely a title to future (real) value, and thus fictitious as value forms per se. Produced within the sphere of circulation by unproductive financial workers, financial assets constituted, in short, fictitious capital embodying fictitious value" (Christophers 2018: 334).

To quote Marx again:

> Titles of ownership to public works, railways, mines, etc., are indeed, as we have also seen, titles to real capital. But they do not place this capital at one's disposal. It is not subject to withdrawal. They merely convey legal claims to a portion of the surplus-value to be produced by it. But these titles likewise become paper duplicates of the real capital; ... the real capital exists side by side with them and does not change hands as a result of the transfer of these duplicates from one person to another. (Marx 1959: 477)

But Marx's analysis is here somewhat unclear. He "goes round and round in circles asking the question, when is an accumulation of fictitious capital an accumulation of real capital. We know it need not be given booms and busts. ... Marx does not answer his question because he cannot; the answer cannot be found in the logical and practical differences between real and fictitious accumulation" (Fine n.d.: n.p.).

Bryan et al. note that Marx was concerned with the effects of the credit system on inequality and potential for crisis, but emphasise that "issues such as securitization and financial derivatives which, quantitatively at least, dominate current global financial processes are transforming capital accumulation in ways that far transcend Marx's era and Marx's own analysis of finance, although not Marx's method. Indeed, the common characteristic of derivatives and securitization is the process of commodification (of risk): a process immediately consistent with Marx's analysis of capitalist development"[2] (Bryan et al. 2009: 459).

To quote Marx again:

> In its capacity of interest-bearing capital, capital claims the ownership of all wealth which can ever be produced, and everything it has received so far is but an instalment for its all-engrossing appetite. By its innate laws, all surplus-labour which the human race can ever perform belongs to it. Moloch. (Marx 1959: 397)

With the final word 'Moloch' Marx signals again the mystification, the fetishism, which conceals the workings of the capitalist system. As discussed earlier in this book, the Moloch has real power—upheld by the shared beliefs and practices of the people.

Financialisation of Everyday Life

In recent years a new interdisciplinary research area—'social studies of finance'—has developed. This includes what is now a substantial body of work on so-called financialisation of everyday life—or, following the title of Martin (2002) *Financialization of Daily Life*. As one much-cited contributor to the literature notes: "The prominence of finance across economy and society is not essentially new, but the present day reach of finance throughout everyday socio-economic life would seem to be of a different order" (Erturk et al. 2009). Only some, not the majority, of the authors whose work I review make reference to Marx.

The following review is based mainly on contributions in the *Routledge International Handbook on Financialization* (Mader et al. 2020) and articles from the *Journal of Cultural Economy*, which was established in 2008. The aim of these authors is to describe and analyse "a host of structural changes in the advanced political economies", which share a common evaluation of how global finance has altered the underlying logics of

[2] One should not ignore what was already happening in Marx's day, as described in the quotation at the head of this chapter: "with the stroke of an enchanter's wand" (Marx 1954: 706).

economic activity as well as the workings of democratic society (van der Zwan 2014: 99). This new phenomenon is well summarised in the following account:

> In the language of finance, the household is increasingly to be seen as a set of financial exposures to be strategically self-managed. Calculations and decisions must now be made about a range of issues. Some such issues have emerged because the management of certain exposures is no longer undertaken by the state: there is now need for private calculation and decisions about such things as health insurance, education investment, and investment in an asset portfolio for retirement. There are also issues that have emerged with increasing competitiveness within the financial sector: decisions about the proportion of (expected) income to dedicate to home loan interest payments; the time profile of loans, fixed or floating rate loans, the management of consumer credit options; the preferred pension scheme. Finally, there is an emerging set of choices to be made in the face of new financial products, in particular the emergence of derivative products that permit people to hedge exposure to risks relating to their employment and the value of their home. (Bryan et al. 2009: 462)

This phenomenon, sometimes described—apparently without irony—as the democratisation of finance, has "pushed poor and middle-class workers into new financialized schemes of survival, often heavily reliant on borrowing" (Sotiropolous and Hillig 2020: 382).

A major issue discussed in the literature is the role taken by household debt that has, in the contemporary era, "become necessary for many households to meet the costs of social reproduction, including food, healthcare, housing, and education" (Predmore 2020: 130). Increased access to credit for consumption has allowed the development of new financial products: "bundling together of streams of future repayments from car loans and credit card debt" has "linked household borrowing with global capital markets" (Pagliari and Young 2020: 142).

Thus, the reach of financialisation processes extends well beyond the productive and corporate economies: "Uninterrupted, and actually deepened in the course of the global financial crisis (Davis and Williams 2017), financialisation processes are now arguably being experienced more widely and acutely than ever (Langley 2020: 89). Workers are increasingly drawn in to financial markets, through pension funds, mutual funds and mortgages. "The proportion of households in the US invested in the stock market increased from 20% in 1983 to 52% in 2001" (Davis 2009: 213) quoted in Sotiropolous and Hillig (2020: 381).

The implications for power relations have been studied, but not usually in Marxian terms. Rather, they "are challenged or nourished with concepts and ideas taken from the wider body of social theory", especially post-structuralists Michel Foucault and Gilles Deleuze (e.g. de Goede 2010; Langley 2020). The cultural economy literature was, according to Montgomerie (2020), initially divided "between cultural economy of Foucauldian governmentality … and the political economy of Weberian agent-centric preferences". But she argues that gender studies had a significant impact. Elias and Roberts' (2016) pointed out "the extensive feminist literature using the concept of the everyday as a gender lens to connect the mundane practices and minutiae of everyday life … to large-scale movements of financialization, crisis and austerity". This, she argues "brings a new conceptual clarity to how financialization occurs at the scale of the everyday, which is largely obscured by the bifurcated political and cultural economy accounts" (Montgomerie 2020: 426).

Predmore (2020) also notes the criticism by some feminist scholars of "the lack of attention paid to household and reproductive labor, despite its apparent compatibility with, and intellectual debt to, feminist inquiry" (130). She spells out the implications of a gender perspective, identifying three main themes: (1) the distributional effects of crises and austerity policies, which are generally more severe for women and people of colour; (2) the hegemonic masculine norms pervasive throughout both "high" and "everyday" finance, along with the women's inclusion initiatives that have emerged in response to criticism of these norms; and (3) the financialisation of social reproduction and "everyday life", two distinct but related concepts (Predmore 2020: 125).

The scholars whose work I am discussing seek to understand, the pervasive, but hidden, power of financialisation: its logic and ethos. Langley (2020: 89) describes it as "a set of voracious processes that crystalize financial logics and values across multiple domains". According to Appadurai (2016: 44), "The machinery for measuring, modelling, managing, predicting, commoditizing, and exploiting risk … has become the central diacritic of modern capitalism" quoted in Aitken (2020: 412).

The challenge of understanding the power of financialisation is in many ways similar to the issue that Marx faced, which I have been discussing in this book: how to understand and communicate the power of the capitalist system and the dominant categories of economic thought.

> This is an ethos where the techniques, metaphors, dispositions, narratives, ideas, ideologies and relational practices we associate with high finance come to have purchase over a wide diversity of other fields of practice, social life and imaginative expression. … This ethos is characterized, in general terms, by the imperative towards speculation, monetary measurement, individualistic competition in which anything and everything of material or immaterial value is transformed into an asset to be leveraged. Importantly, as Randy Martin argues, financialization is distinguished from commodification and monetization by the way it demands a transformation of the imagination towards a mapping of future potentials, the calculative activities of risk management and notions of hedging, leveraging and securitization. (Haiven 2020: 389)

The link between financialisation and neo-liberalism is very close; indeed some see them as effectively synonymous. Harmes (2001: 122) hypothesises that by transforming tens of millions from passive savers into 'active' investors whose personal wealth is tied to financial markets, "the financialization of the economy is vastly expanding the constituency in favour of neoliberal policies such as capital mobility, price stability, low capital-gains tax and shareholder value". To quote Pagliari and Young:

> The financialization of everyday life is a manifestation of a powerful governmental rationality and a range of risk management techniques that regard uncertain financial market circulations in positive and productive terms as vital to securing socio-economic life (Langley 2020: 89). In these works, the link is frequently made between financialisation, neo-liberalism and the state: how the financialization process "may be building its own constituencies of political support". (Pagliari and Young 2020: 145)

The issue is complicated by the fact that individuals may also be benefitting as investors. To quote Harmes (2001): this "creates a potential for a 'split personality' dilemma for political subjectivity under conditions of financialization. In terms of policy preferences, those policies that may benefit an individual or household as investors—such as policies to promote shareholder value maximization in the management of companies—may affect them adversely as workers."

A central element for an understanding of this phenomenon is the significance of risk, which is emphasised by many commentators. According to Boy, Burgess and Leander (2011), quoted in Langley (2020): "financial logics and techniques loom large in the formulation and execution of the contemporary neo-liberal government of social and economic life as problems of security. This is because finance and security share an ontological conundrum—how to confront the uncertain future—and a shared epistemology of risk that is manifest in the deployment of risk management techniques and tools in order to render the future actionable in the present."

As noted by Martin et al. (2008: 121) "risk applies to more than the things traded on the Chicago Mercantile Exchange. Indeed a large extant social sciences literature now exists on the emergence of a so-called 'risk society' (Beck 1992). … In this broader and innately social framework, we need to consider the possibility that finance is now a central conduit of risk shifting and social change."

The financialisation of the everyday has been facilitated by discourses of risk-taking, self-management and self-fulfilment. "In a move away from the security provided by postwar welfare schemes, individuals today encounter a world of risk, in which they themselves are responsible for dealing with the uncertainties of life (Cutler and Waine 2010)". This has an impact on the subjective understandings of one's role within the political economy (van der Zwan 2014: 111). "Finance has become a decentralized form of power … exercised through individuals' own interactions with new financial technologies and systems of financial knowledge. By participating in financial markets, individuals are encouraged to internalize new norms of risk-taking and develop new subjectivities as investors or owners of financial assets. Finance thus becomes, in Foucauldian terms, a 'governmentality'" (van der Zwan 2014: 102).

In summary, financialisation has, in the course of a few decades, and thanks largely to new technology, greatly changed our everyday lives—both our practice and our mindset. Risk—how to cope with an uncertain future—is not new; it is part of the human condition. But one might argue, to put it simply, that while the risks involved in everyday life were, at least in the post-war period, dealt with by the welfare state they are now in the hands of the financial sector. We have entered a new era, requiring new analytical perspectives to comprehend it. As capitalism developed, the individual became a wage labourer, subject to the logic of the market and the power of the capitalist. As financialised capitalism develops, the individual is drawn—not in the world of production but in the world of consumption—into the logic of the financial market and the power of the financier. "As with earlier processes of dispossession to create new horizons for accumulation, capital now dispossesses labour of that haven from market instrumentalities known as private life" (Martin et al. 2008: 130).

Is Finance Productive?

According to Christophers (2018: 335): "For many of those accustomed to seeing financiers as what Marx (Capital Volume 3) himself called a 'class of parasites', the notion that finance could be construed as anything other than unproductive is unconscionable, not least in the aftermath of the biggest financial crisis in over 70 years". In a recent and very instructive debate with Fine, (Christophers and Fine 2020)[3] he does, nevertheless, declare himself "less and less well satisfied with the traditional view that finance in general is unproductive of value".

Christophers is "less and less satisfied with the traditional view that finance in general is unproductive of value". He criticises scholars who—while recognising the significance of the fundamental shift in the weighting of the capitalist economy toward financial forms of revenue and profit—"nonetheless cling to an essentially *un*changed (Marxian) understanding of value". According to such a view "there is productive labour, which produces value, and thus wealth; and there is unproductive labour, which does not. And the finance sector and the labour embodied within it are, in this schema, fundamentally unproductive."

[3] Since this is a debate, I have chosen—hereafter—to identify the speaker rather than give page references to Christophers and Fine (2020).

In response, Fine begins by presenting "the classic Marxist position": that while "labour in finance, and in many other activities, can facilitate the productivity of the labour that does produce value", value "is only produced by wage labour dedicated to the purpose of producing commodities for profit".

Fine's definition of financialisation "sees it in terms of expansion of what Marx called interest bearing capital (IBC), i.e. capital in exchange that expands the production and circulation of surplus value. Whilst not producing surplus value, it at most facilitates accumulation (although susceptible to financial crises)." He regards the proliferation of financial assets, forms of credit and so on as "increasingly complex forms, not determinants, taken by the circulation of value; but their circulation needs to be traced out in how they relate (surplus) value to its forms with real effects". (He notes that there are two differing views within this position, which I will discuss in the next section; both, however, share the view that finance does not produce value.)

Fine recognises that "(V)alue is challenged with every existing and new complexity that capitalism throws at us, financialization or otherwise". But he maintains that Marx's analysis is still relevant. "For Marx, IBC was primarily advanced for industrial development but, under financialized neoliberalism, it has been extended to, and intensified within, more or less each and every aspect of economic and social reproduction—not so much mortgaging or consumer credit as such, for example, as trading in the proliferating types and volumes of assets that can be formed out of these and any other exchange dealings involving (securitisable) streams of revenues." "As such, financialization in this narrow sense is not new—Marx was able to identify it! What is new is the extent to which such financialization has gained purchase over what has been termed economic and social reproduction, financialization of everyday life, as it has been called."

In summary, according to Fine, what is new is only the scale of the phenomenon—which is indeed huge; also, perhaps, a new phenomenon: the financialisation of everyday life.[4]

---

[4] A separate, but in some ways similar, question is whether specific labour conducted in the information economy is productive or unproductive (Smythe 1977).

Christophers asks: "whether we *can* comfortably bracket off value creation from finance (and financialization). Given the weight of profit now generated through financial channels, does a theory—classical Marxism—according to which finance is unproductive of value still hold water; still make sense? Is the value of financial commodities indeed merely 'fictitious', and financial labour thus extraneous to value-producing labour?" He thus again suggests that it is the sheer *scale* of finance that now makes it necessary to reconsider Marx's theory of value. Although he does not fully carry the argument through, this is nevertheless an important and apparently controversial challenge.

Fine responds: "I do take Marx's longstanding theory of IBC as at the heart of financialization, in the narrow sense—in that IBC has expanded enormously both intensively (within existing activities) and extensively (to new areas of applications) over the past three decades". He nuances his argument by saying that many definitions and approaches to financialisation "tend to conflate it in the narrow sense, as IBC, with its effects in the broader sense of being embedded in economic and social reproduction". The latter presumably refers to 'the financialisation of everyday life' discussed above.

Fine identifies some key controversial questions, such as: "Where exactly do the boundaries of (surplus) value creation lie (theoretically as well as empirically/historically)? Which parts of finance are value creating, and which not, and when did this become so? … How do we distinguish between the creation of this (surplus) value and its distribution or destruction (immanent in commodity and fictitious forms)?"

Christophers agrees that there are no easy answers as to where exactly the boundaries of (surplus) value creation lie. "Marx himself found this to be true: his discussions of precisely where productive labour ends and unproductive labour begins were tortured and ultimately a bit unconvincing." But his argument that "the only parts of finance that categorically do not involve value creation are those where commodities are merely being exchanged rather than produced" is clearly only a partial resolution to the problem.

Christophers notes the reluctance of scholars to "think afresh about finance and value more generally" and suggests two explanations. One is that we resist countenancing that finance creates value "because we think of value as something inherently 'good'. But, for Marx, it is not. A commodity can bear Marxian value but have little or no positive social use."[5] His second explanation concerns the "problematic conflation (is) of value and price". "The fact that in many countries today banks and bankers, respectively, make outsized profits and wages does not mean (or mean accepting) that they are disproportionately value-creating. It could instead mean, and I think often it probably does mean, that the market competition required to effect equalization of profit rates across different sectors of the economy is lacking, and has been for decades" (Christophers 2016). This may be true, but does not seem to explain the reluctance of scholars to think afresh about finance and value more generally.

Fine, while reasserting that "(f)inance is structurally part of *exchange*, divided from *value* creation as labour exercised under capitalist production" does nevertheless accept that "Marx is ambiguous and even inconsistent over his (unfinished) work on (un)productive labour".

Fine sums up his position as follows: "From this, all capital (and labour) *in exchange* is unproductive" (my stress). He goes on "but it takes two forms, one of which is subject to a tendency for equalization with the rate of profit (merchant capital for Marx) and one which is not (IBC)". These two elements "profitability and interest … are hard to distinguish in practice. … But this means there is no reason for competition to equalize returns in finance with those in industry." (This relates to the point quoted above, that circumstances have been "prodigiously favourable to finance".)

Christophers, however, sympathises with the view, expressed by Bryan et al. (2015) that contends "that a theory in which finance does not create value is ill-equipped to explain a capitalist world where finance has become more and more central and dominant" (334). In an earlier article, he summarised three alternative approaches to the issue. "There are those who expand the scope of production "to encompass rather than exclude certain financial activities." In other accounts, finance is 'made' productive "by decoupling value-generation from 'production'. The suggestion here is that 'circulation' … can produce value too." The third

[5] The same point was made regarding the comments of eco-Marxists on value, as noted in the previous chapter.

approach is "to focus on risk and to conceptualize the production of financial risk as the production of value". He himself adopts the third approach "following the lead of Bryan et al. (2015) and others" (Christophers 2018: 336).

It is clear that there are problems in interpreting Marx's position. And Fine recognises that the "classic Marxist position" that he adopts is a "narrow way" of understanding value, a "tight notion of value" that has been criticised also "within the Marxist tradition itself". In a recent unpublished text, Fine (n.d.) directly addresses the question "whether Marx's value theory and associated theory of money … remains relevant for contemporary capitalism even if presumed relevant for his own time". Value theory, he says "is about how surplus value is produced and circulated, accumulated and distributed, with dynamic and contested effects and interactions across time and place, in increasingly complex forms, whether these are reflected in corresponding relations, structures, processes or agencies of production, distribution and exchange, and the corresponding powers and conflicts that they engender". His view is "that it does remain valid, subject to interpretation, although it can be better expressed".

Perhaps the central question is whether the changes in finance since Marx's time are so substantial as to necessarily imply that his theory is outdated. Here it is relevant to recall Marx's criticism of economists who did not recognise that the categories they applied, such as rent, took on a wholly new meaning under capitalism. A similar issue perhaps arises today: is modern, financialised' capitalism so fundamentally different that the established analytical categories cease to be relevant? Does the sheer increase in scale of financialisation necessarily imply that this phenomenon cannot be adequately understood according to Marx's stringent categories? I would, however, distinguish between the—admittedly enormous—quantitative increase in the scale of financial activities, and what is perhaps a qualitative change: the financialisation of everyday life. A priori, I suggest, the former does not constitute grounds for rendering Marx irrelevant, but the latter might.

What Kind of Appropriation?

Much of the literature on financialisation is concerned with the injustice and increased inequality that has accompanied this phenomenon. Some discuss this in class terms, perhaps referring to a loosely specified 'financial elite'. Various different terms are used to refer to the relation between the parties involved, sometimes interchangeably: exploitation, expropriation and appropriation.

As discussed in Chap. 5, Marx analyses interest-bearing capital as a relation between capitalists: "Interest ... expresses merely relations between capitalists, and by no means relations between capital and labour" (Marx 1971: 494). Although, as Marx says, interest and interest-bearing capital "express the contradiction of materialised wealth as against labour" (Marx 1971: 477), "this position is turned upside down in the consciousness of men because, prima facie, the *moneyed capitalist* does not appear to have any relations with the wage-worker, but only with other capitalists" (Marx 1971: 476). This is the fetishism of interest-bearing capital.

> the source of profit is no longer recognisable. ... In M-M' we have the incomprehensible form of capital, the most extreme inversion and materialisation of production relations. (Marx 1971: 462)

> One portion of profit, as opposed to the other, separates itself entirely from the relationship of capital as such and appears as arising not out of the function of exploiting wage-labour, but out of the wage-labour of the capitalist himself. In contrast thereto, interest then seems to be independent both of the labourer's wage-labour and the capitalist's own labour, and to arise from capital as its own independent source. If capital originally appeared on the surface of circulation as a fetishism of capital, as a value-creating value, so it now appears again in the form of interest-bearing capital, as in its most estranged and characteristic form. (Marx 1959: 829)

Thus, regarding financialisation, it is necessary to distinguish between the *exploitation* of labour by capital, which robs labour of the surplus value it has created, and the *appropriation* of part of this surplus value by the moneyed capitalist. In addition, it is—certainly in the modern era—relevant to consider the relation between financiers and individual people in 'the financialisation of everyday life', as discussed above. Various different terms have been used to refer to the latter relation. I suggest that this too could be called appropriation. Thus, I would distinguish between:

Appropriation 1: the relation between lender and industrial capitalist. Here, the moneyed capitalist appropriates, at the expense of the industrial capitalist, part of the surplus value that is generated in the production process—through the exploitation of labour.

Appropriation 2: the relation between lender and individual (not necessarily a worker). This concerns not production but consumption, and the social reproduction of the workforce in the financialisation of everyday life. (Note: As I shall discuss, there are similarities here with my categories 'Appropriation 1 and 2' concerning the environment.)

The question—'what kind of appropriation?'—concerns how these two forms of appropriation are to be analysed in Marxist terms. Regarding the former, there is little disagreement; the payment by industrial capitalists to financiers is clearly classified as interest-bearing capital and is understood in accordance with the quotations from Marx above. The situation is, as noted, complicated by the fact that a capitalist may, in practice, take on the combined role of both industrial and financial capitalist; but the theoretical distinction is clear.

More debatable is appropriation 2. The adverse effects of financialisation on individuals are not generally referred to as exploitation in the literature, although they may be analysed in class terms.[6] Thus, Bryan et al. (2015) liken the relationship to that between capital and labour:

> While securitization of mortgages, credit card debt, automobile loans, college loans, and the like compromise ideals of consumer freedom, it also crafts the very forms of interdependence; here, mutual indebtedness, that Marx understood as the basis of class formation. (Bryan et al. 2015: 471)

[6] According to Langley (2020), however, "Foucault and Deleuze prompt recognition that these processes cannot simply be traced to powerful class interests and the constraining actions of elites".

Christophers (2018: 338) likens the insurer to the factory owner; each procures in the marketplace "the power to create financial risk, or widgets, respectively". And, "Just as the factory-owner endeavours to squeeze wages, so the insurer, guided by its actuaries' calculations, endeavours to absorb less risk: stipulating coverage exemptions, raising deductibles, and so forth. And in doing so, it increases surplus value: the gap between what labour is paid and what it generates for the payer; the extent, in short, of under remuneration and exploitation" (2018: 337).

In an article on the 2008 financial crisis, Adorjan (2014) criticises Lapavitsas (2009b) and others for their unduly 'agency' focused analysis and argues that "reductionist interpretations, which conceptualize 'finance' either as a hegemonic group of strategic actors or as a prominent sector in neoliberal markets, may be critically evaluated in the light of Marx's theory of fetish forms" (Adorjan 2014: 285).[7] He refers to Fine (2009) in rejecting the views of those Marxists who "tend to view this entire process through a class-analytical lens" (Adorjan 2014: 309). Lapavitsas and Fine have both written extensively on financialisation, but they take up rather different positions, as I shall summarise. Lapavitsas' views are set out at length in his book *Profiting Without Producing: How Finance Exploits Us All.* (Lapavitsas 2013). (In his writing he uses both terms 'exploitation' and 'expropriation'.) Here he notes that financial profit has grown enormously in the years of financialisation, but claims that "it has not been explicitly analysed by Marxist or other political economy".

> It cannot be overstressed that exploitation occurring in financial transactions is qualitatively distinct from exploitation in production. To be specific, exploitation in financial transactions amounts to a direct transfer of value from the income of workers to the lenders—that is, it stands for a re-division of money revenue streams, typically taking the form of interest. The social factors that account for such exploitation are related to the sphere of circulation, reflecting in particular the unequal position of workers and capitalists in financial transactions. (Lapavitsas 2013: 143)

[7] His article draws heavily on the concept of fetishism: "to draw attention to the ways in which the general 'financialization' of society since the 1970s has by now rendered (late) capitalism more adequate to what Marx called its "most superficial fetish" (Adorjan 2014: 289).

He quotes Marx *Theories of Surplus Value Part III* to conclude that "profit 'upon expropriation' that arises from lending to workers represents a form of exploitation which is independent of surplus value". He quotes also *Capital Volume III*:

> That the working-class is also swindled in this form, and to an enormous extent, is self evident; but this is also done by the retail dealer, who sells means of subsistence to the worker. This is *secondary exploitation*,[8] which runs parallel to the primary exploitation taking place in the production process itself. (Marx 1959: 609) (My stress)[9]

Lapavitsas also quotes the *Grundrisse*, and compares modern era financialisation, as it relates to individuals, to old-fashioned usury.

> In broad historical terms, financial exploitation represents a throw-back to ancient forms of capitalist profit-making that are independent of the generation of surplus value. … In financialized capitalism, however, profit-making that is unrelated to surplus value no longer represents a survival of ancient pre-capitalist relations. On the contrary, it stands for the spreading of new and exploitative relations across society as financial markets grow and as individuals are increasingly drawn into the formal financial system. (Lapavitsas 2013: 146)

In the modern era, "the sources of profitability have changed, shifting toward the sphere of circulation and raising the prominence of financial profit. Finance has been able to extract profits directly and systematically from salaries and wages, thus shaping financial expropriation."

> Note that relations between banks and households are qualitatively different from relations between banks and industrial capitalists. Financial transactions between banks and households do not refer directly to the creation of profit (surplus value) in the sphere of production. (Lapavitsas 2013: 39)

[8] This is a rare occasion where Marx uses the word 'exploitation' to refer to something other than the capital-labour relationship.

[9] For consistency in referencing, I have here used the 1959 Moscow Progress version of this quotation.

Thus Lapavitsas locates appropriation 2 in the sphere of circulation. It is made possible because "workers are typically disadvantaged compared to banks with regard to economic information and power".

Two quotations from another work by Lapavitsas indicate some ambivalence, or perhaps nuancing of his position. He writes (2009):

> Financial expropriation is an additional source of profit that originates in the sphere of circulation. Insofar as it relates to personal income, it involves existing flows of money and value, rather than new flows of surplus-value. Yet, despite occurring in circulation, it takes place systematically and through economic processes, *thus having an exploitative aspect.* (Lapavitsas 2009a: 131) (My stress)

And regarding similarities between financialisation and usury:

> Profit from financial expropriation is reminiscent of usurer's profit. … Interest received by the usurer … is different from interest received by financial institutions for lending to productive capitalists, which derives from profit systematically generated in production. By the same token, advanced financial institutions differ from usurers. *But, in times of crisis, the former can become usurious*, extracting interest out of the capital of the borrower, rather than out of profit. (Lapavitsas 2009a: 132) (My stress)

Fine contrasts his own position with that of Lapavitsas. He argues that appropriation "is primarily from surplus value produced by workers whereas Lapavitsas places more emphasis on the appropriation of wages (value) through exploitative credit relations" (Christophers and Fine 2020).

In another work, Fine (undated) criticises Lapavitsas at some length. What follows is a summary. Central to Fine's argument is variations in the rate of profitability.

> At the core of the dispute … is whether "financial expropriation", as they term it, is a legitimate way of addressing the rise of (abnormal) profitability through provision of financial services (to the working class). In contrast to them, I suggest not, and that, as an aspect of financialisation, the contemporary provision of financial services is better understood as the integration

> of such services with interest bearing capital (for which the rate of profit is not equalised). (Unnumbered)

In his critique, Fine lists several points which I will here summarise. First, he rejects "the parallel, precedent even" that Lapavitsas draws with usury and trucking.

> The problem … is that usury and trucking are proto-, even pre-capitalist, highly individualised, not open to generalisation and the exception rather than the rule. Is it possible that usury and trucking can be general across workers in the context of developed capitalism?

Fine also criticises the links that Lapavitsas draws between financialisation and changes in the forces and relations of production ('technological revolution in information and telecommunications', and 'deregulation of labour and financial markets' respectively). While acknowledging that these are associated he is unconvinced that the connections are necessarily causal.

He agrees that "financialisation in general, and financial expropriation in particular" have emerged on the basis of asymmetrical development between industry and finance" but argues that regarding the outcome of this asymmetry, the advantage to either side is contingent: "Why should corporations be free of the mercy of exploitative credit relations?" "Why has capital not flowed into the sector of personal finance and reduced profitability to normal levels?"

He argues that Lapavitsas perceives financial expropriation as a "new process (usury and trucking apart) and as a deduction from wages but without explaining why financialisation does not reduce such expropriation to normal levels of profitability".

Fine agrees with Lapavitsas regarding "the extent to which items of working class consumption have been commercialised through privatisation and the like". And quotes him approvingly:

> These developments owe much to the withdrawal of public provision across goods and services comprising the real wage: housing, health, education, pensions, and so on. Financial institutions, consequently, have been able to

extract profits directly and systematically out of wages and salaries. (Lapavitsas 2009b: 8)

But he argues that it is important to distinguish between different manifestations of the phenomenon—discussing the housing market at some length and credit cards more briefly. "Yet these are all rounded up into the same undifferentiated category of financial expropriation." In summary, Lapavitsas' analysis "offers no explanation for why such credit should command abnormal as opposed to normal profits".

For Fine, what is at issue "is not simply a matter of the status of the notion of financial expropriation but how this relates more fundamentally to the Marxist theory of finance". The problem, according to Fine, "is the relative lack of grounding of their analysis in the theory of finance, and corresponding concepts, put forward by Marx himself".

Despite their differences, Fine—as noted initially—describes his disagreement with Lapavitsas as one of emphasis. His position is that appropriation "is primarily from surplus value produced by workers whereas Lapavitsas places more emphasis on the appropriation of wages (value) through exploitative credit relations".

To conclude, financialisation has certainly created a renewed interest in Marx's works. Compared to the literature on environment, discussed in the previous chapter, commentators make more reference to Marx's theory of value. Both the two questions I have discussed here—'what sort of appropriation?' and 'is finance productive?'—have generated debate between Marxian scholars. In some cases the disagreements may indeed reflect only differences in emphasis. But some have suggested that a thoroughgoing reinterpretation of the theory of value may be required. In the final chapter that follows, I draw some wide-ranging, somewhat speculative conclusions, based on this chapter, and the previous one on Marx and the environment.

Bibliography

Adorjan, I. (2014). The Fetish of Finance: Metatheoretical Reflections on Understandings of the 2008 Crisis. *Critical Historical Studies, 1*(2), 285–313.

Aitken, R. (2020). 'A Machine for Living': The Cultural Economy of Financial Subjectivity. In Mader, P. Martens D., and van der Zwan N (Eds.) (2020), 412–422.

Appadurai, A. (2016). *Banking on Words: The Failure of Language in the Age of Derivative Finance*. University of Chicago Press.

Arrighi, G. (1994). *The Long Twentieth Century: Money, Power and the Origins of Our Times*. New York: Verso.

Beck, U. (1992). *Risk Society: Towards a New Modernity*. Sage Publications.

Boy, N., Burgess, J. P., & Leander, A. (2020). The Global Governance of Security and Finance. *Security Dialogue, 42*(2), 115–122. Cited in Langley 2020.

Braudel, F. (1984). *Civilization and Capitalism, 15th–18th Century: The Perspective of the World*. Berkeley: University of California Press. Cited in Durand.

Bryan, D. Martin, R. and Rafferty, M. (2009). Financialization and Marx: Giving Labor and Capital a Financial Makeover. *Review of Radical Political Economics, 41*(4), 458–472.

Bryan, D., Rafferty, M., & Jefferis, C. (2015). Risk and Value: Finance, Labor, and Production. *South Atlantic Quarterly, 114*, 307–329.

Christophers, B. (2016). For Real: Land as Capital and Commodity. *Transactions of the Institute of British Geographers*.

Christophers, B. (2018). Risking Value Theory in the Political Economy of Finance and Nature. *Progress in Human Geography, 42*(3), 330–349.

Christophers, B. (2015). The limits to financialization. *Dialogues in Human Geography* 5(2), 183–200.

Christophers, B and Fine, B. (2020). *The Value of Financialization and the Financialization of Value*. In Mader, P. Martens D., and van der Zwan N (Eds.) (2020), 38–50.

Cutler, T., & Waine, B. (2010). Social Insecurity and the Retreat from Social Democracy: Occupational Welfare in the Long Boom and Financialization. *International Review of Political Economy, 8*(1), 96–118. Cited in Sotiropolous, and Hillig (2020).

Davis, G. (2009). *Managed by the Markets: How Finance Reshaped America*. New York. Cited in Sotiropolous, and Hillig (2020).

Davis, L. (2017). Financialization and Investment: A Survey of the Empirical Literature. *Journal of Economic Surveys, 31*(5), 1332–1358.

Davis, A. and Williams, K., (2017). Introduction: Elites and power after financialization. Theory, Culture & Society , 34(5–6), pp. 3–26.

Dore, R. (2008). Financialization of the Global Economy. *Industrial and Corporate Change, 17*, 1097–1112.

Durand, C. (2014). *Fictitious Capital: How Finance Is Appropriating our Future* (D. Broder, Trans.). London and New York: Verso. Oxford University Press.
Elias, J., & Roberts, A. (2016). Feminist Global Political Economies of the Everyday: From Bananas to Bingo. *Globalizations, 13*(6), 787–800. Cited in Montgomerie 2020.
Epstein, G. A. (2005). *Financialization and the World Economy.* Aldershot: Edward Elgar.
Erturk, I. Froud, J., Johal,, S, Leaver., A & Williams, K (2008). Financialization at Work: Key Texts and Commentary. Routledge, London.
Fine, B. (2009). Locating Financialisation. Historical Materialism 18: 97–116.
Fine, B. (2010). Locating Financialization. *Historical Materialism, 18*(2019), 97–116.
Fine, B. (2013). Financialization from a Marxist Perspective. *International Journal of Political Economy, 42*(4, Winter 2013–14), 47–66.
Fine, B. (n.d.). From Marxist Political Economy to Financialisation or Is It the Other Way About? Unpublished.
Froud, Froud, J., Haslam, C., Johal, S., & Williams, K. (2000). Shareholder Value and Financialization: Consultancy Promises, Management Moves. *Economy and Society, 27*(1), 80–110. Cited in Christophers and Fine 2020.
Gershrenkon, A. (1962). *Economic Backwardness in Historical Perspective.* Boston: Belknap Press of Harvard University Press. Cited in Durand 2014.
de Goede, M. (2010). Financial Security. In *The Routledge Handbook of New Security Studies*. Routledge. Cited in Langley 2020.
Haiven, M. (2020). Culture and Financialization: Four Approaches. In Mader et al. (2020).
Harmes, A. (2001). Mass Investment Culture. *New Left Review, 9*, 103–124. Cited in Pagliari and Young 2020: 142.
Hilferding, R. (1990). *Finance Capital.* London: Taylor and Francis. Cited in Durand 2014.
Krippner, G. R. (2005). The Financialization of the American Economy. *Socio-Economic Review, 3*(2), 173–208.
Langley, P. (2020). *The Financialisation of Life.* In Mader et al. (2020), 88–99.
Lapavitsas, C. (2009a). *Financialisation, or the Search for Profits in the Sphere of Circulation.* Research on Money and Finance Discussion Paper no 10. School of Oriental and African Studies, University of London.
Lapavitsas, C. (2009b). Financialised Capitalism: Crisis and Financial Expropriation. *Historical Materialism, 17*(2), 114–148.
Lapavitsas, C. (2013). *Profiting Without Producing: How Finance Exploits Us All.* London and New York: Verso.

Mader, P., Mertens, D., & van der Zwan, N. (2020). *Routledge International Handbook on Financialization*. London and New York.

Marx, K. (1954). Capital, Vol.I, Moscow, Progress.

Marx, K. (1959). Capital, Vol.III, Moscow, Progress.

Marx, K. (1971). Theories of Surplus Value, Part III, Moscow, Progress.

Martin, R. (2002). *Financialization of Daily Life*. Temple University Press.

Martin, R., Rafferty, M., & Bryan, D. (2008). Financialization, Risk and Labour. *Competition & Change., 12*(2), 120–132.

Montgomerie, J. (2020). *Indebtedness and Financialization in Everyday Life*. In Mader et al. (2020), 424–434.

Pagliari, S., & Young, K. L. (2020). *How Financialization Is Reproduced Politically*. In Mader et al. (2020), 136–148.

Perez, C. (2002). *Technological Revolutions and Financial Capital: The Dynamics of Bubbles and Golden Ages*. Cheltenham: Elgar. Cited in Christophers and Fine 2020.

Predmore, S. (2020). *Feminist and Gender Studies Approaches to Financialization*. In Mader et al. (2020), 124–135.

Smythe, D. (1977). Communications: Blindspot of Western Marxism. *Canadian Journal of Political and Social Theory, 3*(1), 1–27. Cited in Fisher, E., & Fuchs, C. (Eds.). (2015). *Reconsidering Value and Labour in the Digital Age*. Basingstoke: Palgrave Macmillan.

Sotiropolous, D., & Hillig, A. (2020). *How Financialization Is Reproduced Politically*. In Mader et al. (2020), 149–160.

Vercelli, A. (2013). Financialization in a Long-Run Perspective. *International Journal of Political Economy, 42*(4), 19–46. Cited in Christophers and Fine 2020.

van der Zwan, N. (2014). Making Sense of Financialization. *Socio-Economic Review, 12*, 99–129.

16

Conclusion

There has been a revived interest in Marx's work in recent years, largely thanks to the 2008 financial crisis and the growing challenge of climate change and environmental destruction. In my review of recent literature in the two previous chapters I have identified issues that appear to be of particular concern to Marxist scholars. With regard to each of the two topics: the key questions turned out to be similar: "Is nature productive?"/"Is finance productive?" and "What sort of appropriation is taking place?" This is perhaps not surprising, for these questions relate to two fundamental issues in Marx's analysis: the production of surplus value and the appropriation of this surplus by capital. The magic of capitalism is that it creates surplus value; and the mystifying categories of bourgeois economics make it appear that it is capital, not labour, that creates this surplus value. This is what the qualitative theory of value reveals. Yet the scholars whose work I have reviewed—especially those writing about the environment—have paid relatively little attention to his theory of value and the associated concept of fetishism.[1]

[1] Regarding the latter, the few exceptions usually relate to fetishism rather than, more specifically, commodity fetishism.

D. McNeill, *Fetishism and the Theory of Value*, Palgrave Studies in the History of Economic Thought, https://doi.org/10.1007/978-3-030-56123-9_16

Marx's theory of value is certainly difficult to comprehend. But, as discussed at length in this book, the phenomenon to be understood—value, in the capitalist system—is indeed complex, and this is compounded by the fetishized categories of conventional economic theory. The theory of value itself and what follows from it—not least Marx's analysis of interest-bearing capital—could no doubt be better expressed. But to what extent have efforts to reinterpret the theory been successful?

I have expressed doubts about these attempts with regard to the environment. Here, the proposals to modify or extend Marx's concept of value are not very well grounded. It is important to emphasise that Marx's work is a critique of the form that value takes under capitalism; it is not an analysis of what human beings value or ought to value. When Marx writes of rent being the return to land, according to bourgeois economics, land is not synonymous with nature, it is an economic category. And what falls under the definition of 'land' under capitalism is determined by the scope of private property.

In the case of financialisation, the main argument in favour of reinterpreting Marx appears to be the sheer increase in scale of financial activities. Financial capital has certainly grown very considerably by comparison with industrial capital, and this, importantly, may have been the cause of reduced investment in recent decades. But I do not see that this is—a priori—sufficient to modify Marx's theory. What may be more significant, I have suggested, is the intrusion of finance into everyday life. This involves not just a quantitative but a very significant qualitative change—with substantial implications for power relations, to the disadvantage of individuals and households.

As my review reveals, there are interesting overlaps and parallels between the recent literature on the environment and on financialisation. First, the two issues are merged in phenomena such as carbon trading and payment for environmental services. As discussed in Chap. 14, nature is being not only commodified but also financialised. Schemes such as Reducing Emissions from Deforestation and Forest Degradation (REDD+), ecotourism and wetlands banking create the basis for financial derivative markets.

Second, and perhaps more interesting, there are parallels concerning what is happening with regard to the environment and financialisation.

To clarify this issue, I introduced the terms 'Appropriation 1' and 'Appropriation 2', which I applied to both. But how similar, in fact, are they? And what conclusions might be drawn?

Appropriation 1: Regarding the environment, this refers to rent; the landowner appropriates from the capitalist a part of the surplus value that is generated in production. Regarding financialisation, it refers to interest-bearing capital; the moneyed capitalist appropriates from the industrial capitalist a part of the surplus value that is generated in production. The similarity is thus complete; these are simply two of the three relationships which Marx refers to in his analysis of the Trinity Formula. (It is worth noting that Marx does not use the term 'fetishism of rent'; but in view of the close parallels between rent and interest-bearing capital, I suggest that it would be not only valid, but quite appropriate, to do so. The 'landowner–rent' connection in the Trinity Formula, discussed in Chap. 5, is just as mystifying as the 'capital–profit' connection.)

There is perhaps another parallel to be drawn. Marx states that, in the capitalist mode of production: "the landlord is reduced from the manager and master of the process of production and of the entire process of social life to the position of mere lessor of land, usurer in land and mere collector of rent" (Marx 1959: 883). By analogy, one might assert that: "the financier is reduced from the manager and master of the process of production … to the position of mere (albeit well paid!) lessor of credit, usurer in interest-bearing capital, and mere collector of interest". The similarity between the situation of the landlord and the financier—in relation to the worker—is, it would appear, rather close.

The situation is more complicated when it comes to Appropriation 2. Regarding the environment, this refers to the institution of private property: the landowner appropriates land from individuals and households. This frequently occurs on terms disadvantageous to those who are removed from the land, thanks to the superior power of the landowner, often with the support of the state.[2] Regarding financialisation, Appropriation 2 refers to the revenues extracted by financiers from

[2] To be more precise there is a combined effect of landowner and capitalist: the loss of land is accompanied by the worker's loss of autonomy in entering the employ of the capitalist, as discussed in Chap. 14.

workers. This frequently occurs on terms disadvantageous to the latter, thanks to the superior power of the former, with the support of the state.

Expressed in this formalized way, the parallels in relation to Appropriation 2 seem very clear. How much are we to make of them? A very radical conclusion would be that financialised capitalism represents a new era of capitalism in which the role of financial capital is sufficiently different as to require reinterpretation, or even modification, of Marx's analysis. A new stage in history is in the making, one might say. In the past, as capitalism developed, the individual became a wage labourer, subject to the logic of the market and the power of the capitalist. As financialised capitalism now develops, the individual is drawn—not in the world of production but in the world of consumption—into the logic of the financial market and the power of the financier. To quote (Martin et al. 2008) again: "As with earlier processes of dispossession to create new horizons for accumulation, (*financial*) capital now dispossesses labour of that haven from market instrumentalities known as private life" (Martin et al. 2008: 130) (my insertion in parentheses).

The argument would thus be that financialised capitalism involves a fundamental change in the social relations of capitalism; and that this requires a new conceptual apparatus. I believe this would be to overstate the case; but valuable insights can nevertheless be derived by analogy. This especially applies, I suggest, to the concept of fetishism. Although commodity fetishism, the fundament of the capitalist system, finds no equivalent here, there may perhaps be similarities with the other forms of fetishism, where appearances deceive—to the benefit of capital. The financialisation of everyday life creates a situation in which one group, financiers, is able to extract massive revenues from another group, households. The injustice of this is concealed, mystified; it appears 'natural' ('There is no alternative'). Marx's concept of fetishism might thus be helpful in conceptualizing what I have referred to as the ethos of the financialisation of everyday life. Marx invoked the concept so as to better understand a complex phenomenon: how the unchallenged, often implicit, modes of thought of people in society can shape their lives—to the advantage of one class and the disadvantage of another. This would appear to be relevant also to what is now happening with the financialisation of everyday life. The scholarly works on cultural economy that I discussed above make little or no reference to Marx's concept of fetishism, but I suggest that close parallels may be drawn. The power of fetishistic categories is akin to "the techniques, metaphors, dispositions, narratives, ideas, ideologies and relational practices" that, as noted in Chap. 15, are associated with, and supportive of, financialisation. I argued, in Chap. 9, that Marx's that "structuralism has more to offer Marxian economics than has so far been extracted from it"; today, it appears from my brief review of recent literature on the financialisation of everyday life, that scholars are now finding inspiration in the work of post-structuralists such as Foucault.

To conclude, Marx is much referred to in recent literature concerning the two major crises of our era. Yet his theory of value is largely ignored, at least as regards the environment. I have argued that his qualitative theory of value does have continuing relevance to twenty-first-century capitalism. And the same applies to the associated concept of fetishism, which could be usefully applied to enhance our understanding of the financialisation of everyday life. It is precisely because his interest in economics was combined with an interest in history, philosophy and the study of society in a wider sense, that Marx still has something to contribute some 140 years after his death.

Bibliography

Martin, R., Rafferty, M., and Bryan, D. (2008). Financialzation, Risk and Labour. *Competition and Change. 12*(20), 120–132.

Marx, K. (1959). *Capital, Vol.III.* Moscow. Progress.

Index[1]

[1] Note: Page numbers followed by 'n' refer to notes.

D. McNeill, *Fetishism and the Theory of Value*, Palgrave Studies in the History of Economic Thought, https://doi.org/10.1007/978-3-030-56123-9

www.ingramcontent.com/pod-product-compliance
Lightning Source LLC
Chambersburg PA
CBHW031700290626
47387CB00001B/3
* 9 7 8 3 0 3 0 5 6 1 2 2 2 *